The
HEART *of the*
MONSTER

The
HEART *of the*
MONSTER

Why the Pacific Northwest & Northern Rockies Must Not
Become an ExxonMobil Conduit to the Alberta Tar Sands

by

RICK BASS
&
DAVID JAMES DUNCAN

Photography by
FREDERIC OHRINGER

Research by
STEVEN HAWLEY

ALL AGAINST THE HAUL
Missoula, Montana

Published and Distributed by:
All Against The Haul
P.O. Box 7213
Missoula, MT 59807

Contact Info:
Email: info@AllAgainstTheHaul.org
Website: AllAgainstTheHaul.org

First Edition, 2010

Printed in the United States of America

ISBN: 978-0-615-42593-1

Design by Ian Boyden
Edited by Camille Hykes
Printed by Lynx Group, Salem, Oregon
Printed with soy-based ink on Cougar® Vellum
All type is Bembo

"The Earth-Shapers" (the Irish creation myth in Duncan's essay) is used courtesy of Sean Kane, and also courtesy of the Save the Redwoods League and the estate of Ella Young. The poems "The Spill" and "Christopher Columbus Discovers the Tar Sands of Alberta" are courtesy of Tom Crawford.

Cover images:
photograph of the blue waters of the Lochsa River by Frederic Orhinger;
photograph of a Heavy Haul in Alberta by Peter Robitaille.

contents

Clearwater River and Highway 12, Exxon's proposed "Heavy Haul" route.
Photograph by Steve Pettit, a forty-year resident of the route.

preface

by David James Duncan

Once there were brook trout in the streams in the mountains. You could see them standing in the amber current where the white edges of their fins wimpled softly in the flow. They smelled of moss in your hand. Polished and muscular and torsional. On their backs were vermiculate patterns that were maps of the world in its becoming. Maps and mazes. Of a thing which could not be put back. Not be made right again. In the deep glens where they lived all things were older than man and they hummed of mystery.
> —Cormac McCarthy, *The Road*

THIS RAPID RESPONSE BOOK EXISTS out of love for things that "cannot be put back, not be made right again." Noble ways of life, forms of life, and beautiful places threatened. Big Government and Bigger Oil—aided in Montana and Idaho by runamok governors and paid off politicians—are out to turn the Northwest's and Northern Rockies' iconic rivers, roads and wilderness into a tentacle of the largest and most destructive petroleum project in history: the Alberta Tar Sands. ExxonMobil is leading the effort to convert 1100 miles of riverways and scenic byways into a "High and Wide industrial corridor" that will connect the Tar Sands to the industrial nations of the Pacific Rim. South Korea, China, Vietnam, and any other country with whom

the multi-national Tar Sands investors choose to do business, will then commence to deliver potential thousands of the largest, heaviest single objects ever to travel even by ship, to Vancouver, Washington, transferred to barges, and shipped up the Columbia and Snake Rivers to Lewiston, Idaho. From there, the mega-loads—230 feet long, some of them, and seven times heavier than the 80,000 pound loads the roads were designed to support—will creep over 600 miles of the most cherished wild river and mountain roads in America, pass into Canada, and join forces with the worst CO_2-spewing operation in history.

These loads are headed for the wild and scenic Clearwater and Lochsa Rivers in Idaho, over Lolo Pass, through Missoula, Montana, over gas lines, sewers, bridges and other fragile infrastructure, up the Big Blackfoot River, over Rogers Pass, and along the Eastern Front of the Rockies to Alberta. The same kind of loads, carried by the same Mammoet trailers coming here, have crashed on level four-lane highways in Canada by simply breaking the steel of their giant trailers. Here they'll be traveling mountainous, icy, serpentine byways in the dead of winter and the dead of night, stopping all other traffic as they scrape alongside sheer granite and basalt cliffs, sending out unprecedented vibrations in avalanche zones that have swept semi-trucks into the rivers. Damage to infrastructure, delay of emergency vehicles, serious disruption of local communities and tourists, and economic loss because of these disruptions, are certainties. Strip-mining gear irretrievably dumped in the Clearwater, Lochsa or Big Blackfoot River is a likelihood. And ExxonMobil's assurances to the contrary carry the weight of smoke. This company's history of environmental debacles, consistent lies and denials, criminal convictions, human rights atrocities, catastrophic oil spills, and junk climate science, speak for themselves.

The establishment of this Tar Sands tentacle will allow any Big Oil or Pacific Rim industrial interests to convert our region's Lewis & Clark Trail, Nez Perce Historic Trail, hometowns, pristine rivers, agricultural

Above: The Clearwater River valley and U.S. Hwy 12. Roughly 180 miles of Hwy 12 between Lewiston and Lolo are 22 feet wide from fogline to fogline, and only two lanes. The Mammoet trailers carrying the Tar Sands modules are 24 feet wide. Photograph by Steve Pettit.

Below: A variety of Tar Sands modules snarling and delaying traffic and endangering highway users in Canada. Photographs by Peter Robitaille.

transportation routes, hunting, fishing, kayaking, skiing, and wilderness accesses into a "High and Wide" industrial shipping route at will, in perpetuity. We will have no local control over what foreign industrialists or Big Oil choose to shunt through our wilds. The first big financial beneficiaries of this hijacking will be ExxonMobil and a South Korean steel company. The first big financial losers will be the American people. And the economic losses pale beside cultural and spiritual losses that economists don't even know how to address.

Worse, ExxonMobil's Northwest invasion is only the beginning: as the Alberta Tar Sands are fully exploited, thousands of miles of dangerous, poorly monitored oil pipelines will be run down through America, crossing hundreds of our most important agricultural aquifers, rivers, wetlands, and farmlands, invading human and wildlife communities. One of the first such pipelines, running from the Tar Sands through Michigan, has ruptured three times *since July, 2010.* The first leak spilled close to a million gallons of oil into the Kalamazoo River and Lake Michigan, creating havoc.

⇉

Growing resistance to Tar Sands madness has sprung up not just regionally, but nationally and internationally. Local resistance in Missoula, Montana is being spearheaded by a group called All Against The Haul (AATH). At the first AATH meetings the group called for an artful, rabble-rousing book to unite opposition, attract media attention, and inform the largest possible audience. I was approached to that end, and confess I first refused: I'm working on a novel with a strict deadline and that novel, compared to this grim topic, is a joy! Seeing the seriousness of this threat, I decided that if AATH got me the enormous help I'd need, I would be willing to sacrifice my cherished annual salmon and steelhead fishing season and help construct a small protest book. I said I'd need a dyed-in-the-wool Montanan like Rick Bass to write the in-state side of the story; an excellent journalist like Steve Hawley to dig up the political, industrial,

Above: A swath of Canadian Boreal Forest slated for Tar Sands destruction. Photograph by Peter Essick.
Below: Syncrude Aurora Tar Sands Mine, one site revealing the impending 44 million acres of destruction. Photograph by Peter Essick.

and legal dirt; a fine art photographer like Frederic Ohringer to capture the power and poignancy of our threatened region; and a state-of-the-art book designer like Ian Boyden to construct the book.

To my amazement (and to the ruin of my fall fishing), AATH "hired" this team. We set to work in good faith because speed, we felt, is of the essence. ExxonMobil had a two year headstart on us, meeting with politicians behind closed doors. Our need for speed eliminated the possibility of conventional publishing, which normally takes at least a year to produce a book. We hoped that, with a crazy-fast writing and design effort, and a first printing by All Against the Haul itself, we could, with incredible luck, have a book of sorts ready by Christmas, 2010.

As it turns out, we do.

Our intent is to educate, to ignite community protest, and above all to remind people how great the Northwest and Rockies are, *as is*, without an invasion by an oil corporation with the heft and power of a major industrial nation. We've heard Big Oil's arguments about jobs and "economic spin-off" many times before—and in Prince William Sound, Alaska and the Gulf of Mexico we've seen the devastating effects of unintended "spin-off." These companies never mention their catastrophic blunders in advance of their invasions. The best data on the Heavy Haul—virtually *all* the data not being produced by ExxonMobil and its accomplices—suggests that thousands of green and tourist industry jobs will be lost regionally if this Tar Sands tentacle goes through. And the jobs Big Oil is creating at the Tar Sands, though lucrative in terms of pure dollars, are devastating in countless other ways. Drug use, alcoholism, depression, theft, suicide and spousal abuse are rampant in the Alberta Tar Sands. According to Andrew Nikoforuk's award-winning book, *Tar Sands: Dirty Oil and the Future of a Continent,* 98 percent of the people working in the Tar Sands have said that they hope to live elsewhere as soon as they've saved enough money to do so.

❧

I've written an essay, "Heart of the Monster," that tries to strike a balance between exposé and spiritual solace. A complete dossier on Big Oil's misdeeds in the Tar Sands alone would fill Yankee Stadium. It overwhelms. My intent in response is to warn of dangers, but also to try to keep hearts—including my own—awake to some of the inviolable sources of balance, creative action, and inspiration.

Rick Bass has amazed me with a full-on novella. "A Short History of Montana" is a haunting portrait of the backward evolution of a once-remarkable political figure as Big Oil and Big Energy's concepts of power begin to stew in his head and eat away his heart.

My book team's performance has astounded me. Our joint effort, broken down, consisted of a month of preliminary research work by Steve Hawley, a month of photography work by Frederic Ohringer, a month of mad writing by Rick and me (fact-checked by Steve and others), and a Herculean three-week effort by Ian Boyden. The result is a book that, whatever its faults, was generated in perhaps one-quarter of the time it normally takes to produce a work of this size and scope.

It was impossible to polish further because our whole concept was: *fast*. As Thomas Jefferson said, "If I had more time, I would have written you a shorter letter." Exactly. But I dare say I am still pleasantly surprised. Because Rick, Steve and I were working on home ground, we were able to let loves and sorrows we've long been living pour onto paper. There may be a little repetition between Rick's and my pieces, because we each worked independently with no idea what the other was doing. But the flavor of our work is so different that I hope the costs of our necessary speed of passage are outweighed by what we were each able to do well.

Steve Hawley's research, fact-checking, and brainstorming have been spectacular from beginning to end. His forthcoming Beacon Press book, *Recovering a Lost River,* is the definitive account of the Columbia/Snake salmon crisis and on the inarguable benefits of strategic dam removal. Steve's energy, wit and high spirits helped keep us going ("Me Tar Sands, You Jane"). Steve is also picking up some of the threads of this rapidfire effort: his next book (after *Lost River*) will give much fuller treatment to the ingredient I most wish this book had: a comprehensive celebration of the spectacular new green energy technologies, local food and culture movements, and anti-corporate-gigantism movements springing up all over the world despite virtually no governmental support.

My invitation to Frederic Ohringer pulled him from the life of a late-starting gentleman farmer and even later-starting jazz saxophonist in New York State. Frederic had to borrow back the cameras he'd traded in for a sax, to help us. He then flew West on almost no notice, commenced demonstrating that he's still a maestro with the camera, showered our efforts with his good sense and contemplative serenity— and, AND!—on the kind of bright sunny day that turns the jaws of anadromous fish into locked bank vaults, Frederic made two casts into the Clearwater—with *my* fly rod and *my* steelhead fly in a run *I* showed him—and on his second cast hooked, fought, becalmed, photographed, and gently released one of the most beautiful wild steelhead I've seen in my half-century marriage to fly rods and rivers. And we've got photos to prove it.

Rick and I consider this the most serious matter we've ever addressed. This is not just a "conservation battle." This is a fight for the cultural, political, spiritual, and conservation autonomy and future of the Northwest and the Northern Rockies. By extension, it is also a battle for the sake of every person, place and creature suffering the effects of climate change or facing impending pipeline dangers.

Hope may not be organized, or pretty in a visible way. But it sure is beautiful when you feel it lifting wings you didn't previously know you owned. For lifting ours, thanks to Susan Estep, Susan O'Connor, Roy O'Connor, the PROP Foundation, Bob Lang and Alice Outwater, and the ever-visionary Patagonia Company. For riding the same thermal with us, thanks to All Against the Haul (especially Spider McKnight, Trish Weber, Zack Porter and Layla Turman). For help wrestling the wild animal that is the English language, thanks to Bret Simmons, Melissa Madenski, Jessie Van Eerden, Lindsay Iudicello, Philip Aaberg, and Paul Hawken. For her editing virtuosity and wisdom, thanks to Camille Hykes. For serving as the first real "David" in this fight, thanks to FightingGoliath.org's Linwood Laughy and Borg Hendrickson, and to Advocates for the West. Enduring gratitude to the Nez Perce people for occupying the high moral ground on the Clearwater for centuries. Enduring gratitude to wild salmon and wild birds. Last and most, thanks to Adrian Arleo, Elizabeth Bass, Kathy Jubitz, Jennifer Boyden, and Jane Taylor, who endured the absenteeism and volcanic passions this effort caused their husbands. We rest in the knowledge that we gave our best and worked out of deep gratitude and love.

—*DJD, on the Heavy Haul Route, November 9, 2010*

The Heart of the Monster

An essay/memoir by

DAVID JAMES DUNCAN

Conservation is not just a question of morality,
it is a question of our own survival.
　　　　　　　　—the XIVth Dalai Lama

The climate record is not debatable. We have to move to the energies beyond fossil
fuels. This is a moral issue analogous to what Lincoln faced with slavery... This is
an intergenerational injustice.
　　　　　　　　—NASA climatologist James Hansen

ExxonMobil is ground zero for climate devastation on planet earth.
　　　　　　　　—Bill McKibben

The dispersants used in BP's draconian experiment [in the Gulf of Mexico, sum-
mer of 2010] contain solvents (that) dissolve oil, grease and rubber... People are
already dying from this... I'm dealing with three autopsies right now. I don't think
we'll have to wait years to see the effects like we did in Alaska (after the Exxon
Valdez spill). People are dropping dead now. I know two people who are down to
4.75 percent of their lung capacity, their heart has enlarged to make up for that,
and their esophagus is disintegrating. One of them is a 16-year-old boy who went
swimming in the Gulf.
　　　　　　　　—Dr. Riki Ott, marine biologist, toxicologist,
　　　　　　　　　　& Exxon Valdez survivor, October, 2010

For the most part we are crisis-management experts. If there is no crisis,
wait a few minutes and one will develop.

After an incident, we add more detail to the procedure and fire the victim.
     —BP employees, Texasville, Texas

The greatest danger man has to face is the power of his ideas. No earthly power
ever destroyed ten million people in four years, but man's psyche did it. And can do
it again... (In response), turn the eye of consciousness inward. See what you can do
in small ways... Obey as fully as possible the divine will within. This task gives
me so much to do that I have no time for any other... If we were all to live this
way we would need no armies, no police, no diplomacy, no politics, no banks. We
would have a meaningful life and not what we have now—madness.
     —C.G. Jung

The Heiltsuk Nation was unequivocal when it told Enbridge, Inc., the world's
largest pipeline construction company, that they will never allow oil tankers on
or near their traditional territory on the British Columbia coast... Their concerns
include risks to the marine environment, food security, livelihood, economy and
culture. Marilyn Slett, Chief Councillor of the Heiltsuk Nation, stated: "We
will not change our position, we stand behind our coastal First Nation neighbors
and the declaration that we all signed that bans oil tankers on our coast. We will
never support the Enbridge project and we will never support a project that has the
potential to destroy our way of life."
     —News Release, November 4, 2010

1. Corporate Welfare for ExxonMobil vs. Rivers, Roads & Wilds for the American People

A CORPORATION," WRITES THE KENTUCKY FARMER and sage, Wendell Berry, "is, essentially, a pile of money to which a number of persons have sold their moral allegiance. It can experience no personal hope or remorse. No change of heart. It cannot humble itself... Its single purpose is to become a bigger pile of money."

Two years ago the pile of money known as ExxonMobil set its sights on the Pacific Northwest and Northern Rockies. ExxonMobil's expressly amoral aim was to convert 1100 miles of achingly beautiful rivers and roads through the heart of both regions into a so-called "High and Wide industrial corridor," or "Heavy Haul route," connecting the Alberta Tar Sands to the industrialized nations of the Pacific Rim. The proposed conduit, if established, will be permanent. Its purpose will be to barge mega-loads of giant strip-mining modules, sand-cooking machines, and refinery gear (outsourced by ExxonMobil to South Korea) through the scenic heart of Oregon and Washington to Lewiston, Idaho, load them onto the most gigantic trailers ever to attempt an American highway, and drag them along some of the most pristine rivers and mountain ranges in Idaho and Montana, then north to Canada and the Alberta Tar Sands, where they will set about destroying the earth. Later mega-loads could come from China, Vietnam, Singapore, Taiwan, or anywhere else Big Oil chooses. And God knows what extractive industries might choose to ship in the opposite direction. The states, communities, river and wilderness users, residents, and wild creatures being invaded will be given no say.

Among the treasures slated to be pierced, bilked, culturally warped and degraded are the Columbia and Snake Rivers, the historic and heartbreaking Nez Perce Trail, the epoch-making Lewis and Clark Trail, the homelands of three sovereign Indian tribes, the steelheaders' paradise that is the Clearwater River, the kayaker's paradise that is the Lochsa River, Montana's Bitterroot, Clark Fork, and Big Blackfoot River of *A River Runs Through It* fame, two formidable mountain passes, *Motorcycle Magazine's* number one rated long-distance American joy-ride, and the federal highway system's number one rated scenic byway. Tourists en route to Yellowstone and Glacier National Parks, or to the largest group of contiguous wilderness areas in the lower forty-eight, or to the Front Range of the Rockies, or to the Sturgis Motorcycle Fest, will now have to wait in line for hours, then dodge their way around police cars escorting 220 foot-long, three-stories-tall loads of Tar Sands strip-mining gear. The safety and character of scores of rural communities and four fabulous states will be seriously compromised. Thousands of sustainable jobs in the two states' leading industry, tourism, will be diminished or lost. The cultural travesties will be equally galling if ExxonMobil is allowed to convert the spirits of Chief Joseph, the slaughtered Nez Perce people, President Thomas Jefferson, and the Lewis and Clark Expedition into Tar Sands lackeys in the Afterlife.

The politicians touting ExxonMobil's Tar Sands tentacle are careful never to mention the international repercussions: the Alberta Tar Sands are releasing so much CO_2 that leading climatologists liken it to an act of war committed by Canada against itself and every other nation in the world. "Conflict-free oil," Montana Governor Brian Schweitzer calls this product. I will eventually dispose of this claim in two ways, but I'll begin with a wake-up call from one of the most respected voices in the world:

Archbishop Desmond Tutu of South Africa has received the Nobel Peace Prize, the Gandhi Peace Prize, the U.S. Presidential Medal of Freedom, and the Albert Schweitzer Prize (very different Schweitzer!). It's worth mentioning that few people alive today have offered solace to more people in the wake of grievous suffering than Archbishop Tutu and his friend, the IVXth Dalai Lama. It's also worth mentioning that, despite having soothed so many sufferers, when Tutu and the Dalai Lama have occasionally joined forces on stage, the sound of the Archbishop's flock-of-ecstatic-birds laughter, harmonizing with the earthquake guffaw of His Holiness, has swamped auditoriums with a delight so infectious that many listeners never recovered and have led lives of wild compassion ever after.

In a fine new Kathleen Dean Moore-edited anthology, *Moral Ground: Ethical Action for a Planet in Peril,* Archbishop Tutu writes:

> Leading environmental scientists predict that as many as 185 million Africans will die in this century as the direct result of climate change. Many more will face untold suffering in other parts of the world... Climate change is real (and) the countries that are least responsible are paying the heaviest price. The average U.K. citizen produces nearly fifty times as much carbon dioxide as any citizen in the developing world... This is a serious injustice. As an African, I urgently call on ordinary people in rich countries to act as global citizens, not as isolated consumers. We must listen to our consciences, not to governments who speak only about economic markets. These markets will cease to exist if climate change is allowed to develop to climate chaos.

Amid the smog of Tar Sands boosterism some phrases bear repeating: *185 million Africans dead from the effects of global warming, this century. Economic markets cease to exist when climate change becomes climate chaos.* Note that Tutu's warning is both altruistic and of dire consequence to good capitalists. The summer of 2010 was the hottest on record in some parts of the world and the wettest in others. A tornado struck Brooklyn and Queens, a flood in Pakistan killed 2000, deadly dispersants joined the rains on the Gulf Coast. And Governor Schweitzer's new friend, ExxonMobil, while committing acts of climate warfare globally, has paid millions on junk science and billions on lobbyists and campaign contributions, causing U.S. lawmakers to lag a half century or so behind the rest of the world in response to global warming. (For a clear look at how Big Oil does this dirty work, see the Pulitzer-Prize winning *Angler: the Cheney Vice Presidency* by Barton Gellman, and *Climate Cover-up* by James Hoggan.)

Why should so many people sacrifice so much to create a Northwest and Northern Rockies Tar Sands tentacle? Here are Big Oil's three favorite reasons:

1) to bloat the money-pile known as ExxonMobil, already the richest company in the world.

2) to employ the Korean steelworkers ExxonMobil chose over Canadian steelworkers, creating the transportation difficulties that have inspired their attempt to cram a Tar Sands tentacle through the greater Northwest.

3) to accelerate, in Alberta, the destruction of the living world at a pace so impossible to describe that I can only refer you again to the Peter Essick photos in the front of this book (p. 12).

Corporations in this country are granted the rights of "persons." Their money is granted the protections of "free speech," and given the power to buy elections via media brainwashing. But the powers that converted the boreal forest in Essick's upper photo into the post-world in the second is neither human nor personal. An assault like this, if attempted by an actual person, would result in that person being arrested and imprisoned—or shot as a terrorist in the act. ExxonMobil's plan to turn the Northwest and Northern Rockies into a tentacle of this destruction is not a form of "speech," nor is it remotely democratic. Every friend and neighbor I have in Oregon, Washington, Idaho and Montana is being not asked, but *told*, to serve the killing power of the Tar Sands by surrendering the rivers and roads of our home. There is a word for this kind of demand from 'on high' and it is not 'democracy.' The people of the Northwest and Northern Rockies are being ordered to serve a dictator named ExxonMobil.

⁊⋲

My power to protest this takeover is limited to a language known as English, a feeble prospect at first glance, I admit. But for all its rough and hypocritical edges, English is a wild sonic animal, dynamic, alive, thought-shaping. And there is an old British word that Americans creatively hijacked, commandeered, and refined to express the well-nigh inexpressible: the word "*wilderness*." The etymology derives from Old English "wildéor," a combination of "wild" and "deer," and in England, and in colonial times here, the stock of this word was very low. For generations of Manifest-Destiny-spewing china-tipping tea-sipping "Empire builders," the root word "wild" meant *out of control, uncivilized, savage, uncultured, rude, pagan, dirty, unreliable, bloodthirsty, bad-smelling, sexually nasty*, and *low grade*—and the innocent word "wilderness" was deemed guilty by association. (John Bunyan: *Woefully I walk the wilderness of this world!* Shakespeare: *Jailed by a wilderness of sea.*)

How handy it would have been for the ExxonMobils, Shells and BPs if things had stayed this way. But the word "wilderness" underwent a transformation in America, and that transformation has done nothing but bear fruit for two centuries. It thrills me in a patriotic, darned near flag-waving way that the meaning of "wilderness" is one that Americans, as a nation, almost singlehandedly managed to transform. Starting with Thoreau, Emerson, Whitman, and the closet wild salmon-lover Emily Dickinson ("*Exaltation is the going of an inland soul to sea*"), achieving a more physical but still spiritual fervor in the rhapsode John Muir, taking on "dominionists" and embracing stewardship via the fearless Rachel Carson, revealing the cathedral-like allure of mountains via the vision of Ansel Adams, increasing in groundedness but maintaining reverence in the Zen hippie Gary Snyder—love of the wild has spread to the grassroots via the voices and work of more writers than I could name in a day. But even more, the love of the wild has spread through direct experience of the American wild itself. As John Muir put it, "Nothing can take the place of absolute contact, of seeing and feeding at God's table for oneself... The Lord himself must anoint eyes to see, my pen cannot. One can only see by loving." The inhabitants of this continent, wandering through its beauty, fell so in love with their particular wild places en masse that they began, under the visionary (Republican!) leadership of Teddy Roosevelt, to preserve the best of our wild places as no nation ever had. What's more, when Americans tossed the old, suspicion-ridden definition of *wilderness* back at Europe, a lot of Europeans cried, "What ze hell were we senking? *Vive le Jean Muir!*", and began restoring the wilds of their own nations.

What is the revamped American definition of *wilderness*? I heard David Brower sum it up rather nicely, just before he died. He said that, thanks to the lifelong influence of the wild, at age eighty-six he was still "just a gee-whiz kid." He then described his incredulity the first time he saw a wilderness spring at age six. He was so mesmerized by the sight of what he called "all that clean clear water coming up out of *dirt*" that, eighty years later, he still sounded gee-whizzy as he exclaimed, "*I couldn't understand how it could do it!*" Like so many wilderness lovers, he couldn't contain himself: "Who invented all this life?" the old man rhapsodized. "All this beauty and mystery! Every wonderful thing that's out there! How did it all happen? Not in a civilization. *In Wildness.*"

An even better testimony than Brower's for the kind of nature love you see in most Americans occurred in a questionnaire given to soldiers returning home after World War II. When asked, "What did you miss most about your life in the United States?", a full sixty percent of the returning GI's (all of whom I expected to shout "Women!") topped the list with their favorite places to camp, hunt, and fish.

❧

In the context of this abiding American reverence for *wildness*, it has been nauseating, recently, to read ExxonMobil's Tar-Sands-tentacle spokespersons gloating about the money they're paying to "upgrade" 600 miles of America's wilderness-piercing mountain roads. This is rather like turning the roads through Yellowstone Park into industrial conduits and asking to be thanked for it. The scenic byways through Idaho and Montana are among America's most beautiful. A crucial part of that beauty is their scale. The deer, elk, foxes, coyotes, eagles, ravens, bear, flocks of wild turkey and quail, moose, and squirrels I so often encounter on these roads survive precisely because the roads are modest, curved, often steep, and must be driven with extreme (but rewarding!) caution. ExxonMobil's self-styled "$67.8 million in economic activity and spin-off benefits" is a ludicrously self-serving description of what it's costing Big Oil to convert gorgeous wild and scenic river-hugging byways into the most schizophrenic-looking industrial obstacle course in American travel.

The first analysis by a non-ExxonMobil economist was done by University of Montana's Dr. Steve Seninger. To summarize: •The expected number of new jobs is small, even according to ExxonMobil's so-called Environmental Assessment of April 2010. •The $68 million in spending is not a "benefit," but a cost of modifying and visually degrading two-lane highways to accommodate ExxonMobil's Tar Sands equipment. •Workers involved in utility line relocations are already employed, as ExxonMobil's impact statement admits. •The actual transportation of the first 220 or so modules will create eighty-two temporary jobs for flaggers, pilot car drivers, and (already employed) police. •Potential job losses in outdoor recreation and tourism outweigh by far every small job gain the big rigs will bring to western Montana households. •In Missoula County alone, annual spending by out-of-state, non-resident visitors to Missoula County and by local consumers for outdoor recreation and tourism was $422 million in 2007. •Even a five percent reduction in tourism and recreation caused by an industrialized transportation corridor could result in the loss of jobs for the (huge) employment base built in Missoula County after years of effective marketing and branding of natural resource attractions.

❧

The Tar Sands mega-loads will not be "trucked." That's why I'll keep using the word "dragged." ExxonMobil's South Korean earth-eating gear will creep along behind super-tractors towing *two* twelve-axle trailers. The loads will be nearly the length of a Fenway Park home run, three stories in height, and will weigh up to 670,000 pounds—seven times the legal federal load limit—a fact so outrageous I may end up mentioning load-

One of three semi-trucks swept into Lochsa River by avalanche, February, 2008. No driver error was involved, the avalanche just took the trucks with it.
Photograph by Richard Walker.

weight seven times! They will block both lanes of our two lane highways through-out the journey, bringing all other traffic—including emergency vehicles—to a standstill. They'll attempt to cross bridges rated for maxi-mum loads of 76,000 pounds six decades ago. They'll try to maneuver 24-foot-wide loads, for 200 miles of the journey, around the tight curves of a byway that, from painted fogline to fogline, is only 22-feet wide. When passenger vehicles containing, say, you and your friends or family, seek to pass a Tar Sands behemoth, you'll be herded by police escorts onto paved outcroppings installed in wild and scenic rivers (in violation of the Wild and Scenic Rivers Act). These detours will occur at night, in the winter, or during spring avalanche season. A frigid river gorge will lie below you. The outcroppings have no guard rails. Much of the year the roads are covered with ice and snow. As the massive loads rat-tle through, there will be falling rock, collapsing road beds, and damaged infrastructure that will not be detected when it occurs. Taxpayers and util-ity-users will suffer the repair costs. There will be accidents, and long road closures due to accidents. People in small towns and rural places who suffer medical emergencies will be unable to reach hospitals during the closures.

Will our conversion into Tar Sands Corridor be hard on the tour-ism that is Idaho and Montana's leading industry, or on the thousands of families who use these roads for daily commerce? ExxonMobil refuses to even countenance such questions. And guess who our politi-cal "leaders" invited to do their own environmental assessment of the effects of the proposed Heavy Haul route, and to include no assessment of the effect on tourism or local economies at all? ExxonMobil. Two of America's most culturally rich, skillfully inhabited, carbon neutral regions are being ordered, by the region's colluding political toadies, to relinquish the democratic process, surrender their defining virtues, and serve ExxonMobil and Big Oil as a conduit to the worst CO_2-spewing operation in history.

Imperial calls this, "Wooing locals with spin-off benefits." As one of the locals being referenced, I'm here to tell you: if this is "wooing," so is date-rape. What ExxonMobil in fact did was sneak into our region in secret, pinpoint the most obsequious political politicians it could find, pay them off to circumvent objective analysis and steamroll its Tar Sands tentacle, then lie that it did no such thing.

Let's dispose of the lie, for starters. This massive "takings" began with insultingly nominal payments from ExxonMobil to elected officials in Idaho and Montana. Here, according to OpenSecrets.org, are the amounts ExxonMobil doled out during the 2008 and 2010 election cycle to herd along the Northwest political contingent: Idaho Senator Mike Crapo: $5,000. Idaho Senator Jim Risch: $5,250. Idaho U. S Rep. Mike Simpson: $3,000. Montana Senator Max Baucus: $5,000. Montana U.S. Rep. Denny Rehberg: $5,000. Washington U.S. Rep. Doc Hastings: $7,250. Idaho U.S. Rep. Bill Sali: $10,000. Washington U.S. Rep. Kathy McMorris-Rodgers: $5,000. This is ExxonMobil's way of "*wooing locals with spin-off benefits.*" The rest of us are simply told to stand back, shut up, and passively endure an invasion of our homes that offers about the same "benefits" as the Soviet tank invasion offered Czechoslovakia in the spring of 1968.

That wasn't quite fair: the tanks that invaded Prague were only 27 feet long, ten feet wide, and nine feet tall, and they left after twenty years. A single ExxonMobil Tar Sands module is the height of three such tanks, the length of ten, the weight of fifteen, and when it arrives in Alberta the havoc it will unleash on Earth's boreal zone, atmosphere, glaciers and low-lying nations will be fatal millions of times over and ongoing for centuries—this according to the hard data of the best scientists and climatologists in the world *and* the EPA, as opposed to the pseudo-data of the think tanks ExxonMobil funds.

The economic injustices of ExxonMobil's invasion of the Northwest and Rockies are even more offensive than their mega-loads. All of the strip-mining and sand-cooking gear could have been manufactured next door to the Tar Sands in Canada. Instead ExxonMobil, in its own words, "crunched the numbers," and chose the Korean steel manufacturer that created its preposterous transport problem. The richest company in history now demands that the citizens of the Northwest and the overburdened U.S. taxpayer solve their problem for them.

To put the outrageousness of this demand into some kind of rational perspective, here are a few numbers ExxonMobil has neglected to "crunch:"

•Eighty-three percent of all U.S. stocks are now in the hands of one percent of the people.

•Thirty-six percent of Americans, meanwhile, are no longer able to contribute a penny to their retirement savings, and forty-three percent have less than $10,000 set aside for retirement.

•America's banks—which we the people were just forced to bail out of a mortgage and junk-derivative crisis the banks themselves created—now own more residential housing than all of the American families and individuals who bailed out the banks, put together.

•The average amount of time needed to find a job in the U.S. is now a record thirty-six weeks. Millions have lost jobs due to "outsourcing" to countries like South Korea and China by companies like ExxonMobil. Millions have lost their homes, savings, and medical coverage.

•The bottom fifty percent of all workers in the U.S.—everybody working those menial but utterly necessary agricultural and service industry jobs—now own less than one percent of the nation's wealth.

•Twenty-one percent of all American children now live below the poverty line.

•In the summer of 2008, as the world faced near economic collapse and millions of Americans suffered, ExxonMobil took advantage of the panic by arbitrarily jacking their gas prices to $4 and $5 per gallon. They reported a second-quarter profit, that year, of $11.4 billion. This breaks down to earnings of about $1,500 per second. Their third quarter profits, after sticking it to Americans in panic and pain, were $14.8 billion, an all-time three-month record.

•ExxonMobil's total annual profit for 2008 was $45.2 billion. Not *earnings*. Pure *profit*. •Their profit for 2005: $36.2 billion. •2006: $39.5 billion. •2007: $40.61 billion. 2009: $19.4 billion.

•An entity whose pure profit, over the past five years, stands at $181 billion now demands that we the people not only donate our rivers and roads to them, but also subsidize them by shrugging off the direct financial damages their invasion of our region will cause.

•The income of the average ExxonMobil exec, compared to that of the average Idahoan or Montanan, is a number so obscene I won't defile this page by setting it down, but what that number boils down to is

clear. The lords of Big Oil are telling the citizens of the United States: "We deserve to own absolutely everything, you deserve to own nothing, and our lobbyists, Supreme Court justices, and price-setting will go on purchasing "your" politicians, perverting your laws, and siphoning dry your wallets at the gas pump till that's exactly the way it is."

This is not just "economic disparity between poor and wealthy": this is the psychotic predation of our nation.

⁂

In light of the fact that the middle class in America has already been ruthlessly preyed upon, and that half of America's work force is already scraping by on one percent of the GDP, the sales pitches for more and greater corporate predation are almost funny. Senator Lindsay Graham of South Carolina, after a recent visit to Alberta, called the Tar Sands "an industrial waltz" that "really blends in with the natural habitat." Should Senator Graham ever ask you to dance, I suggest you show him Peter Essick's Tar Sands photo, then run like hell before the "natural habitat" you call your legs turns up pulverized and missing. But I do congratulate the Senator's physician. Lindsay's happy pills are really working!

As for Montana Governor Brian Schweitzer, the hypocrisy of his attempt to turn the greater Northwest into a Tar Sands tentacle would be the stuff of literature if it were taking place in a Dickens novel. Alas, it isn't. Schweitzer is trying to wrestle his entire constituency into serving the kind of mega-industry that, in the words of Wendell Berry, "thrives on the disintegration of homes (and) subjugation of homelands." And the person who makes a technological choice of this scale, as Berry adds, "does not do it for himself alone: he does it for others. Past a certain scale he chooses for *all* others." Schweitzer is foisting just such a choice not just upon Montanans, but upon America. He began by excluding his electorate. When citizens protested he then began prevaricating about the scale, permanence, and injuriousness of the change he's railroading. In an interview in the May 2, 2010 *Missoulian,* the governor scoffed at fears that the region will become a permanent conduit between the Tar Sands and the industrial nations of the Pacific Rim. "That's not the proposal at all," he said. "This is temporary for 200 loads and nobody's proposed a permanent corridor."

The evidence that the corridor *is* permanent is overwhelming. A mere sampling: •The Port of Lewiston, on their website, states, "If one oil company is successful with this alternative transportation route, many other companies will follow their lead," resulting in hundreds of additional loads. •A printout from a Montana Department of Transportation slide show states that ExxonMobil proposed to create *"permanent* High and Wide Corridors," and in a July, 2009 meeting, MDT head Jim Lynch said outright that the proposed routes will be permanent. •The CEO of the Korean company that manufactured the first 207 ExxonMobil modules has told news agencies that his company expects future orders for additional modules totaling $1.5 billion—which suggests an additional 1200 modules on our rivers and highways. •Bemoaning the loss of Canadian jobs due to the outsourcing to Korea, a Canadian industrial association recently stated, "This route (from Lewiston, Idaho to the Tar Sands) will become the highway for energy-related products from not only South Korea, but even lower-wage suppliers such as China and Vietnam." •In a 2009 letter to the Port of Lewiston, the Idaho congressional delegation stated that, should ExxonMobil's Tar Sands shipments prove successful, "there exists the potential to import hundreds of component modules through the Columbia/Snake River System and Port of Lewiston." •On Oct. 1, 2010, *The Columbian* newspaper in Vancouver, Washington noted, "The Port of Vancouver's role in handling the oil equipment is connected to a three-year contract it signed last year with South Korea's Dong Bang Transport Logistics Company, which is shipping the Korean-built equipment to the port's Terminal 2."

A three year contract for a one-time one-year corridor? A $67.8 million investment by ExxonMobil in a one-time one-year deal? All this evidence suggests that Schweitzer is lying. The question is why. And the flagrant reason our research has uncovered is that ExxonMobil's Tar Sands tentacle is the first move in a series of Big Oil moves that could change the nature not just of our region, but of the United States. When the full repercussions of this change begin to be understood by the residents of the thirty-two states targeted, citizens won't stand for it. Tar Sands boosters are snowing people for as long as possible so that, when the grim consequences of the long-range plans start raining down, it will, they hope, be too late for the public to rise up and stop them.

Not only has Schweitzer fallen into dismal company, he's belligerent about it:

James Cameron, the Canadian director of "Titanic" and "Avatar," was recently invited by First Nations people at Fort Chipewayan to visit the Alberta Tar Sands. The tribes called on Cameron because they've been stricken with loss of livelihood due to a toxic Athabasca River fishery, and with a cancer epidemic due to Tar Sands-tainted groundwater. As an artist making movies about indigenous struggles and a Canadian citizen to boot, Cameron answered the call. But he gave equal time to Tar Sands developers—and he was surprisingly circumspect when he departed. First Nations people, he told a press conference, should be included in policy decisions since they can no longer trust their water. And Canada should slow its run on the Tar Sands until it learns "how to extract this resource in a safe manner."

These mild assertions caused Schweitzer to go ballistic. He called the press and said he was sick of environmentalists and Hollywood celebrities "blowing smoke" about the Tar Sands. If Cameron's views upset the governor to this degree, I fear he may have popped like a weasel if he had to sit through the 2008 Democratic Convention listening to a speaker *by the name of Brian Schweitzer.* During his greatest fifteen minutes of fame, Schweitzer told the nation: "We face a great new challenge, one that threatens our economy, our security, our climate and our very way of life. Until we meet that challenge our problems will only get worse... CO_2 emissions are increasing global temperatures. Sea levels are rising and storms are getting worse. We need a new energy system that is clean, green and American made."

The same man who in 2008 thought no Tar Sands oil should be extracted in any manner at all now excoriates Cameron for daring to suggest that the dirtiest oil on earth should be extracted in a less destructive manner. The late great Montana poet, Richard Hugo, once wrote a letter to a pal from an Idaho bar. In it he remarked, "One thing about politicians, they can never be whores, they're not honest enough. They screw men in ways that only satisfy themselves, (then) wonder why no one believes in the system. What system? The cynical lean with the wind, whatever one's blowing."

We stand at a crossroads. We can heed the warnings of people like Archbishop Tutu, the Dalai Lama, the First Nations people who stand in defiance of the Tar Sands juggernaut, and the wilderness lovers, hunters, hikers, fisher folk, and business people who serve them. Or we can lean with the cynical and go with the Big Oil bluster.

⁂

The politicians' glib introduction of mega-corporate power into our midst has left Idahoans and Montanans stripped of rational analysis of true costs. Secret payoffs and backroom conniving are about to turn genuine love for and defense of home and country into potential "crimes of resistance." When concern for human, animal and avian neighbors, ecological health, peaceful coexistence, global well-being, personal safety, and sustainable work and play becomes a crime, it's a pretty sure sign your region is ceasing to be a democracy and is rapidly becoming a Petro-state. ExxonMobil's bargain purchase of regional politicians *is* the political modus operandi of that Petro-state. Those corporate campaign contributions led directly to lack of rational outside analysis and democratic due process. This same lack of voice or freedom is about to drive some citizens to acts of protest that, amid the upsidedown politics of Big Oil, will be defined as "unlawful." Yet ExxonMobil itself (as this essay will show) is a repeatedly proven lawbreaker on a massive scale.

The good news is: a powerful grassroots resistance movement is taking shape nonetheless. At this writing the Idaho resistance is fighting a heroic legal battle to force some objective economic and environmental impact studies into the picture. Here in Montana, lawsuits, both state and federal, are brewing, and a voter initiative banning Tar Sands gear from crossing our state lines is in the works. Informed Idahoans and Montanans are grumbling that the string-ties and shit-howdy Western repartee of their governors would be less offensive if they heavy-hauled their high-and-wide asses to South Korea and went to work for those to whom they're trying to give our roads, rivers, and jobs.

The Northwest and Northern Rockies thrive economically, biologically, psychologically, and spiritually *because of our quality of life.* This—not backroom payoffs or "spin-off benefits"—is our priceless source of shared wealth and health. The residents and the millions of annual visitors to our regions enjoy some of the cleanest air and water and some of the wildest places left in the world. We live in the company of magnificent birds, wildlife, and *hell yeah* trout, salmon and steelhead. We cut free firewood on public lands. Our small towns and country roads are quiet. Our daily bread is given amid stunning scenery, in proximity to glorious National Parks, and offers a plethora of outdoor delights ranging from poking around for chanterelles and morels, to summiting peaks, to skiing down them, to downing three beers too many while floating downriver in an inner tube on a blazing August day.

These daily gifts are vouchsafed by hard-won protections such as Wild and Scenic River designations, All American Road designations, wilderness designations, cultural and historic designations. ExxonMobil demands that these designations must suddenly mean nothing. We are simply being ordered to serve them as a mega-industrial strip. This servitude will break the laws that create these vital designations, permanently cancel them out, and cost us all the financial and cultural benefits we now enjoy.

The Northwest and Northern Rockies can't be everything to everyone. The phrase "*A River Runs Through It*" means something here because a Tar Sands tentacle does not run through it. ExxonMobil's industrial corridor through the heart of our region is not "economic stimulus." It's a corporate hijacking of the very essence of our beautiful states.

Right: Explosion of the oil pipeline in Bellingham, Washington, June 1999.
Photograph courtesy of City of Bellingham.

2. A Dream of Earth & Oil Execs

IN JUNE, 1999, A PETROLEUM PIPELINE burst in Bellingham, Washington. The line had a history of damages that its corporate ownership, for its own economic convenience, chose not to repair. 300,000 gallons of fuel spilled from this "cost-saving" maneuver.

No one and nothing at Corporate were harmed. The harm, as usual, befell an American city, an ecosystem, and human beings. The fuel from the ruptured pipe cascaded down a tiny rivulet into Whatcom Creek, the trout, salmon and steelhead stream that bisects downtown Bellingham, creating a wild haven in the heart of the city. Two ten-year-old boys were playing near the ravine through which Whatcom flows. Anxious for the approaching Fourth of July, the boys had a tiny bottle rocket which, being boys, they naturally wanted to see take flight.

They struck a match to light it. Hundreds of Bellingham residents thought the explosion, an instant later, was nuclear. The mushroom-like cloud rose 27,000 feet into sunny June skies.

The blaze that ensued was so savage it boiled Whatcom Creek to its underwater cobble and sand, killing every living thing in the stream down to its Puget Sound terminus. Nothing could save the two young boys. But they had unintentionally prevented a far greater catastrophe. Because the explosion and fire so ferociously devoured the fuel, the vast quantities of polycyclic aromatic hydrocarbons (PAH's) in the fuel were devoured as well. The same disaster that harrowed the city saved the city from the athsma, cancer, hardening of the arteries, low birthweight, heart malformation, developmental delays, suppressed immune systems, and DNA damage to which PAH's can lead. Because the elements of fire and air had worked their violent purge, other ancient elements could go to work as well. Water began bathing wounds, washing away the dead and damaged, resurrecting and reintroducing species as only water can. The element of earth, leavened with ash, then worked its own small miracles and moss, lichens, weeds, flowers, shrubs, trees, rose from the ruins of former selves.

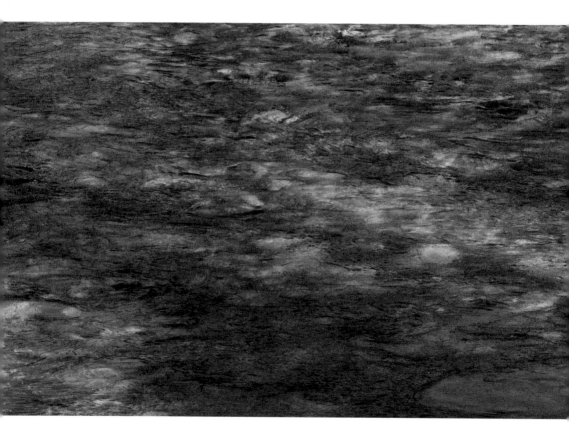

⁂

The Bellingham pipeline tragedy took place 600 miles from my home. I may not have learned of it for months had there not been a third victim. Eighteen-year-old Liam Wood was a fly fisher who, it turned out, had read and reread my novel about a fly fisher, *The River Why*. Liam was fly fishing Whatcom Creek when the pipeline rupture occurred. He'd just graduated from high school. On the floor of his room he'd left his diploma, my book, and a note to his parents saying he'd be home for dinner. The spill was so voluminous that fumes overwhelmed him before he could flee. He passed out, fell face-down in the stream he loved, and drowned before the fire reached him.

Two years after his death I met Liam's mother and stepdad, Marlene and Bruce. I'd heard stories about their efforts to make politicians aware of the dangers posed by pipelines. Sensing how heartbreaking it must be, amid deep grief, to try to instill awareness in politicoes hedged in by lobbyists, I had an idea. What if something were done to simply celebrate Liam's passions? He'd been an uncanny fly fisher and a white-water kayaker, and he aspired to write about the wild world he loved. Putting our heads together, Marlene, Bruce, other friends and I hit on the notion of starting a little fly fishing and river restoration school in Liam's honor. Thanks to dozens of people who've worked far harder at it than me, The Liam Wood Fly Fishers & River Guardians is now in its tenth year, with a thriving branch in Bellingham and a modest wing here in Montana, too.

A thousand stories have accrued over a decade. A favorite: two young Hispanic gang members, along with a fly fishing padre they'd met in jail, got into the Liam Wood School. In the somewhat alien company of Anglo college students, this duo not only excelled as fly fishers and fly-tiers and worked hard on stream restoration, they visited the Skagit River on their own after "graduation," deployed their fly rods uninstructed, and caught pink salmon on flies. Juan, a one-time gang leader, turned out to be a natural caster who can rifle a fly ninety feet and look relaxed doing it. Towering, paradoxically gentle Teddy, to his own surprise, liked Norman Maclean's *A River Runs Through It* so much that he composed a rap song that struck me as the first real advance in Maclean criticism in decades. Better yet, at a fundraising performance that Sherman Alexie,

Jeffrey Foucault and I did for the Liam School, Teddy walked out in front of a thousand people, nailed his *River Runs Thru It* rap cold, and brought down the house.

A favorite feature of the Missoula branch of the School is quieter. Six years ago a dozen custom fly rods were built for and donated to our students. At my request, and with Marlene's permission, legendary Montana rod-builder, Glenn Brackett, customized the twelve rods by inscribing sentences Liam had penned in a sort of fishing journal the year before he died. Most of our Missoula students come from broken families and live in group homes. I love watching these kids step into Montana streams each summer with their Mohawks and tattoos, bright green or blue hair, in pursuit of a first fly-caught trout. So far they have all managed to catch fish. And every summer they're casting nine-foot blue rods upon which Glenn's deft calligraphy gives a little afterlife to Liam's writings. Some of my favorite inscriptions:

The Metolius looks like it should contain olives instead of trout.
　　　　—Liam Wood

I remember the sun and the feeling of water on my legs.
　　　　—Liam Wood

Just to sit and listen to the river talk.
　　　　—Liam Wood

I was just a pagan fisherman until Liam came along.
　　　　—Liam's fishing pard, Evan

The smells of pine trees and dry earth, mosquitoes and powdered Gatorade.
　　　　—Liam Wood

As his fly was swinging back to shore the rod was almost torn out of his hands.
　　　　—Liam Wood

I got to share one of the most beautiful places on earth.
　　　　—Liam Wood

❧

In 2003 Marlene sent me a little vial of Liam's ashes. For seven years I kept them in a sort of makeshift shrine, letting Liam's molecules commune with small spiritual treasures in which I place love and trust. In the spring of 2010 I somehow felt this communion was complete, and called Bret Simmons, one of the co-founders of the Liam School. Bret had been a fishing buddy of Liam's. When we started the school he became a fishing pard of mine. As we made plans for our annual September excursion, we decided to spend our first day hiking into a tiny cirque in the Selway Bitterroot Wilderness of Idaho, to release Liam's molecules.

❧

On July 26, 2010, shortly after Bret and I had made our plan, a pipeline burst in Michigan. This line was owned by a Canadian-based corporation, Enbridge Inc., the largest pipeline construction company in the world. The line was carrying oil south into the U.S. from the Alberta Tar Sands. 840,000 gallons poured from the rupture into the Kalamazoo River, then out into Lake Michigan, introducing millions of Americans—and billions of hapless life-forms—to the term "Tar Sands oil" for the first time.

Five facts haunt me:

•Local residents reported the leak for thirteen hours before Enbridge's "failsafe" leak detection system in Edmonton, Alberta, finally shut off the appropriate valve.

•Enbridge still considers their system safe.

•At this November, 2010, writing, the same pipeline has ruptured twice more *since July*.

•Other Enbridge lines have leaked or ruptured a *hundred times in the past decade.*

•The spill created havoc for birds, fish, wildlife, aquifers, humans. Corporate sent out a clean up crew and launched a PR campaign to assuage anger. Enbridge now calls the spill "cleaned up." *But no explosion or fire purged the PAH's from this spill*, as happened in Bellingham. The people of Michigan, like the people around Prince William Sound in Alaska, will now learn the hard way, via asthsma, cancer, hardening of the arteries, low birthweights, heart malformations and so on, that the phrase "cleaned up," in Corporate Speak, means that the company sopped up enough oil to ease it into the safety of a legal gray zone wherein illnesses, deaths, and damages no longer result in lawsuits.

Another set of facts haunts me even more:

•Over the next decade, Big Oil intends to run many thousands of miles of Tar Sands pipelines across all ten Canadian provinces and thirty-two American states. Some will reach to Maine, some to California, some to Florida, others to the already-hemorrhaging Gulf.

•Infamously dangerous and under-monitored, the lines will pump highly pressurized oil by the millions of gallons over, under or through America's crucial agricultural aquifers, rivers, wetlands, farmlands, and towns. Lines will rupture. Spills will attack aquifers, marshes or rivers, cause the evacuation of farms and towns, oil animals and birds. After more "clean-ups" and corporate PR campaigns, PAH's will invade human and wildlife communities, human food, human fetuses, DNA.

•Even without ruptures, this vast web of lines—in the name of "energy security"—will turn thirty-two states into one of the world's biggest and easiest terrorist targets. A kook with a rifle, a disgruntled teen with a jug of kerosene and a match, could raise hell.

•Even without ruptures, a vast web of Tar Sands pipelines will erode the unique qualities of the American West, Northeast, Deep South, Great Lakes, Heartland, causing each distinct region to bear ever more resemblance to a hapless third world Petro-state.

⅔

Over the course of the same summer of 2010, a group of Exxon-Mobil and Imperial Oil reps visited a few towns along their proposed Tar Sands tentacle through the Northwest and Rockies, steadily approaching my own home town. It grew hard not to feel stalked. The reps carried charts, graphs, and that self-righteous air of condescension that corporate employees assume when their purpose is a snow job. What color tie do you choose as you prepare to send hundreds of mega-loads of strip-mining gear through an economically strapped region?

I was happily sequestered away from all of this, writing a novel, when I received word that, in the tiny Clearwater River town of Kooskia, Idaho, the reps ran into trouble. First, in a city of just 634 residents, 300

Kooskiites showed up for ExxonMobil's Dog & Pony Show. Attendees included loggers, hippies, vegans and carnivores, gun nuts and constitutionalists, droves of fishers and hunters, Earth-loving evangelicals, bikers (as in Harleys), bicyclists (as in Trek, Kona Cadabera, etc.), realtors, entrepreneurs, butchers, bakers, kayak-makers, school teachers, Tea Party zealots, whitewater guides. And to the dismay of the ExxonMobil reps, not one of them looked happy to see Big Oil pimping a Tar Sands tentacle. The suits chanted their trusty mantra of "economic activity" and "benefits" (the grand prize being a job holding the Stop & Slow flagger sign for the Canadian road construction companies ExxonMobil again outsourced after "crunching more numbers"). The Kooskiites bought not a word of it, and presented a bristling, unified front of opposition.

Growing uneasy, the reps said there could be no Q & A or public comments, because there was no P.A. system over which questions and comments could be heard.

Having foreseen this possibility, Kooskia's own Linwood Laughy—who looks a little like Santa Claus and is equally, puckishly disarming—began setting up a P.A. system he just happened to have brought. The dreaded Q & A and comment period could not be dodged by the oil reps. Worse, Mr. Laughy is a Lewis and Clark scholar who can recite chapter and verse proving that a Tar Sands tentacle for ExxonMobil is an infinitely far cry from the "Northwest Passage" Thomas Jefferson had in mind when he sent the Corps of Discovery out to chart the natural wealth of the West. And worse yet, Laughy and his equally scholarly and tenacious wife, Borg Hendrickson, founded a ferociously well-informed anti-Tar-Sands-tentacle website known as FightingGoliath.org that has become one of the biggest thorns in ExxonMobil's side since the terrible publicity of the Exxon Valdez spill.

When the P.A. fired up and the comments began, the Kooskiites, to a man woman and child, saw Big Oil's proposed corridor as the invasion it is and opposed it so vehemently that the suits not only left town in a hurry, they changed plans. They'd intended to drive up the harrowing curves of the upper Lochsa River and over Lolo Pass to their next Dog & Pony Show, at the Lolo Montana Community Center—my town. That meeting also promised to be well-attended and emotional. ExxonMobil cancelled, and in the months since has gone back to making unfounded claims of "spin-off benefits" from behind locked doors at Corporate.

A friend who attended the Kooskia meeting—this book's esteemed researcher, Steve Hawley—phoned me the same night and gave an account so moving it dove deep into my psyche as I went to bed.

ϿϾ

In the small hours that night I dreamed that four oil company execs were driving a black luxury sedan through the dark roads of wildest Idaho, when their headlights lit upon a naked woman walking down the center of the road. The four suits braked in astonishment, then eased their sedan up close.

The woman stopped walking and turned to face them. She was stunning. Full hipped, full breasted, dark-haired, unafraid. The men lusted instantly and ferociously. They were four. She was alone. But something in her eyes—an agelessness; extreme dignity; the lack of fear—prevented them from even making cracks about what they'd each like to do.

As they silently eye-raped her, another thing changed: they began to notice scrapes and bruises on her body, and an unhealthy pall on some of her skin. Fear of contagion bled into their lust.

The four men climbed out of the sedan and gathered, shoulder to shoulder in their dark suits, white shirts, silk ties. The woman stood across the car from them, totally vulnerable, yet totally calm. The men did not offer help. The woman did not ask for it. But, seeing the way they kept eyeing her injuries, it was she who broke the silence. In a calm low voice, without a hint of accusation, she said, "I am for you, as I am for all living things. All your lives I have moved with you in your every breath, as you have moved through me. From me you arrived, and to me you will return." She looked at her own body slowly, with the detached air of a physician, or mortician. "These wounds," she said, "have been inflicted by you."

That took care of one threat: the execs no longer hoped for sex. They knew too much about what had been done to her. Sex would be far too dangerous.

They decided to see what they could get by bartering. Since she carried nothing and wore nothing, robbery was not going to produce. But oil execs have their methods.

One of them ducked into the car, produced a chessboard, set it on the dark hood of the sedan. They challenged her to a match. When she merely gazed at them in response, it grew clear that she was passive before any human proposal. She had no choice but to play.

The men swiveled the board to give themselves the white pieces, and the first move. She didn't protest. The suits consulted in low whispers. One of them then slid forward a piece that looked like a white drilling platform. The moment the piece moved, a genuine drilling platform appeared in the Gulf—and a multitude of bruises appeared not so much on as under the woman's bare skin. She shuddered. But her voice was calm as she said, "You may do as you wish. And I will do as I must."

She made a counter-move, sliding forward a black piece made of countless tiny carved fish, birds, marine mammals. As the piece arrived in position she sent a ray into the minds of the men, giving them a vision of what their move and her counter-move had wrought: in the Gulf, sperm whales, bluefins, dolphins and sea turtles by the thousands, billions of shrimp and fishes, and millions of birds disappeared from the planet in a writhing black mass.

The four men gaped till the vision faded, then looked nervously at her. She gazed back without expression.

Less sure of themselves, but still determined, they put their heads together. One of them reached for a piece that looked like some kind of steel earth-eating device. When he touched it, an engine audibly started, then rose to a roar. He slid the piece forward into boreal forest.

The woman reeled slightly, coughed up a little blood, but her face remained calm and her hand steady as she made her counter move. She touched a piece that looked like a black queen. The queen became a small black cloud. The woman slid it forward. Vast tracts of forest vanished, machines and modules roared, smoke spewed, land and lakes were devoured, sludge reservoirs appeared. The woman coughed more blood, wiped it away, kept sliding the black cloud/queen forward. White pieces flew from the suits' side of the board. Hurricanes and tornadoes spun over the world. Insane skies rained oil, dying fish, pieces of houses, shattered birds. Pipelines appeared at the speed of thought, ruptured over farmland, ruptured in cities. Earth's Poles turned to slush. Coastlines and islands vanished under rising seas. Refugees from inundated lands swarmed over borders by the millions, overwhelming hard-pressed countries. Glaciers vanished from every mountain range and more millions swarmed down from the highlands. Ocean gyres reversed direction. Trees died by the billion. Nations went to war over water, over hunger, over dearth.

The execs gaped till the vision faded, then turned to the naked woman. She was breathing hard. There was blood at her mouth corners. Her body was a mass of contusions and burns. But her eyes were still clear, her expression calm, and her breasts, hips, flesh, at least in patches, were still lovely to behold.

The execs put their heads together, preparing their next move.

The woman breathed, and waited, prepared to do as she must.

❦

I took Liam's molecules into the Idaho wilds in the company of our shared friend, Bret. Our destination was a tiny creek in a glacier cirque that has long since lost its glacier. It's one of the few creeks I know that remains so pure I'll still drink from it. A few hundred yards from its origin-spring, the creek dives over a thousand foot decline, vanishing into the most remote part of the Selway Bitterroot Wilderness. I love this vanishing point. It feels like, looks like, *is,* a gateway into the unknown. Liam had long since passed through such a gate. It felt nothing but right to allow his molecules to follow.

There is an inscription on the box containing the Buddha's ashes, placed there by his lovers. It reads, *Atha dipa, Ana sarana, Anana sarana.* *("You are the light, You are the refuge, no shelter but You.")* I spoke these words over Liam's molecules, then stood to say the most powerful prayer I know, one long ago learned by heart, brought home from India. It was a mild day, but as I was reciting the prayer a remarkable wind came down and swirled round Bret and me so fiercely that I had to gulp air to keep the prayer coming. I thought of the broken pipeline that took Liam's breath. I had the fleeting sense of a Breath inside the breath, rushing in at the sound of prayer to restore what had been taken. I felt an ease, despite the wind's power. Felt a deep welcoming.

In the midst of that opening I released the molecules, and watched them go. As with previous releases, I was a bit surprised by how substantial ashes are as you pour, and how long you continue to see them, flowing with the water among the weeds, wildflowers, underwater beds of moss. I was a little surprised, too, by the many bits of bone, and found myself brushing them from the moss, thinking or maybe whispering aloud, *You go now too.* This urging brought to mind a line from *The Upanishads*—the line a victorious and departing soul speaks, joyously, back to those still in human bodies: *Whoever gives me away helps me the most!*

I pray this is so. Felt it is so.

Photograph by Steve Pettit.

I realized that, over the course of ten years, an eighteen year old boy I never met and never can meet had nevertheless become my friend. How? A thousand shared intimacies with things, places, people. I too have shared some of the most beautiful places on earth, many times with people dear to Liam himself. I too, when I daydream of fly fishing, think first of the sun—*always*—and the feel of water on my legs. And the Metolius! How did Liam nail *that* one? That crazy spring-born river looks *exactly* as if it should contain olives instead of trout!

I felt more and deeper ease.

Bret and I embraced, and hiked the long, satisfyingly wild way out.

The road home, not yet ExxonMobil's, was wild, too, and beautiful every mile of the way.

3. Jobs in Hell vs. Home on Earth

I AM ABOUT TO DESCRIBE A RELENTLESSLY gruesome industry because there is a problem up north that is so dire it needs addressing. But I promise this piece of writing won't stay in Dire Mode. I love this Earth like the mother she has in fact been to me, and feel adoration is as powerful a tool in her defense as exposé. Keeping weary minds open and good-heartedness intact, serves life, and levity is a form of light that can also dispel darkness. Once I've waxed dark, I'll return to all the light I can kindle.

That said—with profound thanks to Alberta's own Andrew Nikiforuk for his staggeringly upsetting book, *Tar Sands: Dirty Oil and the Future of a Continent* (Greystone Books)—here is all I can bear to say about what the Tar Sands portend for America and the world:

❧

•Alberta's so-called "Saudi Arabia" consists of what oil execs and biocidal politicians call "the last great oil field remaining in North America." But the Tar Sands are not an "oil field" at all and the difference is fatal. The Tar Sands are a vast deposit of bituminous sand from which tar and, much later, oil, can only be derived at staggering cost to Earth's atmosphere, ecosystems, freshwater supply, polar caps, glaciers, atolls, coral reefs, fish, birds, boreal forests, and all the humans who depend thereon.

•Alan Greenspan's adolescent infatuation with the econoporn writer, Ayn Rand, joined to international fantasies of "unmonitored free markets," recently led the industrialized world to the brink of financial collapse. The world is not close to recovering. Canada's oblivious prime minister, Stephen Harper, doesn't care: he is overseeing an old-fashioned econoporn "unmonitored free market" fire sale on bitumen. His entire nation—and the world—is reeling as a result.

•The handler of America's unique Supreme Court-appointed president, George W. Bush, was of course the admirably villainous (in the Shakespearian sense) Dick Cheney. Cheney has headed powerful corporate positions, political offices, and "energy task forces" since the Nixon presidency. Throughout his career he has worked hard, and successfully, to castrate democracy's ability to monitor or slow any form of energy development. His legacy thrives in the bureacracies and three houses of government in Washington, D.C., in Canada, and overseas. A few outcomes of Big Energy's gung-ho power: Five hundred U.S. mountaintops have gone missing and the streams beneath each mountain's ghost are dead or poisoned as a result. "Fracking," a decade ago, was a way to approximate the F-word on the TV show, "Battlestar Galactica"; today it is one of the most polluting forms of extraction in history, and millions of wells, scores of vital aquifers, and the very air are poisoned as a result. And of the BP Gulf disaster, what more need be said?

Not just American but *North* American government, from Mexico to the Arctic, is rife with Cheney-Think. Democrats are as implicated as Republicans. And ordinary citizens are beginning to see that democratic government and Petro-states have never coexisted and never will. In America's rapid slide toward becoming a bribe-driven, backroom-governed, post-democratic shadow of its former self, I know of no more dangerous lubricant than the oil being squeezed from the Tar Sands.

•International investment in the Alberta bitumen bonanza now totals well over $200 billion (U.S.), making the region the largest energy project, largest construction project, and largest industrial capital venture on the planet. The Tar Sands are also the dirtiest and most damaging industrial project in the history of the planet, and the show is just getting started. If Alberta continues to be stripmined until its bitumen is gone, a boreal forest wilderness the size of Florida (66,000 square miles: 44 million acres) will become a Mordor-like wasteland and industry's largest-ever contribution to climate chaos will be a fait accompli.

•Quick correction with regard to Florida: if the Sands are fully exploited, a quarter of present day Florida could vanish under water, so we'd best imagine the Tar Sands as a post-biological chaos the size of Pennsylvania and Ohio combined.

•The bitumen strip-mining process begins with the clearcutting of boreal forest, but this is too easy to say. Bitumen mining begins by obliterating millions of trees from one of the two great lungs of the living Earth. Tropical rain forests comprise the other great lung, but boreal forests sequester *twice as much carbon* as rain forest in their permafrost, peat bogs, and living timber. This entire carbon load is being blasted into the atmosphere as the industry clearcuts the trees, rips up the peat and permafrost, and creates its vast toxic bogs—all of this before the bitumen even begins to be heated with natural gas, or "upgraded," or refined, and *long* before a drop of gas reaches our car engines.

•The resultant release of CO_2 is so massive that climatologists liken Tar Sands development to an act of war against all other nation, as said, but it's an especially egregious war against the hundreds of millions living in countries dependent on vanishing glacier water for agriculture, or the hundreds of millions living in places of low-elevation like the Netherlands, Bangladesh, Florida Keys, Marshall Islands, Maldives, Kiribati. Most of the inhabitants of these places have no place to go. What good are global communications if we don't use them to communicate. It is our duty as communicators to imagine how these people feel. The coastline of Bangladesh is moving inland, threatening to make refugees of tens of millions of people. At least 1.3 billion people are threatened by loss of the glaciers that, each summer, provide all of the water for their crops. Maldivian culture is ten thousand years old. Their written culture is two thousand years old. Their entire country is 1.5 meters above the Indian Ocean. A three degree rise in the atmospheric temperature eats the entire country. They have nowhere to go. Big Oil, Otter and Schweitzer, the industrial waltzer Lindsay Graham, Prime Minister Harper, and all the Cheney wannabes plundering the Tar Sands, haven't offered to fund a new homeland for the millions of impending refugees. The Maldivians are desperately constructing a synthetic island that is two meters higher than their ancient homeland. Imagine how it feels to haul in rock and dirt, bury your own home and your grandparents' homes beneath it, and try to live on top of the result. Archbishop Tutu: *"We must listen to our consciences, not to governments who speak only about economic markets."* There are 2,500 energy lobbyists in D.C., four per congress person, chanting, *Forget the Maldives, forget Africa, forget millions of impending refugees, forget the intergenerational injustice being inflicted upon your own children.*

•In lowland nations globally, trees are dying as freshwater turns to salt. In the North American West, thirty million acres of lodgepole and whitebark pine stand dead, beetle-killed due to the same general atmospheric cause. The Canadian government glosses over its war on Earth's atmosphere by running folksy ads in any periodical shameless enough to print them. A recent ad likened Tar Sands devastation to a good neighbor loaning ol' Uncle Sam a cup of sugar. I'd like to offer Canada's PR hacks a more realistic metaphor: Tar Sands exploitation is more like stealing an enormous supply of cold meds to whip up the world's most gigantic batch of crystal meth, selling *that* to Uncle Sam, and turning a vast swath of Canada into the equivalent of a meth house in the process.

•Meth and cocaine use, by the by, is epidemic among Tar Sands workers.

•Once Tar Sands mining begins, two tons of earth must be excavated to make a barrel (42 U.S. gallons) of tar. Next the tar must be steamed out of the sand and converted, by extreme heat, into crude oil. The natural gas burned to steam out the tar is a comparatively clean fuel. Bitumen-derived oil is as dirty as fuel gets. Burning massive quantities of natural gas to produce Tar Sands oil is as counter-intuitive as, say, raising factory-farm chickens by feeding them wild elk and salmon. The sole reason for this squandering of natural gas is that ExxonMobil, Imperial, Shell and so on are the "chicken farmers" in the equation. As Kurt Vonnegut's Kilgore Trout used to say: "Up your ass with Mobil gas!"

•By 2008, the amount of natural gas the Tar Sands industry used to heat bitumen daily, was equivalent to the amount needed to heat four million homes. The industry has since doubled in size. At the current rate of growth, forty percent of Canada's natural gas reserves will be gone by 2030, bringing on a continental natural gas crisis. Which states, ranchlands, and neighborhoods will the Tar Sands oligarchs choose to frack and poison then? How will even the Tar Sands-enriched flee the biocide, pollution, and social chaos they will have caused?

•Bitumen-mining is the most water-intensive process in the history of petroleum exploitation. The industry, back in 2008, used as much water daily as a city of two million. This amount has since doubled. Each barrel of bitumen consumes and defiles three barrels—that's 126 gallons—of fresh water. The small percentage of poison water that is "recycled" (usually just once) has caused money-drunk Tar Sands boosters to declare that their industry is "sustainable." To this I can only add that death is "sustainable," too. Death really works as it recycles healthy living organisms into corpses, then into carbon.

•Canada has no national water policy and is one of the worst polluters among industrial nations. Alberta's farcical monitoring of the release of pollutants into the atmosphere, rivers, lakes, and groundwater has been repeatedly proven in court to be frauds. The greenhouse gasses emitted by bitumen mining alone are now equal to the round-the-clock revving of roughly two million passenger car engines—this before the natural gas even turns the bitumen into crude oil, or the crude is refined into gas and the gas burned in a car.

•The tailings ponds located along the Athabasca River leak millions of gallons of pollutants into groundwater, daily. For the last decade the First Nations people downstream at Fort Chipewyan have been contracting rare cancers caused by this leakage. According to the Natural Resources Defense Council, a thirty percent rise in rare cancers has occurred since the creation of the Tar Sands waste reservoirs.

•Tar Sands exploitation, according to ornithologists, is going to kill a minimum of six million and maximum of 166 million North, South and Central American birds in two to three decades. (I will address this topic on its own, shortly.) The same industry is rapidly destroying the third largest watershed in Canada.

•Then will come the thousands of miles of pipelines, crisscrossing thirty-two American states, as Big Oil continues to "triumph" over democracy, human culture and biological life.

Ѫ

Frack my soul. I could use a rap by a Liam Wood School alum! Big Teddy! Help me out!

> *See, sometimes I feel like a cockroach*
> *an incomplete metamorphiss* (sic!)
> *instead of a butterfly*
> *that's all pretty an' gorgeous*
> *The other day I tied a fly*
> *usin' hair from elk an' horses...*
> *Besides that I read a book*

called A River Run's Through It
To me flyfishin's like a language
but not bein' fluent
I'd still rather cast a rod
then sit in streets shootin' bullets...
Like Paul I'm a bad boy
with an Indian girl
but even Paul had a peaceful
and beautiful world.
That was fly fishin' the river
that splashed an' swirled.
That's a book I read
by Norman Maclean
He still found peace fly fishin'
Through all the stress an' the pain.

Yeah. That's what I'm talking about. Teddy. Liam Wood School. Fly rods. Rivers. *Thanks.*

Oregon, Washington, Idaho and Montana, *"through all the stress an' the pain,"* remain the region of the United States most capable of becoming truly carbon neutral. For such a region to become the "Tar Sands Tentacle States" for ExxonMobil makes a cruel joke of our idealism and subverts our potential example to the world. Millions of Northwesterners lay their hands daily upon the tools that will rebuild a living earth. As a cultural norm, an inordinate number of Northwesterners recycle, invest in innovative green energy, devise ingenious practicalities like Seattle's car-lending program, defend endangered species like Puget Sound orcas and wild salmon, work like heroes to resurrect damaged estuaries, neighborhoods, soils, green spaces, creeks. They carpool and bike and drive electric or high mileage cars to work. They insulate, choose green products, support local food and culture, grow gardens. The politicians forcing this constituency to collude in rampant Tar Sands growth are forcing their violence upon us all. Your family and mine, like it or not, could soon be helping Big Oil—over the dead bodies of birds and First Nations cancer victims— convert planetary lung-tissue into a greenhouse gas explosion.

The Alberta Tar Sands are a BP Gulf disaster, and worse, unfurling in slow motion. Our children *already* face crises no politician or Tar Sands booster can even begin to foresee. The great hope of the Northwest and Northern Rockies, and our greatest possible contribution to the living world, is that we become our ever more localized, mutually supportive, naturally abundant, sustainably green selves.

❧

Those calling for a clean, green and compassionate energy future are hardly a "splinter group." Financial, moral, intellectual, spiritual, and political support for this mainstream movement is streaming into the world from thousands of faith leaders, from universities all over the country, from literally millions of nonprofits and NGO's, from the wealthiest man in America (Bill Gates), from activist rockers like Bono and Eddie Vedder, and from an award-winning director despised by Brian Schweitzer for believing energy can and should be clean (James Cameron). The coalition includes past and current presidents and CEO's, millions of grassroots rabble-rousers, artists, student organizers, and social justice organizations of every size and kind, many of whom have realized that our most pressing conservation issues and our public health concerns about smog, dying oceans, PAH's, befouled beaches, defiled food, defiled birds and animals, are the same one issue.

The clean green energy advocates also include a group of investors who hold the purse strings to more than $421 billion in assets, much of it already invested in clean tech and green energy. These well-informed capitalists are making the case that if America does not charge whole-heartedly into the burgeoning effort to wean the planet of fossil fuel, China and Europe will widen their lead in green development, and millions of the best new jobs will pass the United States by.

4. The Ease of Killing Birds by the Thousand vs. the Hard Work of Saving Birds One at a Time

The Brown Pelican didn't take part
in the Industrial Revolution.
It just wanted to go on being a pelican.

Unable to fly, it waddles down the beach,
dragging its useless dip-net throat
while the ocean serves up more tar-balls
and plastic spoons.

You want a happy poem,
everything to be put back right?
That was the Romantic Period.

Even as we sleep
and dream our dreams,
ships are raking their black nets
across the floors of the ocean.

—from "The Spill," by Tom Crawford

The Tar Sands of Alberta are displacing one of the last great planetary preserves of avian fecundity with a second Gulf-like disaster to the north, making the lives of hundreds of species of South, Central and North American birds an impossibility in a doubly-defiled migratory corridor.

Every bird dependent on boreal forest and the Gulf is now the proverbial "canary in a coal mine." The "coal mine" itself is the emerging North American Petro-State.

A massive Natural Resources Defense Council study (*"Danger in the Nursery: impact on birds of tar sands oil development in Canada's Boreal forest"*) concludes that in the next two to three decades the Tar Sands could kill as many as 166 million migratory birds. "Virtually every facet of Tar Sands oil development has the potential to harm boreal birds," writes lead ornithologist Jeff Wells. ExxonMobil, Imperial, Shell, Syncrude, and the other Big Oil giants invested in the Tar Sands are paying nothing—$0.00—in recompense for the vast habitat damage and direct damages they're wreaking upon birds.

As if inspired by Big Oil's complete lack of accountability, Senator Orrin Hatch, Representative Joe "I Apologize, BP" Barton, and other oil industry servants now want to lure the giants of bitumen-mining to the Desert Southwest and set about the destruction of Utah, its people, wildlife, birds, and its nearly nonexistent waters.

ೋ

A single example of how strip-mining for tar kills birds is all my heart can bear.

Step one: Consider again the Essick photos of boreal forest, and of what replaces it.

Step two: Imagine a bird, expecting the world in the first photo, trying to land, rest, feed, and drink amid the post-world in the second.

On April 8, 2008, the bodies of 1,606 dead waterfowl were scooped from a Syncrude tailings pond. Syncrude's effluent "pond" is formed by the second largest dam on earth. The massive sludge reservoir this dam encloses is perched at a higher elevation than all the surrounding water. Gravity, of course, is constantly forcing the poisons into the ecosystem, and the reservoir itself is Poison Central. The reservoir is located amid the ancient nesting grounds of millions of waterfowl and other birds. During a blinding early morning snowstorm the birds were forced to rely on migratory memory, and landed on the death lake. Birds (need I say it?) are about as discerning as human toddlers. The death lakes are a ceaseless offering of poison Halloween candy. The industry's idea of a "warning system:" when a flock of waterfowl flies close to the biggest reservoirs, a cannon might fire. Thousands of dreck ponds possess no such cannon.

On the morning of the 1,606 duck kill, the cannon didn't fire because it was snowing. A Syncrude spokesperson later acknowledges, on film, that the actual number of birds killed that morning, or any morning, is impossible to determine because mired birds sink fast in the sludge. The bodies of moose and bear have been found in the same sludge. In May, 2008, the same "pond" was responsible for the death of at least 500 ducks, but the kill was not reported by Syncrude. It only became known after it was discovered by passersby. The number of incidents like this in the Tar Sands are incalculable.

ExxonMobil's ads celebrate their willingness to go after the "tough oil." This is way beyond "tough." To reward a migratory bird that has survived the Gulf oil devastation with a breeding ground replaced by Tar Sands effluent is a cruelty worthy of the Dark Lord of Mordor. A few of the birds in increasing crisis due to Big Oil's love affair with tar: *Bohemian waxwings. Canada warblers. White-throated sparrows. Blackpoll warblers. Gray jays. Bay-breasted warblers. Boreal chickadees. Dark eyed juncos. Evening grosbeaks. Rusty blackbirds. Olive-sided fly-catchers. American robins. Swainson's thrushes. Golden plovers. Buffleheads. Short-billed dowitchers. Horned grebes. Lesser yellowlegs. White-fronted geese. Ross's geese. Lesser sandhill cranes. Canada geese. Canvasbacks. Greater and lesser scaups. Western grebes. Mallards. Sandhill cranes. Whooping cranes.*

Whooping cranes.

Are we to pray that ExxonMobil suddenly discovers human kindness and a Franciscan regard for birds despite the corporate by-laws that make it illegal to do so? Are we to pray Syncrude's cannons "successfully" scare every duck and shorebird off the death ponds for the next thousand years? Are we to pray that blizzards at dusk will magically cease to be blinding? Are we to seek a house of worship with a God so dumbed down that He might deign to answer such stupid prayers? Or does the Dalai Lama nail it? *Prayer is good, as is meditation—but we also need prompt action!*

❧

In the coming few weeks ExxonMobil hopes to parade its monstrous modules past my home. If the Idaho resistance weren't battling so bravely they would already be passing. Our home is passive solar. The south-facing livingroom wall is double-paned glass from floor to ceiling. A wide eave keeps sunlight out in summer, when the angle of the sun is high, but lets sunlight all the way through to the interior north wall in winter. The design serves us well—but we've had to learn to close the Venetian blinds in some seasons, to keep birds from flying into the glass. In mating season, when males are setting up territories and chasing each other around in a blind passion, we still have a few collisions.

When my daughter Celia was eleven, a pine siskin flew into the window, then hung upside down in the bushes below, looking dead. She ran out and fetched it. The bird was still breathing. I sat down and showed her a sort of "procedure" I've learned from a life of bird-worship. My Warm Springs Indian friend, Liz Woody, discovered the same procedure, and had recently described it to me: when a bird hits a window and is knocked unconscious, you improve its chances if you hold it to your heart. Right up against the beating of it. (That's right, Syncrude: this is what it takes to actually serve a living bird.)

You hold it against your chest (I showed my daughter where, and she sheltered the little siskin). Then you promise the bird—silently or aloud: I prefer aloud—to be its steadfast guardian. *And you have to mean it.* You vow to sit still for as long as it takes, no time limit, letting the unconscious bird feel your pulse, your determination, your solid protection. You wish the little bird soul well no matter which world it decides to enter, ours or the other.

As Celia held the siskin I emphasized that it doesn't matter how busy you think you are. The bird's helplessness changes that. Unless someone is going to die while you're guarding it, don't worry. Give yourself completely to that bird. If we claim to 'love nature,' anything less is hypocrisy, because anything less is not love. I have been such a hypocrite, I told my daughter, and I have also been faithful. Faithful to me means: you sit with the bird in a gateway that leads beyond time and let the Unseen decide which way it will fly.

Last spring I held a male Downy woodpecker I felt sure would die. It had smashed the window so hard I checked the glass for breakage. I went out, gathered it up, cradled it, then sat in a chair on the back deck—in bright early spring sunlight—holding it to my heart. I began breathing my favorite prayer word onto the bird. Murmured spontaneous stuff, too.

I told it was okay to die, if that's what needed to happen, but that it's also beautiful to be a woodpecker. As I spoke, its tongue was lolling—and a Downy's tongue is a marvel. It is striped, black and off-white, and nearly three inches long though the entire bird is only seven inches long. What a *tool*, you realize as you gawk at the thing. No grub or beetle stands a chance.

The Downy's eyes stayed shut for close to an hour. Its neck looked ruined the whole time. But as it lay up close to my heart, warm in my hand, it kept breathing. So I worked with it, said my prayer word, held steady in the gate.

Then felt something. A slight quickening. The bird's *being* arrived from who knows where. It happened so fast. The limp body turned electric, the bird sprang back to consciousness, and its ruined neck—suddenly, *impossibly*—was fine.

I didn't even have time to stand. I just opened my hands. The Downy took one look at me—totem red, black and white, obsidian eye, a lightning look—then was off like a shot.

My daughter, too, held steady in the gate that day. And after a quarter hour her pine siskin filled her hands with the quickening. Opened its eyes.

Celia opened her hands. Received the lightning look. Away the siskin flew.

And my daughter's face as it winged away! When a bird falls into the unknown, lies against your heart, wakes and returns, flies from your hands, something in *you* quickens, awakens, and knows it too can fly.

⁊⋩

Widgeons fly about 45 miles per hour when nothing's troubling them. Grebes and buffleheads are faster, despite smaller wings. A red-breasted merganser was once clocked doing a hundred by the airplane that was chasing it. Teals—blue-winged, green-winged, cinnamon—doesn't matter—are thought by hunters to be the fastest ducks because of their rapid wing beat, but they are actually among the slowest: a mere thirty miles per hour. Phalaropes are of a different order of being altogether, flying with a tirelessness that carries them from Pole to diminishing Pole, suggesting that it is blithe innocence, not strip-mining and fracking, that produces the most vital forms of energy.

All these species pass through the boreal funnel. All seek water to feed and rest. All now negotiate, or fail to negotiate, the ponds of death. No flight speed, slow or fast, can help them if they land. Need I add, to the story of my daughter and a heart-held siskin, that when birds seen or unseen die by the thousand and the skies slowly empty, something in us dies as well?

Syncrude. Imperial. ExxonMobil. Blithely moving their chess pieces. Checkmating ducks, swans, cranes, crossbills.

Naked Earth. Calmly gripping her black pieces. Making the counter-moves she must.

❧

The chess-piece-black ravens I see over my home river valley are usually traveling from high mountains in the south to high mountains in the north. They never seem in a hurry. They weave, circle, chase each other, play games with hawks or crows. They peer down at my place from hundreds of feet overhead. When I hear their unmistakable call I rush out and call back sometimes, attempting to speak their language. I'm bad at it, but not shy about it, because every spring I hear the raven's fledglings, and they don't speak Raven either. In their youth they're total hacks at their own language! But I hear the patience of their parents. Hear how those big hollow *klooks* take practice. So I keep practicing, too.

What's been great about this practice is: if I've got a cold, so there's a little googy in my throat, my calls bring an occasional raven spiraling down from on high, in search of the unidentified caller. And what good-humored *kuk-kuk-kuks* they make when they spot the featherless, flightless me, grinning at them.

In the First Church of Birds we hold that any bird peering and calling down, and any human peering up and calling back, encourages greater care of the skies. Rilke names it:

Fling the emptiness of your arms into the spaces we breathe.
The birds will fill the air with more passionate flying.

I don't speak Loon, either, but never stop trying, because every loon I've heard for six years has sent a bolt to my heart. Here's how the first bolt struck:

Six years ago, driving home from Seattle, I saw a black plastic tarp lying in the fast lane on Interstate-90 near the St. Regis River in Montana. The tarp flapped, as the truck in front of me passed it, in a way that caught my eye. As I too passed, the "tarp" turned into a loon, lying by the truck-tire groove in the fast-lane. It had been rainy the night before. The bird, a young female, mistook moonlit freeway for water, and crash-landed. Loons must run on water to get back into the sky. There was no such water. So she had lain all day on cold concrete, saving herself, over and over, by dodging semi tires in the manner of a black flapping tarp.

I pulled over, threw it into reverse, backed up like a maniac, grabbed my winter coat, and sprinted across two lanes of freeway as a convoy of semis approached in the loon's lane. There was no time for gentle introductions: I threw my coat over her head, pulled her to my chest, and jumped into the grassy meridian just as the convoy reached us. That's when the bolt struck: as the coat-blinded bird felt this small, strange lift-off, she let out a full Far Northern tremolo that pierced, without stabbing, my skin, ribs, bloodstream, heart, day, life.

I drove her to a rescue center two hours away. Several times, en route, she let out more tremolos. How gratefully I swear I will never be the same.

"The bird rescue lady" (as my daughters called her) examined the I-90 loon, found no injury except a slightly chipped upper bill, and deftly replaced that bit with an eighth-inch-long minnow-catching tip sculpted out of epoxy.

We let the bird test her repaired beak in a water tank stocked with feeder goldfish. An hour after her freeway ordeal she was out-swimming the fish, gobbling one after another. A day after her ordeal she joined a flock of loons on Placid Lake, near Seeley Lake, Montana. There, too, she was fishing in no time.

In late spring this year, 2010, a loon arrived at those same lakes, visibly oil-damaged, almost certainly by the Gulf. There is no means of knowing how many Montana loons and other birds failed to survive the Gulf this year, and that's heart-breaking. But here's what my loon-pierced heart keeps saying about the paralysis such heart-break can engender:

Don't succumb. Don't kiss the rancid ass of despair. Wild birds still live with an integrity and courage that eludes humans, and when we make room for them in our lives, at our feeders, in our coats, cars, rescue centers, their integrity and courage awaken our own. Yes, these very awakenings are among the things Big Oil is killing. But the best revenge, the best defense of the remaining birds, is to awaken to your own integrity and courage even so.

Birds aren't the only winged ones in the inner wild. "The natural property of a wing," Socrates says in *The Phaedrus*, "is to raise that which is heavy and carry it aloft to the region where the gods dwell." This includes us. Flying up into integrity and courage takes effort. Flying at Big Oil in defense of Earth does, too. But the birds are still here to help us. Jesus' adage "*Consider the fowls of the air*" is not a complicated commandment. It means that when the male goldfinch or lazuli bunting dress to the nines to wow their womenkind, we should feel free to shout *Wow!* It means that when the bar-tailed godwit flies six thousand nautical miles in six days and nights without resting, we are perfectly entitled to compare that miracle to Muhammad's horseback ride to heaven or Jesus's stroll upon the sea. It means that when a bird calls down to you and the spirit moves, *call back to it.* The very sky is served by blithe inter-species conversation. Bird-to-human and human-to-bird contact touches the place in us that lives beyond space and time. Nothing has changed since the eighth century moment that caused Li Po to write:

> *The birds have vanished down the sky.*
> *Now the last cloud drains away.*
>
> *We sit together, the mountain and me,*
> *until only the mountain remains.*

Nothing has changed since the 13th century moment that moved Dogen to say:

> *The migrating bird*
> *leaves no trace behind*
> *and does not need a guide.*

Nothing has changed since the 20th century instant that caused Rilke to write:

> *The inner—what is it*
> *if not the intensified sky,*
> *hurled through with birds?*

The sky never ages, and birds, all their lives, pierce this timelessness. The sky makes room for sunlight, thunderheads, F-16's, the concertos of Mozart, the blat of Senate Gulf oil spill hearings, the hell fumes of Alberta, the bemused tunes of small children forging a life amid fumes—and birds fly all their lives through this spaciousness. "What Seymour loved most about the Bible was the word, 'Watch!'" wrote J.D. Salinger. And till the eyes fall from my head, I will. Birds save nothing, carry nothing, horde nothing, live song to song, seed to seed, sky to mouth, and the place they call to within us is recruiting more Tar Sands Resisters by the day.

My fellow bird-worshipper, Tom Crawford, has written our
Resistance a poem:

CHRISTOPHER COLUMBUS DISCOVERS
THE TAR SANDS OF ALBERTA

How did it happen
he got so far inside us?
You shave and you shave
and he still grows back
as wilderness caved in
under the iron shoes
of his horses.

The rumble we hear now,
the coming of giant modules
on flatbeds down our roads,
assaulting our towns,
our families.
They're not in the stars
dear reader but in ourselves,

and what's this new plan
five hundred years later
once they crawl their way to Alberta
on these Mammoets?

We're going to build a fire,
then we're going to cook the earth
'til it pukes its oil,

and if we have to—
that's right you're in the kitchen
on this one—I mean if we have to

we'll deep-fry 160 million waterfowl
and song birds in their summer
nurseries and nesting grounds.

How to save what's left?

Hard work.

You'll have to pull the Columbus in you
out from behind the wheel, America.

All good poems are hard work.
They say, *change your life.*

Change your life.

5. Destroying Democracies for a Big Oil Paycheck vs. Where To Live Once You're Paid

B RIAN SCHWEITZER AND OTHER BOOSTERS like to call Tar Sands oil "conflict-free" because it doesn't come directly from a petro-dictatorship. But history teaches, brutally, that democracy and oil extraction are mutually exclusive. History also teaches that the more expensive the oil, the faster and more thoroughly democratic freedoms vanish—and Tar Sands oil is the most expensive oil in the history of the industry. *New York Times* columnist Thomas Friedman has written about this powerfully, calling the ratio between oil price per barrel, and loss of freedom, an axiom of our age. "Thinking about how to alter our energy consumption patterns to bring down the price of oil," Friedman writes, "is no longer simply a hobby for high-minded environmentalists, or some personal virtue. It is now a national security imperative."

Brian Schweitzer and Butch Otter are in way over their heads. Henry Kissinger was not whistling "My Home's in Montana I Wear a Bandana" when he said, "Control oil and you control nations." Alberta's environmental minister, Rob Renner, manifested Kissinger's dictum and history's harsh pattern when he defended rampant Tar Sands development with the words: "It's not the role of Alberta Environment to advocate on behalf of the environment." Coming from a man responsible for the health and safety of Canadian citizens, this statement reveals a collapse of the democratic system.

Another mistaken belief of Tar Sands boosters is that supporting the ruin of Canada will cure the United States of its addiction to oil. According to the U.S. Energy Information Administration, the U.S. consumes 18,771,000 barrels per day, half of that to fuel cars and trucks.

That's roughly one-billion-two-hundred-million gallons. To maintain this level of consumption a supertanker must dock somewhere in the U.S. every four hours. As Andrew Nikiforuk points out in *Tar Sands: Dirty Oil and the Future of a Continent*: "To replace Persian Gulf imports alone, the United States would have to drain *all* of Canada's projected (Tar Sands) crude production by 2016: 3.8 million barrels a day." The Tar Sands, in short, will do next-to-nothing to make America energy independent. Oil imports from the Middle East and South America will continue as long as the U.S. remains addicted to fossil fuel.

The boosters also claim that neither the Tar Sands nor the proposed pipelines that would crisscross thirty-two American states will require a military presence. These are half-truths at best. Tar Sands development, like rampant oil development in any petro-state, has dragged Alberta away from genuine democratic representation, not the other way around. Boomtown chaos reigns in Fort McMurray and has spread to Edmonton and Calgary. Police forces and emergency services are overwhelmed. The military is being called in to help. Alberta's enviably civil society of past decades grows less civil by the day.

This has been the case almost everywhere that Big Oil has done business. The Tar Sands tentacle through Oregon, Washington, Idaho and Montana is already using homeland security operations on the Columbia and Snake River barging corridor, and will soon deploy police escorts as the giant modules creep through our comparatively mild states. Later, the thousands of miles of Tar Sands oil pipelines headed for thirty-two American states could become targets not only for organized terrorists but for any disgruntled and armed person, any vandal, any kook. Military or police presence will greatly increase. And even with those freedom-reducing forces in place—as my friends Bruce, Marlene, and Liam unforgettably demonstrate for me—the safety of pipelines are a national scandal and their history of catastrophe is unending.

The only way to achieve genuine "national security" and true "energy independence" is to strike out in the bold new green direction that Brian Schweitzer, of all people, recommended, to the greatest cheers he ever received, back in 2008.

The $200 plus billion spent on Tar Sands development could have worked wonders for that industry. Instead, it has created contemporary Alberta.

The Tar Sands capital of the world, Fort McMurray, is sometimes known now as "Fort McMordor," but is most commonly known as "Fort McMoney." U.S. companies have poured about sixty percent of the $200 billion invested in the city and its neighboring Sands so far. Billions more have come from France, Norway, China, Japan, the Middle East. The labor pool comes from Mexico, Hungary, India, Romania, or the Atlantic coast of Canada, where cod fishermen became unemployed after government policies destroyed fish stocks. The same government is now destroying the fish stocks of northern Alberta with Tar Sands poison. When labor gets short, oil companies fly in temporary "guest workers" from China. Every oil giant in the world including the Abu Dhabi National Energy Company, Syneco Energy, the national oil company of China, the national oil company of South Korea, Norway's Statoil, Japan's Canada Oil Sands Limited, and the usual suspects—Shell, Chevron, BP, ExxonMobil, Conoco Phillips—are invested in the Tar Sands. What these investments and "spin-off benefits" have created is a sneak preview of what a Tar Sands tentacle could do for the Northwest and Northern Rockies:

•Alberta's school drop out rates and divorce rates are now the highest in the nation.

•Alberta's women suffer the highest level of spousal abuse in Canada.

•Drug abuse has also skyrocketed. The Tar Sands boom has created fantastic opportunities for the Hell's Angels, Indian Posse, and other entreprenurial drug dealers. By some estimates as much as $7 million worth of cocaine now travels up Highway 63 every week on transport trucks. According to *The Economist*, "about forty percent of the Tar Sands work force test positive for cocaine and marijuana use in job screening and post accident tests." Health food stores can't keep enough urine cleanse products in stock for workers worried about random drug trials. There is a black market in clean urine.

•Alberta's premier, Ed Stelmach, calls such facts "the price of prosperity." Welcome to Big Oil's idea of prosperity.

•Fort McMoney reports five times more drug offenses than the rest of Alberta. Ordering crack cocaine at a work camp is said to be easier than ordering a pizza. Contractors claim they'd lose half their crews if they did drug testing. The first question ambulance crews ask men with chest pains is "Are you on cocaine?" •Fort McMoney has an 89 percent higher rate of assault and a 117 percent higher rate of impaired driving than the next-most-dangerous city in Canada. •The price of a single-family home has risen from $174,000 to over $600,000 in a decade. Even a mobile trailer can cost $300,000. In wintertime, many tradespeople plaster a vacation trailer with bubble wrap, tarps and insulation then camp out in minus-40 degree weather. •Fort McMoney has become a frigid urban nightmare. Its infrastructure deficit was $2 billion in 2008. Inflation is rampant. A recreation facility budgeted at $23.4 million in 2005 ballooned to $200 million by 2008. The water treatment plant went from $39 million to a staggering $218 million in the same three-year span.

•A local named Ted labored in the bitumen industry for years. He once worked ten hour shifts for 24 days straight before getting four days off. One employer offered Ted $50,000 a month if he would deal cocaine at work camps. He refused. In 2002, after all his hard work, he was able to buy a house in the Tar Sands suburb of Timberlea. The pollution from the Sands was so severe that it corroded his brass door and fixtures and left a constant film of soot on his windows. Ted was ill almost constantly, until he moved away.

I could go on to describe the psychological and sociological symptoms of boomtown devastation. I could depict the purportedly "reclaimed" areas amid the Tar Sands wastelands that amount, in the words of Andrew Nikoforuk, "to little more than putting lipstick on a corpse." But the aforementioned statistic really says it: 98 percent of the people working in Fort McMurray say they want to move away as soon as they've saved the cash to do so.

❧

Brian Schweitzer's claim of "conflict-free oil" is not only blind to Alberta's growing social disasters, it is inviting the same disasters into our region, daily lives, roads, hospitals, homes. Schweitzer's claim is blind to Archbishop Tutu's cry on behalf of the millions of Africans (and others) facing death due to the effects of global warming. And it is a political chimera:

Nearly every stable democracy in the world remains a democracy because it *lacks major oil reserves.* The United Arab Emirates, Iran, Kuwait,

Iraq, Iran, and Saudi Arabia—the petro-superpowers—are none of them open, free or democratic. Only Kuwait sports an elected parliament—and it is all male. In Central and South America, only oil-free Costa Rica has avoided dictatorship since World War II. The oil-producing countries to our south have been, or still are, ruled by oil-rich despots. As for East Asia: oil-less Japan was the first democracy after World War II, followed by Korea, Taiwan, and the Philippines. Meanwhile, sitting atop their sizable oil reserves, Indonesia and Malaysia declined—or were prevented—from entering into the process of democratic reform.

Oil oligarchs are diverse, ranging from the Sultan of Brunei, the General Secretary of the Communist Party of China, the King of Saudi Arabia, the Mexican Party of Revolutionary Institutions (PRI), and Iran's Shiite clergy, to Dick Cheney. But all are oligarchical by definition—which is to say, all use oil and gas revenues to purchase and dominate their country's respective political systems. They also, unanimously, perpetuate poverty to serve their dominance. The U.N.'s Human Development Index (HDI) ranks countries' ability to provide basic education, health and welfare to their citizens. Chile, Jordan, Panama, Uruguay, Mauritius and Jamaica, despite lower per capita incomes, all have higher HDI ratings than the United Arab Emirates, Iran, and Iraq. India's HDI ranks far above oil-rich Nigeria's. Costa Rica, with its per capita income of just $1,100 per annum, is a better place to live than any major oil-producing country, boasting a life expectancy of seventy-five and a literacy rate of ninety-three percent.

Yes, Western democracies run on fuels sold by despotic regimes—and Tar Sands boosters point to this fact with indignation. But if we look at the history of every nation that has become a petro-state—including Canada today—we see that oil despotism steadily corrodes even Western governments. Big Oil has overrun our northern neighbor's democratic institutions. The government now funds bribes for regulatory officials, establishes slush-funds for pseudo-scientific PR to reassure the public that living in hell is good for our health, and underwrites lavish rewards geared most often to the military and, of course, the corporate elite. This is the kind of governance preferred by Big Oil the world over, and it is repeatedly established and maintained. History teaches this again and again. Two telling examples:

In the 1950's British Petroleum overthrew Iran's democratically elected prime minister, Mohammed Mosseddegh, when he made good on his promise to nationalize Iran's oil fields. The CIA orchestrated the coup. New oil contracts were divvied among American oil companies, the puppet Shah (Richard Nixon's pal) was installed as Iran's leader, and he ruled brutally until the Islamic revolution ushered in the era of mullahs.

In the 1960's, Iraqi leader Abdul Kassim helped found OPEC as a means of loosening the West's stranglehold on Arab oil revenues. Like Iran's Mossedegh, Kassim was about to nationalize the British-owned Iraq Petroleum Company, when he was overthrown in a coup orchestrated by U.S. and British intelligence. Saddam Hussein was placed in power, toting a hit list created with the help of the CIA. Kassim was killed. Five thousand doctors, lawyers, teachers, and professors were rounded up and summarily executed.

When Western intelligence agencies refuse to uproot democracies for Big Oil, the companies sometimes take on the job themselves. Governor Schweitzer has been trying to boost the Tar Sands by saying that the U.S. should avoid doing business with countries as chaotic and damaged as Nigeria. What he would be saying if he knew his history is that the U.S. should avoid doing business with Shell Oil after what it did to Nigeria. A civil war in the 1980's—again, over the flow of oil revenues—caused the death of more than two million Nigerians, mainly civilians. Shell oversaw that conflict, gaining control of oil production in the Nigerian Delta. Oil pollution then began killing the mangrove ecosystem on which life in the Delta depends. In the 1990's, democratic opposition to Shell's poisoning reached critical mass. The Ogoni people native to the Delta started a powerful protest movement against Shell's assault on Nigerian waters. Massive demonstrations led to the democratic election of a new Nigerian president. The Nigerian military countered by voiding the election, installing a dictator general, destroying twenty-seven Ogoni villages, murdering 2,000 people, and rendering another 30,000 homeless. Ken Saro-Wiwa and other Ogoni leaders were arrested, tried, and executed. After intense scrutiny by the press, Shell admitted to importing guns used for the military takeover. Shell also underwrote the costs of the operation and paid bonuses to those who made it happen.

Governor Schweitzer now points to the wretched condition of Nigeria as reason to rush Tar Sands oil into the States and establish an ExxonMobil tentacle through our region. Connect the dots, Governor! These are the same brand of corporate powers that overthrew Nigerian democracy.

The overlords of petro-states undermine or attack democratic government because democracies sometimes serve their citizens, not just oil companies. This is why ExxonMobil has tried to prevent any objective environmental and economic assessment of their Tar Sands tentacle. And it is why there is no more important defense of democracy in our region today than to hold our leaders to their sworn duties and boot ExxonMobil's Tar Tentacle out. The dictatorial moves of oil oligarchs have no place in rural Idaho and Montana.

※

Two last examples of why ExxonMobil cannot be trusted:

Four days after the Exxon Valdez spill of 1989, ExxonMobil spokesman Don Cornett said to Cordova, Alaska fishermen and citizens, "We're doing the best job that's ever been done on an oil spill. And watch. Just watch. You have had some good luck, and you don't realize it. You have ExxonMobil, and we do business straight."

•The 38 million gallons of "good luck" spilled by "ExxonMobil, doing business straight" then proceeded to kill roughly half a million seabirds, 5,000 sea otters, 300 or so harbor seals, and billions of young salmon and herring fish eggs and juvenile fish. It was the largest animal and fish kill in history. •The health of clean-up workers and residents was inadequately protected, as in the Gulf. And the damages from the spill, to humans and scores of species, *continue to this day.* •Fishermen impoverished by the spill were promised compensation checks that in many cases, after 23 years, have still not been paid. •In 1994 a jury ordered ExxonMobil to bay $5 billion in damages to 33,000 plaintiffs. •ExxonMobil appealed the verdict. In 2006, the ninth circuit court cut the damage award in half, to $2.5 billion. •In June of 2009, the U.S. Supreme Court cut that to $500 million—about four days' worth of ExxonMobil profits. (Flashback: *You have ExxonMobil and we do business straight.*") •In the years since, fifteen of twenty-four species have not fully recovered from the spill, and herring, one of the foundations of the food chain, have never returned at all. A report marking the twentieth anniversary, put together by the Exxon Valdez Oil Spill Trustee

Council, states, "The remaining oil will take decades and possibly centuries to disappear."

Final example of how deadly ExxonMobil's power can be, and of how little the supposed "transparency" of corporate business practices can do to lesson the danger:

In Indonesia in the late 1990's, ExxonMobil made security arrangements with the military and police to support their oil venture there. These hired forces were soon responsible for civilian massacres and human rights abuses. In May 2001, one Radhi Darmansyah traveled from Indonesia to the United States in a desperate attempt to plead for mercy with ExxonMobil's then-CEO, Lee Raymond, at a public and "transparent" stockholder meeting. I acquired a text of the meeting transcript from the socially responsible investment firm, Trillium, who holds a little ExxonMobil stock so they can attend shareholder meetings and try to cultivate justice and compassion in the proceedings. A telling bit of transcript:

Radhi Darmansyah: "While you made $26 million as a CEO last year Mr. Raymond, more than one thousand six hundred of my people were killed, maimed or tortured around your facilities in Aceh. I am here to ask for your help. We, the Acehnese, are asking that ExxonMobil stop working with the Indonesian military for its security forces, because the military is murdering its citizens in Aceh. Murdering my brothers and sisters. Raping and keeping schoolgirls as sexual slaves. I ask you today to please issue a public statement that you will not return to Aceh until my land is free of these human rights abuses and my people are free."

ExxonMobil CEO Lee Raymond: "I believe your time is up."

By my watch, reading the words over, Radhi Darmansyah's speech took perhaps 45 seconds. He is entitled to three minutes at such meetings. He continues pleading for his people.

Raymond butts in: "I'm sorry, you'll have to come back another time. Sister Pat, I think we're about to move on to the next item. You have three minutes."

Darmansyah continues pleading for his people.

Raymond blares: "Sister Pat, he's using *your* time... I think you should turn off the light of Number 1 please. You understand you're out of order?"

Darmansyah, of course, continues pleading for his devastated people.

Raymond: "Sister Pat, please! I'm getting ready to move on to the next item."

Darmansyah, bless him!, continues pleading. Raymond ignores him. Raymond also fails to call on Bianca Jagger, who is standing at a microphone ready to support Darmansyah's claims. Instead, the ExxonMobil CEO blusters: "Sister Pat has the floor. Thank you."

On the contrary: no thank you, Lee Raymond. I repeat: the silent, dictatorial moves of oil oligarchs have no place in Idaho and Montana.

I understand *realpolitik*. I understand that, from the perspective of a Beltway insider, it is a kind of mad naiveté to refuse to abide by the Supreme Court verdict that grants "personhood" to corporations and equates election-purchasing by multi-national corporations with the "free speech" of mortal, and increasingly poor, Americans.

But I also understand the word *compassion*. It means "to suffer with another." Both the Buddha and the Christ are considered the apotheosis of this essential human quality. In defense of this human quality we must be clear in our minds that when an ExxonMobil CEO speaks as Lee Raymond did to Radhi Darmansyah, a conversation between two human beings has not unfolded. This is the silencing of what it means to be a human being.

A corporation is not a "person" in any genuine sense no matter what the Supreme Court claims. As the late Daniel Moynihan liked to say, "Everyone is entitled to their own opinions, but no one is entitled to their own facts." The deaths and damages in Aceh, Indonesia and in Nigeria are facts, the deaths and damages in the Tar Sands are facts, the deaths and damages in Prince William Sound, Alaska are facts. If we who are human wish to remain so, such facts cannot be smothered or denied. To explain away events this dire is to smother the essential elements of human life, human freedom, human breath.

6. The Road

Wᴴᴇɴ ᴛʜᴇ ɢᴏᴠᴇʀɴᴏʀs ᴏғ Iᴅᴀʜᴏ and Montana jumped on board the Let's-Be-A-Tar-Sands-Tentacle band wagon, locals began asking whether Big Oil's industrial corridor through our regions and neighborhoods would at least be physically safe. The answer is a resounding *No*. Truck wrecks are so common on the 203 miles of Highway 12 joining Lewiston, Idaho to Lolo, Montana that the Swift Trucking Company of Lewiston no longer uses it. I have a collection of small pieces of crashed semi-trucks, cars, and motorcycles I've plucked out of the Lochsa and Clearwater Rivers while fishing along the exacting curves of Highway 12. A pair of black leather Harley bags complete with tattered fringe, filled with river sand. East Coast license plates with stonefly husks stuck to them. The half-crushed horn of a semi-truck I call "The Horn of Boromir," after the bugle used to warn of danger in Tolkien's *Lord of the Rings*. As a former cornet player I can get a pretty heinous sound out of that truck horn. When I'm feeling random I sometimes scare the crap out of friends, or my dogs, by blowing the thing out my study window and yelling, *"Boromir's in trouble!"*

If Boromir were a Tar Sands module-mover headed for Idaho and Montana Highways 12, 200, 287 and 89, he'd be in trouble indeed. Avalanches, icy surfaces, falling rock, torrential rains, blinding blizzards, and landslides all take out semis and cars on these roads. In several cases (including the wreck in the earlier photo of the avalanche on the Lochsa) the drivers who end up in the rivers or canyons made no error at all. And, as you see below, Tar Sands modules like those headed for our very challenging byways have crashed in Alberta on four-lane straightaways, simply because their tremendous weight collapsed their steel trailers.

Accident involving a heavy haul module on August 31, 2010, just north of Breton, Alberta. Photograph courtesy of *The Western Review*.

This is my road. I know it intimately. Big Oil is asking its drivers to drag 650,000 pound loads over highways rated for 80,000 pounds, and over bridges made of aged creosoted timbers (at Lolo Hot Springs in Montana), and over aged concrete and steel rated for 76,000 pounds (at Fish Creek in Idaho). In the towns of Orofino, Kamiah, Kooskia, Lolo, Missoula, Choteau, the rigs will be crossing underground sewers, gas lines, power lines, water mains. When damage occurs it will be unseen till the loads are long gone, so it's locals who will suffer the consequences and pay for repairs.

The Two Stooges of Tar Sands Assurances, Butch Otter and Imperial Oil, claim to have addressed the public's concern, but this line of work is clearly not their forté:

•When asked at a public meeting about potential damages to U.S. highways from 300 ton loads, Butch Otter stated, "The impact to the highway probably won't be any more than a one-ton pickup." The next question should have been: "Governor Otter. Which of the two—pickup or Tar Sands module—would you prefer to have drive over your foot?"

•When asked how Imperial Oil would deal with a tip-over and dumping of a module into the Lochsa River, IO spokesman Dan Johnson told the public at the ill-fated summer meeting in Kooskia, "We could have a crane here from Spokane in ten hours." What Johnson failed to mention is that no crane of this size is available in Spokane; that a five-hundred-ton crane is an even more problematic transportation problem than the module it would set out to retrieve; that such a crane would require a 45-by-45-foot reinforced level pad on a highway that for eighty percent of its length is only twenty-four feet wide; that a frigid river gorge lies on one side of this twenty-four foot ribbon and sheer granite cliffs or massive mountains forbid construction on the other side; and that even if construction were possible, a crane can only tilt twenty degrees from vertical, so it couldn't reach out over the river to retrieve the module anyway. (Google "best crane wrecks" to see evidence of this. It's almost fun, like watching heavy industry's version of rodeo bull-riding. "Huge Crane Tips Over" is a multi-cultural YouTube classic, though I must give it a severe R rating, for language.)

࿐

Another rocky topic: *topography*. When ExxonMobil's bean-counters were "crunching the numbers" that sent ExxonMobil first to Korean steel factories, then to the Northwest in search of a solution to their self-created transport problem, any fifth grade geography student could have saved the company potential millions by showing them a contour map. Those squiggly lines on contour maps, the child could have explained, indicate *elevation changes*. A whole bunch of these lines in a small amount of space—as when you approach Lolo Pass on the Idaho/Montana border, or Rogers Pass at the top of the Big Blackfoot—means the terrain is *really steep*. Dense contour lines are, so to speak, the fingerprints God leaves behind as He sculpts the world. The highway traverses these sculptures. Not even the most expensive televised PR bulljive alters God's sculptures. It dumbfounds me each time I say it: ExxonMobil wants to drag many hundreds of the heaviest loads in highway history over six hundred miles of some of the most dramatic topographical sculpture in America.

The Wall Street Journal, bless its cosmopolitan heart, recently tried to grasp the apparent insanity of ExxonMobil's first choice for its Tar Sands tentacle route. In an October 22, 2010 article, a *WSJ* pundit conceded that the upper Lochsa River and Lolo Pass looked tough, but then he wrote, "From Missoula, the modules can be hauled across flatlands to the U.S.-Canada border at Sweetgrass, Montana." As a former recycling truck driver who remembers fondly the camaraderie between truckers, I urge ExxonMobil/Imperial mega-load drivers to purchase a good topo map *before The Wall Street Journal kills you.* The upper Lochsa, brother or sister trucker, is impassable to start with on *many* days of the year. *Please,* especially if you're married with kids, check out Milepost 157 in advance. Look at that cliff! Look at that river canyon! Look at the asphalt sloughing into the river on the highway side, *your* side, of the guard rail!

Lolo Pass could take you out if the Lochsa doesn't. And your troubles aren't even close to over. On the Montana portion of ExxonMobil's Tar Sands tentacle (should you make it through Missoula without being stopped by grandma-and-grampa to grade-school-aged activists), you'll be dragging your 650,000 pound loads, through the dead of night in the dead of winter, over a *Wall Street Journal* "flatland" consisting of another two hundred miles of very hilly and curvy road (Highway 200) running dangerously close, in places, to the world famous Big Blackfoot River. You will then have to surmount another *WSJ* "flatlands" feature known to the rest of us as *the ROCKY MOUNTAINS*, where you'll attempt a tortuous crossing of the CONTINENTAL DIVIDE over 5700 foot Rogers Pass, home of the coldest temperature ever recorded in the lower forty-eight. (And the thermometer *broke* at minus 70°.) We who have driven and hiked such terrain all our lives don't consider it fussy to warn that wintry mountains rife with "God's fingerprints" are not "flat," and will not let ExxonMobil's mega-gear pass on to the Tar Sands without putting up a hell of a fight.

Last thought: maybe Fed-Ex or UPS are hiring!

❧

One of the most annoying facts underlying ExxonMobil's insane choice of transportation route is that the modules they hope to ship, barge, and drag from Korea, through the Northwest and Rockies, to the Tar Sands, could have been fabricated in Nisku or Leduc, Alberta. Workers there are furious that ExxonMobil and Imperial outsourced this massive contract. But it's an old story: by going overseas, Big Oil can break the price structure of Canadian module fabricators. Soon Canadian workers will be begging for jobs at South Korean wages. ExxonMobil's profit, the year that happens, could be $9,875,412 billion. Invest now!—if you don't believe in karma, the afterlife, Dante Alighieri, or those wild Buddhist "guardian demons" who follow condemned spirits around on the blazing hot iron floors of Buddhist Hell, jamming molten copper balls into their mouths over and over, which balls plow down through their intestines and burst, still scalding, out their anuses, but alas, in that realm it's impossible to die, so as soon as it is over it happens again.

Where was I? Oh yeah: the galling thing about ExxonMobil's corporate ball-busting games in Nisku and Leduc, is that the richest company in the world now demands to run their union-busting gear, like a molten copper ball, through the Northwest and Northern Rockies. Are we to agree with them that America has become a Buddhist hell? Is ExxonMobil our divinely appointed guardian demon?

I don't think so.

The Lochsa River. Photograph by Steve Pettit.

※

I can joke about topographical stupidity and gubernatorial arrogance. I can even half-joke about ExxonMobil's resemblance to the demons of both Christian and Buddhist hell realms.

I cannot joke about how offensive ExxonMobil's Tar Sands tentacle will be for historical and cultural reasons if it is established. Big Oil's CO_2-spewing cargo will creep through a National Historic route established in honor of the generosity, and later sufferings, of the Nez Perce people. This legendary and still sovereign nation saved the lives of the Lewis and Clark Expedition not once, but twice. Their kindnesses were later rewarded with one of the most unjust treaties ever imposed on an Indian nation (which is saying something), illegally negating a far more favorable treaty that had been signed and validated eight years before— an injustice uncorrected to this day. The route Chief Joseph and the Nez Perce traveled as they were forced to flee their homeland—the route they took en route to the Big Hole battlefield, where sleeping women and children were slaughtered before dawn—will now be traversed by strip-mining behemoths headed for a Tar Sands travesty that is demolishing the lives and lifeways of more First Nations people at Fort Chipewyan. And don't forget: ExxonMobil is also usurping the last best salmon river in the West—the Columbia/Snake—to float their modules to Idaho. Nez Perce lifeways—so contingent upon the wild salmon guaranteed to them in perpetuity by treaty—will be demolished by the Tar Sands' fifty-year demand for the salmon- and steelhead-killing lower Snake River dams.

※

Enough madness. I need to turn to what sustains the heart of me:

There are cedar groves along ExxonMobil's proposed Heavy Haul route that are three-thousand-years old. These groves bathe you, the instant you step beneath their canopy, in a green, fragrant, almost watery light that creates its own coolness on even the hottest summer day. People don't call them "cathedral groves" for nothing.

The Devoto Grove on the Crooked Fork of the Lochsa is one such wild church I favor. There is a particular three-thousand-year-old cedar there that I feel I'm getting to know. Its bole looks like the hoof of some ancient god. Its trunk looks more like a cliff-face than flora. A hundred feet in the air this giant divides into three spires, each living steeple bigger than the tallest pines in my yard at home. A tree this old is a visible history of the integrity of its own being. It reaches deep into the era of the Nez Perce, the Blackfeet, the Salish Kootenai, the Palouse. It was five hundred years old at the time of the Buddha, a thousand years old at the time of the Christ, and more than two thousand years old before "America" was even named. And to this day—if one stands quiet in its company—this tree reveals something silent but towering about the antiquity and integrity of Buddhist, Christian, Sufi, Vedic, Hebraic, Druidic, mystical, and indigenous traditions.

When I visited the cedar, alone, in September, I lay in the ferns beneath, looked up into the three spires, thought about the proposed ExxonMobil invasion just sixty or so yards away, and some kind of eddy inside me started to spin. In an ancient Haida myth, a naked young woodpecker seeing a white and barkless place high on the trunk of an ancient tree, claws its way up, and starts pecking at the bald wood. Inside the tree, an extra-natural being, Old Man White-as-a-Gull, says: *Your father's father asks you in.* The young woodpecker enters. Inside the dark hollow, Old Man makes his presence known, sees the bird's nakedness, and recognizes its need. He picks up a box, inside which is a smaller box, inside which is another, box after concentric box. In the fifth such box Old Man finds what he's seeking: *feathers.* He presents the fledgling with the plumage and colors that become its protection, its power of flight, its very identity.

In the unseen eddy beneath a three-thousand-year-old cedar I remembered Old Man's invitation: *Your father's father asks you in.* Then heard a Jesus sentence, *In My Father's house are many mansions.* Then a Buddha sentence, *Better than a thousand hollow words is one word that brings peace.* The green water light sifted down. The tree shed its ancient patience. The eddy spun. By banging on the hollow of a tree a naked woodpecker was clothed and empowered. By sitting decisively down beneath a Bo Tree, Prince Gautama discovered all Truth hidden in the depths of Self, became the Buddha, and showed millions a Way. By calling bread his body, wine his blood, and asking his lovers to break that body and spill that blood, Jesus foretold his death on the arms of a tree, forging another Way.

Native elders, versed in natural and extra-natural patterns and in outer and inner forms of light, refer unceasingly to unseen but life-giving intelligences and powers. Upon contact with Europeans the names of these intelligences got translated into English words like "totem spirit," "animal essence," "god." Hearing such words, the conquistadors, missionaries, and executives of Dominion, oblivious to natural patterns or inner light, began telling indigenous people: "You've got it wrong. There is one God, Jesus is his only son, stop worshipping your false nature gods, forget ancient tree spirits, totems, concentric boxes and feathers, come sit in a Box of Worship every Sunday. We'll sing Rock of Ages, teach you about our Dominion over you, and on the six days that aren't Sabbath we'll clearcut your forests, sterilize your salmon streams, knock down your totem poles, sell them to the British Museum, and it'll be highly profitable for us and maybe not so great for you, but your souls will be saved no matter how terrible the world becomes as we go on saving it."

The sermons of Dominion have encircled the world for 500 years. ExxonMobil, come to the Northwest, is just the latest rank preacher. The root of the word "indigenous" is the Latin *indigen,* meaning *a genuine need.* Like the needs for air, fire, healthy soil, water, food. The industrial exploitations preached by Dominionists have no more to do with the indigenous blessings bestowed by God on the first page of Genesis, by Buddha in the Sutras, by Jesus in the Gospels, or by indigenous elders in their myths, than thralldom has to do with complete freedom. If the Dominion-blinded truly see, in the devastation of the Tar Sands, an "industrial waltz" that "really looks good in the natural habitat," let them move there.

St. Catherine of Sienna said, *"All the way to heaven is heaven."* The Buddha said, *"Count nothing as one's own."* The Book of Leviticus says we're all renters, not owners. St. John of the Cross said: *"The soul's interrogation of wild creatures is the consideration of the Creator, through those creatures. This divine reflection onto creatures, and our observing that they are things made by the very hand of God, strongly awakens the soul to love."* Amen, says a three-thousand-year old cedar, a newly feathered woodpecker, and me. We have passed through our five-hundred-year Missionaries-of-Dominion phase. It is all over but the shouting. Every person of sense I know, every non-thrall, realizes humanity is dying for lack of the extra-natural wisdom that can pass on, intact, a world wild and vital enough to sustain our children and "awaken the soul to love."

Sunrise through fog on the Clearwater River. Photograph by Steve Pettit.

Pilgrimage to these vital points of contact does not take place in a vacuum. The natural mysteries and forces that create, restore and beautify this crucified world thrive on wild and scenic rivers, along wilderness byways, on high mountain ridgelines, and in the muted light and silence of cathedral groves. The preservation of these points of contact *is an end in itself.* It's what these places are for. The United States was astoundingly prescient to establish sanctuaries of natural pattern and wild wisdom. To run these sanctuaries through with hundreds of Tar Sands modules is a betrayal of the sacred driven by the same venal logic that leads to the slaughter of native peoples, the destruction of countless species, the death of Deltas and boreal forest, and the death of Jesus himself.

I am in love with a three-thousand-year-old cedar on the Crooked Fork in Idaho. No matter how this fleeting fight with ExxonMobil goes, that cedar will go on towering with integrity, rooted in pre-America, breathing in the Now. Our wilds are a living holiness. They are intact archives of the most sustaining forms of knowledge to which we have access. Held in reverence, these places whisper truths that, heeded, would circumvent Gulf oil blow-outs, boreal bird-slaughter, and Arctic ice sheets the size of Montana falling into the seas. For all my love of solitude I pray millions more enter the living cathedrals, that hearts may find rest and lives find direction there. *Your father's father asks you in. In My Father's house are many mansions. Better than a thousand hollow words is one word that brings peace.*

7. Natural Pattern, Natural Compassion, & Humanity's Hope

THERE IS A WILD OF INFINITE dimension that exists outside of us, and a wild of infinite dimension within us. Paul Valéry: *There is another world, but it is in this one.* Jim Harrison: *There is an invisible world out there—and we're living in it.* People focussing upon this cusp between inner and outer wild are addressing the world's wounds, and humanity's needs, more effectively than they've been addressed in centuries—an enormous cause for hope.

There are subtle patterns in nature that correspond to subtle patterns within our deepest self. When we explore the wild world alertly, we perceive these patterns, feel resonations, and make vital discoveries. For five hundred years and counting—and with unparalleled violence in the past quarter-century—industrial humanity has too often attacked nature. But for aeons before the age of attack, nature *partnered* with humanity. A great many astute men and women, looking anew for such partnerships, are discovering wondrous things. Velcro, to cite a first quick example appealing to the capitalist in us all, resulted from careful study of the wild burr—and you should see the Grand Rapids, Michigan mansion of the guy who figured that out. A quick sampling from among thousands of old and new natural partnerships:

•The alkaloids of Madagascar periwinkles (*Catharanthus roseus*) are used in chemotherapy for Hodgkin's disease and some forms of childhood leukemia. •Steroids derived from the Mexican yam are now used for everything from easing asthma to hitting technologically-dishonest home runs. •The popular drug Echinacea, extracted from Narrow-leaved Purple Coneflower, was used by Plains tribes to treat toothache, sore throat, and rattlesnake bite and is now used to ease the common cold. •Pharmaceutical companies now routinely send researchers after native elders to help find the plants that may provide the bases of possible new drugs.

Gigantism, in the creation of energy, is invariably violent. There are thousands of more intimate technologies that could end this violence— and do, when people dare to free themselves from the greed-driven gigantism of Corporate-think:

•There are wind generators so small and efficient that they could stand by the million atop telephone poles or rooftops, powering us sans coal, never harming a bird, never dumping mercury in a river or acid rain on a forest, never creating autism in a child. •There are hydro-electric cylinders that could spin in the current of tidal zones and rivers, never harming a fish; in vast numbers they would facilitate the removal of unnecessary dams, sending thousands of would-be organic farmers forth to re-settle the millions of acres of fertile farmland now lost beneath slackwater reservoirs. •There are buoys that are capturing the incessant energy of ocean wave action, providing power to small coastal cities without harming a single living thing.

•There is a fabulously inexpensive form of solar power on its way to us from legendary green entrepreneur, Paul Hawken, scientist John Warner, and the Bitterroot Valley's own Janine Benyus, compliments of careful meditation on the ordinary deciduous leaf.

•Janine also co-founded the Biomicicry Institute, "biomimicry" being "the science and art of emulating Nature's best ideas to solve human problems." The successes of this new discipline are both financially lucrative and poetically moving. A few breakthroughs:

•The Shinkansen Bullet Train in Japan is the fastest in the world, traveling 200 miles per hour. The problem? Sound! Air pressure changes, when the train shot from a tunnel, produced virtual "thunder claps" that traumatized the people who lived within earshot. Eiji Nakatsu, the train's chief engineer, is an avid bird-watcher. Perusing the unwritten library of nature for a shape that shoots quickly but smoothly between two different mediums, Nakatsu noticed how the beaks of kingfishers enable them to dive from air into water with barely a splash. Modeling the front-end of his train after a kingfisher beak resulted not only in a much quieter train, but in the use of fifteen percent less electricity, and a ten percent increase in speed.

•One of the most water repellent leaves in the world is that of the Lotus. The microscopic crevices covering the leaf's surface entrap a maze of air upon which water droplets float. The slightest breeze or tilt of leaf then causes this water to roll cleanly away—and the departing droplets take dirt particles with them. Eureka! Biomimics began adding microscopically rough surface-additives to a new generation of paint, glass, and fabric finish. These finishes greatly reduce the need for cleaning. GreenShield, for example, a fabric finish based on the lotus effect, achieves the same water and stain repellency as conventional finishes but uses eight times less fluorinated chemicals to do it.

•Fans and other rotational devices are major users of power. Humans have been building fans since at least 100 B.C., but not till biomimicry did we build them as Nature does. Nature moves water and air in the same logarithmic, exponentially growing spiral commonly seen in seashells. Anyone who's ever watched a redtail hawk ride a thermal has witnssed this. The same pattern shows up in the curl of elephant trunks, tails of chameleons, pattern of swirling galaxies in space, and cochlea of your ear. PAX Scientific Inc. applied this geometry to human-made rotary fans, mixers, propellers, turbines and pumps for the first time. The resulting designs, used in a multitude of ways, reduced energy usage on average by a up to eighty-five percent over conventional rotors, and reduced noise by up to seventy-five percent.

• The work of Northwesterner Paul Stamets with mushrooms and fungi is revolutionizing the way we deal with toxic wastes. The mushrooms we see in woods or fields are just the fruit of the *mycelium*, an underground network of root-like fibers that cover much of the earth and frequently stretch for miles. The largest living organism on the planet is a mycelial mat in Oregon that covers 2,200 acres and is more than two thousand years old. No plant community could exist without the mycelium, because its exquisitely fine filaments absorb nutrients from soil, and trade them with the roots of plants in exchange for some of the energy the plant has gleaned from photosynthesis. There is a benign capitalism operating under our very feet—and it is *not corporate!* Fungi actively connect different parts of a forest to other parts, transferring nutrients from species that have nutrition to spare, over to species that need more. Working with this live network, Stamets and others have discovered that fungi are incredibly good at breaking complex, often poisonous substances down into nontoxic components.

•Some fungi take apart the hydrogen-carbon bonds that hold petroleum products together. •Others show potential to clean up nerve-gas agents, dioxins, and plastics. Stamets is using fungi in Fort Bragg California to clean up dioxins and other wastes left by a defunct Georgia Pacific plywood plant. (•New plywood, by the way, is being made nontoxically with an adhesive discovered after study of the way ordinary Pacific Coast mussels attach to rocks.) •Stamets is using fungi in Washington State to clean up toxic chemicals left behind by highway projects and mining. •In a classified study on how to destroy chemical warfare components, Battelle Laboratories, working with Stamets, has tested twenty-six strains of fungi against sarin, soman, and VX, which Saddam Hussein used against the Kurds. Two of the fungi tested were able to break down VX. •In 1986 a nuclear reactor melted down in Chernobyl, in the Ukraine, and spewed deadly radioactive cesium-137 into the atmosphere. Ukrainians later discovered that one type of mushroom, though it continued to thrive there, was absorbing more than ten thousand times more cesium-137 than the background level of contamination. By *nature*, fungi decontaminate the world for the benefit of other species. They are God's Poultice.

A burgeoning library is being written about the plethora of natural partnerships that produce clean, green, ancient, endless energy. I can't catalogue these technologies here, but I urge skeptics to seek them out. The Biomimicry Institute and the Rocky Mountain Institute websites are good places to start. *We no longer require devastating forms of energy*. We have moved past them. Our broken politics is merely failing to move with the innovation. It is also worth mentioning that the mere search for natural partnerships throws us into states of revery and wonder that are a pleasure in themselves, and lead the individual soul to what wisdom traditions call "good karma," "merit," or "kingdom," whereas brute technologies like Tar Sands exploitation stupefy, generate addiction, break down civil society, and undermine democracies for the sake of little more than investor greed.

The sensitivity of humanity to nature's gifts holds the power to heal the earth if we stir some spiritual powers into the mix. Three such powers are love, empathy, and compassion. In an essay called "Justice: Four Windows," Jane Hirshfield describes how compassion is rooted in bird and animal behavior. She writes, "Recognizable conceptions of morality and justice begin with the rudiments of a sense of a separate self and of self's 'place'—that is, with the social order of birds, fishes, and mammals. The experience of a 'correct order,' or of a dismaying disorder, becomes possible only if order is innately present..." (*There is an invisible world out there—and we're living in it.*) "Discomfort over who eats or mates first, last, or not at all, is a precursor to our... feeling that each human being should know freedom of body, spirit, and mind; know security from arbitrary power; know love more than hunger; curiosity and ingenuity more than fear. Among social animals we see the beginnings of visible mercy."

Some examples of these innate precursors to mercy:

•Red foxes bring food to other, injured foxes that are not their own young. •Elephants bring edible branches to dying elephant elders unable to rise. •Scientists videotaped a humpback whale repeatedly lifting another, dead whale to the surface, the way a newborn whale is lifted to the surface for its first breath. The whale carried the corpse to the surface over and over for five hours, before giving up. •A crow, my mother recently told me, adopted an orphaned kitten and was videotaped feeding it and caring for it for weeks. •A man, Hirshfield recounts, attempted suicide by leaping from the Golden Gate Bridge in San Francisco, but was brought to the surface by a seal—a salvation he found so unnerving that he spoke of it to no one for three years. •Many surfers have reported being saved from shark attacks when dolphins formed a protective circle around them.

•My dog Gus, as I set down these words, is sitting on a stump just outside our horses' fenced paddock, literally grinning while our big Andalusian geldings, Cosmo and Tino, lean down over the fence and groom him with their tongues. They do this most every day. Some days twice. When the grooming is over, it is Gus's turn to lightly nibble the horse's chins. To get the particular itch they want nibbled, the geldings swivel their huge heads this way and that, then hold steady, not quite audibly sighing, *Ahhhhhhhhhhh...*

"These acts of empathy and compassion extend interspecies," writes Hirshfield "and underlie our faith in the possibility of a life not ruled by chaos, force, and fear."

"At the bottom of the heart of every human being, from earliest infancy to the tomb," adds Simone Weil, "something goes on indomitably expecting—despite every crime committed, suffered, or witnessed—that good, and not evil, will be done to us. It is this expectation, above all, that is sacred in every human being."

Spawned-out Chinook on the lower Clearwater River. Photograph by Steve Pettit.

8. Junk Science & Realpolitik vs. Restoring America's Greenest Region in One Stroke

PACIFIC SALMON AND STEELHEAD HAVE been the most important food in the Northwest for thousands of years. Salmon caught and preserved by the Nez Perce tribe saved the lives of the Lewis and Clark Expedition twice. Hundreds of species of flora and fauna including human beings, Puget Sound orcas, the sea lions of Oregon's north coast, the eagles, kingfishers, otters of Idaho's Sawtooth Mountains, the best chefs in Portland and Seattle, and those three-thousand-year-old cedars near Montana and me, continue to depend on the delectable flesh of tiny wild salmon fingerlings, the six- to ten-inch smolts that set out for the sea, the Omega-3-rich adult salmon that rove the Pacific then migrate inland to mountain birth houses, and the nitrogen-rich carcasses that feed soils and rise up into the forest canopy after they've spawned and died.

Salmon and steelhead are more than food. They are the treaty-guaranteed daily bread and Eucharist of the tribes. Their life-sustaining self-sacrifice creates direct, time-defying connections between the ancient and the contemporary Northwest. They embody in flesh what only clouds, rains and snow embody otherwise: the way the Pacific makes love to the Rockies.

The most vital wild salmon stronghold in the lower forty-eight consists of more than five-thousand miles of rivers and streams in the Interior West. Roughly the size of Colorado, this vast refuge contains a stupendous number of salmon-friendly waters. When the media talk about a "Snake River salmon crisis" and appear to confine the crisis to that river alone, it's frustrating to those who know this vast region: the lower Snake is only the gateway to the salmon's great refuge, not the vast wild palace itself. The Interior West salmon stronghold includes the Imnaha, Grande Ronde, Wenaha, Lostine, Minam, Wallowa, and Powder Rivers in Oregon, the South and Middle Clearwater, North, South and Middle Salmon, Selway, Rapid, and Lochsa Rivers in Idaho, many more rivers in Washington, and nearly countless smaller tributaries in all three states. A few salmon tributaries on the ninety-mile Lochsa alone include the Crooked Fork, Pack Creek, White Sand Creek, Big Sand Creek, Killed Colt Creek, Brushy Fork Creek, Spruce Creek, Warms Spring Creek, Lake Creek, Sponge Creek, Hungry Creek, Boulder Creek, Old Man Creek, Fire Creek, Fish Creek, Deadman Creek. And the Lochsa web is small compared to the Clearwater web, the vast Salmon River webs, the Grand Ronde and Imnaha webs.

Because of their comparatively high elevation, these Interior West waters comprise the most global-warming-resistant nexus in the Pacific salmon's range in the lower forty-eight. At a time when ninety percent of the ocean's fisheries have been compromised or lost, there is no more important refuge outside Alaska. With a modicum of stewardship, these salmon could thrive as far into the future as we short-lived mortals are able to peer.

That stewardship is not taking place. The Interior West's salmon have been under assault for decades by a federal bureaucracy known as the Bonneville Power Administration (BPA), assisted by the Army Corps of Engineers, and, now, the National Oceanic and Atmospheric Administration (NOAA). Worse, NOAA, the agency responsible for stopping the BPA and Corps depredations via the Endangered Species Act, is not only colluding in the salmon's destruction, it is being dominated and paid by the two agencies it's supposed to stop. Our researcher Steven Hawley's *Recovering A Lost River*, coming in 2011 from Beacon Press, includes an up-to-date account of this fiasco. Here, I'll be brief:

There are 227 massive hydroelectric dams in the Columbia/Snake system. I have nothing to say about 223 of them. But four dams on a 130-mile stretch of the lower Snake River are killing untold millions of juvenile salmon annually as they attempt to migrate to sea. Their survival rate is shockingly low. The "benefit" most often cited to excuse the ongoing salmon slaughter, up to now, has been the hydropower the dams provide. The second most extolled benefit has been the reservoirs created by the lower Snake River (LSR) dams, which allow barges that once traveled 320 miles up the Columbia to the port of Tri-Cities, Washington, to travel an additional 130 miles inland to the "port" of Lewiston, Idaho.

These benefits were protested from the beginning, due to the damage they were certain to inflict on a multi-billion dollar fishing industry, on treaties guaranteeing salmon to the tribes, and on the farms and farming communities slated to be flooded in the Snake River Valley. The LSR dams were opposed by President Dwight Eisenhower, by every fisheries biologist and fishing community, by many farmers in the region, by every regional tribe, by millions of Americans, and even by the Army Corps that was ordered to build them. They were commissioned, over that protest, by a 1955 Congress, to power the Hanford Nuclear Works in eastern Washington. Hanford City became a radioactive ghost town forty years ago, eliminating the LSR dams' original purpose. The four dams were constructed anyway. Boosters promised they would not harm salmon. A government dam spokesperson said at a public meeting in Lewiston that a horse could pass safely through the turbines. No horses were forced to attempt this. Every salmon had no choice.

Salmon and steelhead began dying by the millions. Treaties were broken, the tribes cheated and impoverished, and fishing families and communities from Stanley and Riggins, Idaho to Portland, Astoria, Seattle, Puget Sound began to suffer. The Cold War ended. The four dams continued to diminish the Northwest. The Columbia/Snake system, according to an ambitious new study of the historical data, used to return thirty to fifty million adult salmon to hundreds of streams annually. Some of the LSR dams' effects on this number: •All of the Idaho, Oregon, and Washington coho dependent on the Snake River migratory corridor have now gone extinct. •The once voluminous sockeye salmon runs to Idaho have become so seriously endangered that in the years 1990 to 1999 only twenty sockeye, total, returned to the system. •All surviving Snake system salmon and steelhead are now threatened or endangered. •Nearly the entire 2001 outmigration of juvenile chinook salmon was slaughtered at the dams by the BPA when, in the wake of the Enron scandal, they unlawfully managed the system for maximum hydro to make a killing, selling power to California.

"& Etc.", as William Blake used to say.

The hydropower from the LSR dams provides less than three percent of the region's total. This benefit has cost U.S. taxpayers roughly $10 billion to try to make the Columbia/Snake system less deadly to salmon via a variety of "techno-fixes." The barging extension from Tri-Cities to Lewiston is paralleled by highways and railroads that could carry the same cargo. Federal subsidies (consisting of more taxpayer dollars) have given barges an advantage over trucks and trains. The same subsidies, given to farmers to defray any added cost of converting to trucks and trains, would consist of a small fraction of the billions lost to dam techno-fixes and AWOL salmon revenue.

The LSR dams are "run of the river" and provide no flood control: the reservoirs must be kept within a yard of full capacity, the entire year, so that barges can negotiate the locks. As for irrigation, only one of the four dams provides it, to less than twenty farms. That irrigation would be replaced at no cost to the farmers, in the event of dam removal, by pumps and pipes drawing water from a free-flowing river.

ॐ

The LSR dams have never provided truly "green energy." They have provided Extinction Power, and apartheid, and economic harm to a great majority. The price already paid for a 130-mile barging extension is about to become drastically worse in two ways.

The first: every year the Snake River delivers well over a million cubic yards of sediment, on average, to the reservoir adjacent to Lewiston. There the silt settles as the current slows. During the thirty-five years of Lower Granite Dam's existence these sediment loads have raised the riverbed higher every year. A levee had to be erected by the Army Corps to protect downtown Lewiston from being flooded. The levee makes the city look like the prisoner of its own small port—which, increasingly, it is. Another thirty years of silt build-up will breach the levee and downtown Lewiston will flood—but there's a more serious wrinkle: In 2008 the Army Corps said that even a ten-year flood event could breach the levee. And a twenty-, or fifty-, or hundred-year flood will turn downtown Lewiston into a smaller New Orleans, circa Katrina.

The Port of Lewiston knows of the city center's crisis, but once a pork barrel bureaucracy is created and snouts are in the trough, they just keep feeding till somebody drives them off with a stick. To add insult to impending injury, despite thirty-five years of federal and county subsidies, the port is effectively bankrupt. Until recently it employed five people as it spiraled toward insolvency. A recent earnings chart from the Port's own website:

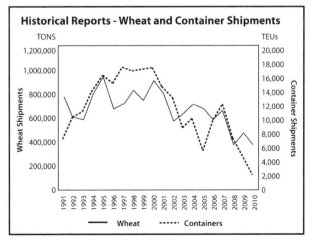

The doom of downtown Lewiston is now one of the costs considered acceptable by the Port and the BPA that maintain the 130-mile barging extension.

An even more serious cost is about to be added:

ExxonMobil—lured to the Northwest by a Lewiston-dooming Port that employed five—proposes to convert the Columbia and Snake into a Tar Sands tentacle leading to the most greenhouse-gas-intensive industrial project in history. This direct link would damage not just a region but the entire earth, overwhelming the controversial "benefits" of these long tragic dams. Anything good for the Port of Lewiston has, historically, been bad for the rest of the Northwest, but to add the ruin of Alberta, the impending devastation of millions of birds, a CO_2 holocaust, melting glaciers, and inundated lowland nations, brings the Port's malfeasance to a cosmic level. Again, what good are global communications, or the dire warnings of exacting climate science, if humanity heeds neither? It is time for the Northwest to replace and *improve* the transportation system of every barge-dependent farmer, replace and improve the irrigation system of every dam-dependent farm, disband the Port that has punished so many taxpayers and regional communities, and set the lower Snake River free.

❦

A brief overview of how corrupt federal science works to preserve the Columbia/Snake salmon extinction status quo:

Juvenile salmon migrating from the Interior West nexus, to the Pacific, need river current to make the journey. Eight dams have turned 450 miles of Columbia and Snake current into slackwatered reservoirs. Every year the BPA's hydro industry tries to horde maximum current for power generation, waging war on the out-migrating salmon smolts. A smolt spilled over a dam has a ninety-eight percent chance of survival. A smolt blasted through BPA turbines has a forty percent chance. Between the salmon rivers in the Interior West, and the Pacific, stand eight giant dams. A million healthy smolts, forced to pass through even four turbine powerhouses or a NOAA "fish passage system," become roughly 160,000 traumatized survivors and 840,000 corpses. The ambulances in this war on salmon are a group of barges that collect dazed or wounded smolts at each dam. The smolts are in bad condition because, when they reach

each dam, they're forced eighty feet below the surface on the upstream side of the concrete, sluiced through a high-pressure tube, deposited in a fish-processing station where they are weighed, measured, marked or tagged by BPA/Corps/NOAA "scientists," then shunted into a barge. After a 300 to 400 mile ride in the barge to the free-flowing Columbia below Bonneville Dam, thousands of smolts become food for a waiting horde of terns, cormorants and warmwater predator fish. As many as sixty percent more vanish before returning as adult salmon, because their crucial bond to the river has been broken by all the processing, and by the ride in the barge.

The Columbia/Snake River system and its dams belong to the American people. The BPA, the people's servant, does not own the rivers. We all do. The BPA is bound by law to give equal consideration to the generation of electricity, and to the ongoing welfare of Columbia/Snake salmon. The agency has turned this crucial balance into a joke. To gain an understanding of salmon migration through this hydro-power corridor, see the objective data generated by the Fish Passage Center of Portland, Oregon, or Steven Hawley's forthcoming *Restoring a Lost River*. Educate yourself with nongovernmental data before you make the mistake of trusting NOAA's "salmon science." Here's why:

The BPA is the endangered salmon's number one enemy, but you'd never know it to hear them talk. The agency tries to control all the salmon science, all the hard data, and all the media discussion of salmon in the Columbia/Snake watershed. In their efforts to exert spin, the BPA's four LSR dams alone have occasioned the most prolific outpouring of bogus science since American tobacco industry "medical science."

NOAA is the agency in charge of implementing the Endangered Species Act (ESA) for the sake of salmon. But during the Bush administration, as a purely political, anti-scientific, neocon-crowd-pleasing move, all 227 dams in the Columbia/Snake system were declared "a natural part of the river." The administration, primarily through the BPA, forced NOAA to back this inane declaration up. The agency responsible for implementing the ESA thus began (along with the BPA and Corps) to worship dams as golden calves and to hell with the legalities and the salmon.

Dams that turn flowing rivers into slackwater are, of course, the very opposite of a river. In the desert climate of the lower Snake these waters become superheated in summer, and deadly to juvenile salmon. Under Bush and Cheney, the very NOAA scientists who prostituted themselves sabotaging salmon were rewarded with job protection and promotions into positions of greater influence. Many of the salmon scientists now working for NOAA were formerly employed by the BPA, the Army Corps, or both. This is like inviting mob bosses into city hall and putting them in charge of cleaning up the mob.

A classic example of the corruption: the head of the Office of Protected Resources at NOAA is a position of almost as much influence as the NOAA directorship held by Jane Lubchenco. The position is held by a Bush-era opportunist named James Lecky. In 2002, Lecky was the salmon scientist overseeing the Klamath River in northern California when, despite a severe drought, the river received its annual fall run of 70,000 adult salmon. Meanwhile in Oregon, Republican Senator Gordon Smith was in a close race. Vice President Dick Cheney had an idea: to publicly demonstrate that Smith was "for the farmers, not the fish," he arranged a media event where Smith and Bush's Interior Secretary, Gale Norton, would divert the drought-stricken Klamath into farmers' fields. James Lecky is the salmon scientist who signed off on Cheney's stunt. Smith was elected, only to lose in 2008. The lasting result of Cheney's maneuver and Lecky's science was the largest adult salmon kill in U.S. history. All 70,000 chinook and coho—that year's entire Klamath run—died in the hot, algae-choked pondwater that replaced the ransacked river. Millions of juvenile salmon were also destroyed. For a political stunt.

From that debacle Lecky moved on to the Sacramento River system, where he amended existing scientific plans and increased water withdrawals from the river system, preparing to kill more salmon. Fortunately, federal judges found the recommended withdrawals and amended science illegal. For his assaults on two major salmon strongholds Lecky was promoted by Bush/Cheney, in 2006, to a third salmon stronghold: the Columbia/Snake.

When Barack Obama's administration announced a return to "open government" and "genuine science," it was assumed that salmon hit-men like Lecky would be retired. They were not. Lecky still wields tremendous influence over the fate of wild salmon.

꙲

When President Obama appointed Jane Lubchenco head of NOAA and announced a new era of genuine federal science, salmon lovers were ecstatic. Lubchenco was a career scientist who understands the needs of threatened and endangered marine species.

Before Dr. Lubchenco could alter any of the corruption or junk science at NOAA, a secret gag order was placed upon her by Washington State Senators Patty Murray and Maria Cantwell, backed up by Lubchenco's boss, Commerce Secretary Gary Locke (the former governor of Murray's state). To keep her job (a decision the wisdom of which I question), Dr. Lubchenco was forced to abandon the trajectory of her entire career and begin defending the oxymoronic term "Bush Salmon Science." This move left every salmon lover feeling punched in the gut— and millions of salmon doomed to death. The Obama administration, at Murray's and Cantwell's urging, turned an enormous opportunity into a tedious further chapter in the Bush/Cheney-concocted prostitution of federal science.

NOAA Fisheries employees claim that a "firewall" exists between their salmon science and the BPA's drive for maximum hydro profits. This "firewall" is nonexistent and the proof (gathered by Steven Hawley after he was denied a Freedom of Information Act request and successfully sued the Obama administration to acquire the information) is in the paychecks. From 2000 to 2010 (the Bush/Cheney *and* the first two Obama years) the U.S. Army Corps of Engineers and the BPA have unwritten NOAA Fisheries in the Pacific Northwest to the tune of $134.5 million through "soft money" contributions. The BPA has contributed the lion's share, $83 million. Together, the Corps and the BPA pay seventy-seven percent of the operating budget for the NOAA offices responsible for the federal plan to save the Interior West's endangered salmon. I repeat, the very agencies from whom NOAA, in the Columbia/Snake region, is supposed to be protecting endangered salmon, pay seventy-seven percent of NOAA's salaries. The BPA is like a drug cartel employing the task force appointed to break up its operations.

This rigged science was established under Bush/Cheney, but the Obama administration, thanks to the bad advice of the Washington State senators, has taken it on completely. When Obama reached out to Murray and Cantwell to find out what the burning science issues were in our region, their private political agendas made a scapegoat of the president. Obama's appointment of Dr. Lubchenco at NOAA shows he was attempting his declared return to real science. The senators and Locke immediately tied Lubchenco's hands. Salmon lovers cannot forget or forgive this derailment.

Aware of the dismay her stilted behavior was causing, Dr. Lubchenco held a series of "listening sessions" with salmon advocates in 2009. But beforehand she had been ordered, like a child, to do nothing at these sessions except listen. The one-sided *non*-exchanges with Obama's "real science" salmon recovery leader made salmon advocates very grouchy indeed. The absurdity of the situation shows in a May, 2009 email sent by Lubchenco to her staff:

"Our decision to meet w only sovereigns, as per the VERY strong guidance from the WA senators, is making it look like we are not transparent and that we are meeting selectively w only government officials... Part of the problem is that we are not telling the public what we are doing which only invites conspiracy theories... We cannot keep people from coming and demonstrating and excluding them fuels the fire and craziness."

It is neither a "conspiracy theory" nor "craziness" to point out that the "VERY strong guidance from the WA senators" was anything but "transparent," and that Lubchenco's defense of "Bush/Cheney Salmon Science" is unconscionable coming from a scientist. Dr. Lubchenco's acumen was never allowed to take up residence at NOAA: it was immediately withered by a politics so toxic that she became a scripted or misinformed maker of inane public relations statements. I could illustrate this with some of her pitifully unscientific statements about the Gulf oil spill. I won't. As a born Oregonian who shares mutual friends with Dr. Lubchenco, I prefer to show her the mercy denied to her by the senators who sacrificed Lubchenco's reputation to their personal political agendas.

❧

I don't wish to malign Senators Murray and Cantwell, either. But I do mean to warn their constituents that the Northwest situation has changed radically: Now that Exxon and the Tar Sands industry is commandeering the Lewiston barging corridor, the D-WA senators' defense of an eastern Washington status quo based on paranoia and pork troughs has become a betrayal of every forward-thinking innovator and green energy proponent and nature lover and locavore and humanitarian and internationalist and fly fisher and child in their region.

In March 2009, when NOAA's botched salmon science was on trial in the federal court of Judge James Redden in Portland, Oregon, the Obama administration's lead defense attorney, Coby Howell, testified that even though endangered juvenile salmon are being slaughtered by the LSR dams barring their way to the Pacific, no more water could be spilled over the dams to help them because every drop of water that is spilled means more fossil fuel, hence more CO_2 in the atmosphere. Over the same spring and summer, LSR barges were hauling millions of gallons of diesel and gasoline to Lewiston. This gas is being stockpiled to drag ExxonMobil's earth-mauling equipment north to convert boreal forest into CO_2, squander natural gas, cook Tar Sands oil, and create wastelands the size of Ohio and Pennsylvania combined. If there were a higher number than 100% for the degree of hypocrisy in Coby Howell's statement, here would be the place to deploy it. Obama's administration—not George Bush's, Obama's—stands to dowse downtown Lewiston, starve out Seattle/Tacoma's orcas for lack of wild Idaho salmon, go down in the books as the worst salmon stewards in U.S. history, *and* collude in unprecedented climate devastation—all compliments of the bad advice of two senators.

A final irony: Senator Cantwell is chair of the Senate Subcommittee on Energy. As such, she plays a pivotal role in moving green legislation through Congress. Again, by assisting in the creation of a Tar Sands tentacle running through her home state's rivers and Idaho's and Montana's iconic wilds, the green energy chair stands to become one of the most hypocritical policy makers in her region since Coby Howell flew back to Washington, D.C.

ExxonMobil is the fifteenth most powerful financial entity in the world. This entity is about to prop up the increasingly damaging and expensive lower Snake River navigation system. ExxonMobil will be a permanent anti-salmon player, with a single focus: adding to its mountains of profit. ExxonMobil will endeavor to take over the Columbia/

Snake system. It will resist all attempts to renew lost balance, restore genuine science, and promote regional justice. Exxon's presence will further institutionalize the economic apartheid the BPA practices against the Tribes. The Northwest's vital but home-grown tourist and salmon fishing economies will be roadkill for a company of this size and ruthlessness.

If NOAA were a genuinely scientific body with a commitment to restoring wild salmon and salmon science, it would be deeply involved in analyzing the threats posed by a dam-ratifying barging route linking the Pacific Rim to the Tar Sands via the greatest salmon river in the lower forty-eight. NOAA is doing nothing. Thanks to Senators Murray and Cantwell, the Obama administration isn't either.

Given the fact that there is no other world in which our children and grandchildren can live, I consider it neither "crazy" nor "conspiratorial" for Northwesterners to seek to love, and lovingly tend, this world. Such a love could fairly be called *scientific*. It is clean air, edible food, water flowing down from glaciers after cold winters, vast stands of living trees converting CO_2 into oxygen, that allow even politicians to play their little games.

The Washington State senators face a monumental choice. They can sell out the region that elected them to Tar Sands industrialists, or they can serve the Northwest, the nation and the world by apologizing to Obama for bad advice, freeing Dr. Lubchenco to institute real salmon science at NOAA, and working to stop the Tar Sands tentacle through their state.

It is gospel fact, appreciated by many farmers in eastern Washington, that Jesus, Peter, James and John were commercial fishermen. It is a gospel fact that the miracle feast served after the Sermon on the Mount was loaves *and* fishes. Not one at the expense of the other, but both. It is a fact that when fishers farm, and farmers go fishing, there is no telling us apart. What a crime if, due to junk science and a fleeting notion of *realpolitik*, these thousands-of-year-old traditions vanish from our region on our watch.

Lost River

I dreamed the people who fished the river never knew want, seldom knew confusion, & with the salmon's self-sacrifice to guide them they could always find love. I dreamed I obeyed the river so gratefully that the name of every rapid, fall & riffle engraved itself on my tongue, & the salmon came back to us again & again, & I never once doubted they would bless my family's table forever.

I dreamed Big & Little Dalles & Methow & Priest Rapids & Lodgepole & Entiat Rapids. I dreamed Coulee Bend & Kettle Falls & beautiful Celilo. I dreamed Chalwash Chilni & Picture Rocks Bay & Spanish Castle & Victoria & Beacon Rocks. I dreamed Black Canyon & Deschutes & Klickitat Canyons & Rocky Reach & Ribbon Cliff. I dreamed I fished by the peach groves of the place called Penawawa, drunk on the river's sweetness within the fruit.

I dreamed I fell asleep to the sound of water, & when I woke a cloud had enveloped the minds of the ruling pharoahs, & they had attacked the river as if its song & flow were curses. I dreamed 227 dams clogged the river & all that I knew was submerged.

I dreamed the salmon young lost strength & direction in the slackwaters, couldn't reach the sea, & when they no longer brought the ocean back to us we grew as lost as they. I dreamed my people stood shoulder to shoulder in casinos

the way we'd once stood by the river, our fists full of quarters, our minds full of broken hope & smoke.

I dreamed I asked why the salmon had to die & the pharaohs told me, "So wheat & Tar Sands modules can ride the slackwater in barges." I dreamed I tried to reason, telling them of wheat shipped by railroad, & of climate chaos & suffering. The pharaohs laughed & marched off to conduct business impossible to distinguish from war.

I dreamed I led the last salmon people out into the wheat fields, & in a golden light we launched our dories, & we went fishing in the stubble. I dreamed I cast the Spey of a Nez Perce named Levi, & the beauty of hidden salmon gleamed in field & sky, & our fishing became prayer. But still the pharaohs ruled the water. I dreamed the one who reads even lost rivers then said, "It is finished," & the last salmon floated by us as a cloud above us.

I dream I am an old man, & Levi & the farmer whose fields we sailed sit with me at Penawawa beside a river finally freed. I dream we hold rods in one hand, sweet peaches in the other, & our lines run true as prayer into the shine. But whether the salmon come, whether they bring the lost ocean back to us, my dreams, like the river, refuse to say.

9. Heart of the Monster

To reach Alberta, ExxonMobil's Tar Sands cargo will creep within fifty feet of an ancient basalt formation known to the Nez Perce people as "The Heart of the Monster." I had heard for years that this formation, according to Nez Perce cosmology, was considered to be the birthplace of the entire tribe. Though intrigued by the notion, I drove past the formation countless times without stopping, because it lies within sight of a fly fisher's river of rivers. I find the Clearwater so seductive that more than a few people will not ride in a vehicle I'm driving when that river is in sight. But when I learned that ExxonMobil would be dragging 650,000 pound strip-mining weapons within fifty feet of the birthplace of the Nez Perce, I hung up my fly rods, forgot about steelhead and, in early October, 2010, drove to the ancient site to see what I could see.

The Heart of the Monster turns out to be a mound of basalt rubble about the size of a large but collapsed airplane hangar. An expansive riverside lawn surrounds the formation, looking like a golf fairway that, instead of arriving at a putting green, leads to this ruinous-looking basalt heap. I've spent my life in the land of columnar basalt formations. I have never seen a more eerily smashed, anti-geometrical, godforsaken-looking heap of this orderly rock than The Heart. That this rubble is the most important piece of mythological real estate in Nez Perce country was bewildering. Basalt formations tend to dominate large landscapes, visibly underlying and connecting with one another. The Heart has no discernible relationship with the land around it. This rubble pile looks more as if a dumptruck the size of a ship descended from the heavens, dumped the basalt where it now lies, and drove away into the stars. I tend to mutter to inanimate things that interest and puzzle me. I found

myself asking the big black heap questions like: *How did you end up here,*
old monster heart? How did you get so wrecked-looking? Why do you look like
you don't belong here at all?

The Nez Perce, it turns out, anticipate these kinds of questions and
offer us mutterers help. About a hundred feet shy of the Heart-heap—
pitching wedge distance—the fairway led me to an unexpected object:
a steel obelisk about the size of hotel room refrigerator, installed in the
ground. This object, too, set me muttering. And again, the Nez Perce had
anticipated my reaction: Etched in the steel on top of the obelisk was a
small coyote. And next to the coyote was a push-button.

This button startled me. In a place so isolated, by a basalt Heart so
imploded, the button gave me the feeling that, if I pressed it, somewhere in the world something might actually implode. It says a lot
(maybe too much!) about my trust of wild things like rivers, basalt
rocks, and coyotes that—despite this feeling—I reached out at once
and pushed the button.

I waited for the sound of rumbling, near or distant. I heard nothing. But—strange to say—I felt a change. In a way I can't describe, I flew
out in front of myself, and sensed that something had indeed begun to
implode. Something huge and dark. Something bigger than a Tar Sands
module, even bigger than the Tar Sands itself. Something so huge that,
even though I sensed that its implosion had begun, the complete collapse
of this thing will take years.

Then a man's voice began to speak. Nothing mysterious. The button
had activated a tape-recording in the obelisk. The man had the easy-going,
uninflected, g-droppin' accent of a tribal storyteller. He was telling the
story of The Heart of the Monster. This is what he said:

> *This all happened many years ago, long before the people came,*
> *when all the animals lived here.*
> *Once upon a time, Coyote was building a fish trap on the river,*
> *when he learned that a Great Monster was eating all the animals.*
> *So Coyote set out to see what he could do. Along the way, he took a*
> *bath, then dressed up to make himself look tasty to the Monster.*
> *Climbing up the ridges, Coyote looked out over the land.*
> *Suddenly, he saw a great head nodding off into the distance, behind*
> *a huge body. Coyote had never seen anything like it before. The*

Monster could not see Coyote, because he was painted brown like the swaying grass.

Using rawhide ropes, Coyote tied himself to three big mountains: Pilot Knob, Cottonwood Butte, and the Seven Devils. Then he called out to the Monster.

"You are the one who swallowed all the animals! Why don't you swallow me too, so I won't be lonely?"

The Monster did not know that Coyote carried with him a fire-making kit, and five stone knives.

The Monster inhaled, making a mighty wind. He inhaled so hard that the ropes broke, and Coyote was carried right inside the Monster's gaping mouth.

Coyote looked around as he walked down the wide throat of the Monster. Seeing many bones, he thought, "Many animals have been dying." Just then Hohosne, the Grizzly Bear, rushed at him, roaring and growling.

Coyote said, "So, you make yourself scary only to me?" And he hit the bear hard on the nose. That is why Grizzly has a short nose.

As Coyote continued along toward the heart of the monster, Wactushna, Rattlesnake, rattled at him threateningly.

"So. Only toward me you are vicious," said Coyote. Then he stepped on the snake's head, making it flat. It is still that way today.

As Coyote walked further, the animals began to greet and follow him. When he finally reached the heart of the Monster, he built a fire with the flints he had brought, then sawed some fat from the heart so that the animals could eat.

Smoke drifted up through the Monster's eyes, ears and nose. The Monster didn't much like it. The animals ate the fat and watched.

With his stone knives, Coyote began slicing out the Monster's heart. It was hard work. One by one, his knives began to break. But Coyote kept on cutting. Kept the fire going, too.

When his last knife broke, Coyote grabbed the heart and tore it loose with his bare hands.

At that moment, the Great Monster died, and all the animals ran out the openings of its body, according to Coyote's directions. Muskrat was last to come out. Everyone had stomped on him, as he was caught by his tail. That is why, to this day, the muskrat has no hair on his tail.

Everyone helped carve the fallen Monster into large pieces. Coyote threw these pieces outward in every direction. Wherever they landed, nations of people sprang up. Coyote named them: Cayuse, Blackfeet, Couer d'Alene, Yakima.

When he finished, Fox came up and said, "What is the meaning of this, Coyote? You have used up the entire body of the Monster, and given it all to far away lands. Is there nothing left for this place?"

"Well," said Coyote. "Why didn't you tell me this before? Bring some water."

Coyote washed his bloody hands and sprinkled the drops on the ground, right here. From this watered ground came the people Coyote named the Nimipoo, the Nez Perce.

The heart of the Great Monster, now turned to stone, still lies here to mark the place of our beginning.

The man in the obelisk fell silent. I looked at the exploded stone heart before me. My earlier questions—*How did you get here? Why are you so incongruous and wrecked-looking?*—began to feel answered. The creation myth I'd heard, on the signage in the park and in guide books, is called "an origin tale." But I was swept up by the feeling that it is also prophecy. Even a prophetic set of instructions. I felt my father's father asking me in; felt I stood on a cusp between an imploding world, and an emerging one. I did not feel afraid. I felt immense possibility.

Remembering the dark thought-forms that held that Africans could be ripped from their homes, enslaved by Europeans, and sold with impunity; remembering the thought-forms that told a self-styled demi-god known as 'White European Man' he had the right to steal the world, lives, and lifeways from indigenous people everywhere; remembering the thought-forms that put Galileo on trial in the same way that neocon think tanks have put NASA climatologist James Hansen on trial, continuing (even after Magellan circumnavigated the globe!) to hold that the Earth is flat, I fully recognized the darkness that had led me to the Heart of the Monster:

It was the corporate darkness. The one that holds that Earth's resources are inert and endlessly abundant as opposed to finite and vibrantly alive; that Earth's delicate looms of life have no greater purpose than to serve a monetary bottom line; the darkness with 2,500 lobbyists telling elected leaders that commercial ventures can target, take, and plunder living places, creatures, cultures, without guilt or karmic consequence.

I looked at the imploded Heart of the Monster, and felt that an age of the world has come full circle. Another seemingly unstoppable darkness, I believe, has created a situation so dire that a kind of divine desperation has begun to fuel those who oppose it. This desperation is the source of the immense sense of possibility that filled me—the possibility I still feel. Faced with a unified wall of divine desperation, I believe the Monster will, in the end, implode.

When there is no scientific doubt or moral question that humanity must change its *modus operandi* and eliminate carbon emissions, why oh why, people of good heart wonder, are BP, ExxonMobil, Shell, Peabody Energy, Koch Industries, the coal companies of China, the frackers and mountain-removers, stomping the pedal to the global-heating metal? Why would the Energy Giants go suicidal on us at the very moment when humanity can least afford it?

The answer is simple when you're standing by the Clearwater River in front of the imploded Heart of an ancient Monster.

The Giants aren't suicidal at all: merely monstrous. What is killing us is what feeds them. Monster-think is spiritually bankrupt, but voraciously logical. For Big Oil and Energy, producing salable products for entrapped consumers—products that lead to ocean dead zones, species extinction, dying forests, dying citizens, lost democracies, climate refugees, biocide, deicide—is still profitable at the moment. The threat of climate chaos means nothing to a feeding Monster. The warnings of Desmond Tutu and the Dalai Lama mean nothing. A thousand more Copenhagen and Kyoto climate summits would mean nothing. To expect the piles of money known as corporations to exert humane, sustainable or visionary leadership is against the Monster's own laws—and the nature-blind, lobbyist-rife thinking in Washington D.C., under the Monster's aegis, has become a self-referential downward spiral with both the inarguable logic, and the inexorable trajectory, of a toilet flush. Those 2,500 energy lobbyists pay a fortune to build tyrannical limitations into political thought processes. Entire regions, ecosystems, peoples, Nigerian deltas, a Colorado-sized expanse of Northwest salmon birthhouses, can be flushed without remorse. To cry "Stop this!" in Washington D.C. is to be scoffed as a country rube ignorant of *realpolitik*. To shout "Where is your humanity?" at corporate headquarters is to be treated the way the former Exxon CEO treated Radhi Darmansyah.

Corporate personhood is the Monster that is swallowing us all. In the words of Exxon Valdez survivor and marine biologist, Riki Ott: "Ecosystems are broken, communities are broken, the election system and our democracy are broken, all for the same reason. *Corporate personhood.* For a hundred years corporations have hijacked our government and remade the world in their own image... We can no longer accept the ruling that corporations are people and money is speech." In the words of Wendell Berry, the Monster "can experience no personal hope or remorse. No change of heart. It cannot humble itself." In the words of James Howard Kunstler, corporations, though granted personhood, are "devoid of any human qualities of ethics, humility, mercy, duty or loyalty that would constrain their rights." In the words of Bill Moyers, "You will hear it said, 'Come on, this is the way the world works.' No, it's the way the world is *made* to work. This vast inequality did not just happen... Early this year the five reactionary members of the Supreme Court ruled that corporations are "persons" with the right to speak during elections by funding ads like those now flooding the airwaves. This was the work of legal fabulists. Corporations are not people; they are legal fictions, creatures of the state, born not of the womb, not of flesh and blood... Yet thanks to five activist judges they have the privilege of "personhood" to "speak"—and not in their own voice, mind you, but as ventriloquists, through hired puppets. Does anyone really think that's what the authors of the First Amendment had in mind?"

Standing by The Heart of the Monster, I could find no reason why those of us living outside the dominant paradigm should plead any longer with those by whose logic we're being so completely misled. To ask corporate Earth-killers to stop the killing leaves the decision to the killers' tyrannical thought processes.

The vast possibility—the hope I feel and see—is in decisive, massive, compassion-fueled action by the grassroots. The decision to stop killing the Earth can be imposed on those who have not made such a decision, by those who have. Tall order? Extremely! Am I overreaching? Of course. But how can we seek a solution to our quandary if we fail to address the real problem? The playing field upon which corporations and we the people are playing is a vertical cliff. To attempt to turn the planet sideways to level the cliff is impossible. The way forward is to insist on a new playing field entirely.

Every human being feels the wrongness of corporate personhood in their bodies, lungs, gut, whether or not they choose to recognize it in their minds. It is those with lungs and a heartbeat who are persons; those who, exposed to a stew of dispersants or PAH's, suffer the health consequences; those who breathe, need clean water, and possess fragile bodies and ineffable souls that, in the after-worlds, reap the spiritual consequences of their actions. To call an entity that suffers no physical or spiritual consequence a "person" and give it the most powerful voice in a democratic system simply destroys the democratic system.

What, then, is the source of the wave of possibility I felt and still feel? In reading my friend Paul Hawken's tour de force book on the divine desperation sweeping the world, *Blessed Unrest,* I was stunned to learn that there are more than three million NGO's, nonprofits, churches, sanghas, faith groups and activist businesses fighting to save various wild or cultural treasures, expose particular corporate crimes, start up an ingenious new energy technology, save a school or historic building, a wetland, an indigenous people, a social freedom, a dying language. But it also struck me that the isolated efforts of all these groups—like the isolated roar of Grizzly, hiss of Rattlesnake, guile of Fox—are taking place inside the bowels of the Monster. If these same millions joined together with a single coordinated priority—to unmake the "personhood" that lies at the heart of the Monster swallowing our world—they would be a force like nothing history has ever seen.

I do not feel we will say a "day of reckoning" so much as an increasing revulsion toward the powers that are destroying life, and an ever more vital love for the powers that are breathing new life into the world. Coyote, for all his mischievousness, is a god of boundless compassion. At the Nez Perce origin site, He drew whole tribes of noble human beings from the very ruins of the Monster's body and heart. A fresh wave of boundless compassion, I felt by a mysterious pile of heart rubble in Idaho, is even now in the act of doing the same. A heart-fueled rebellion against the dominant paradigm is in progress. It is fueled by empathy, natural compassion, deep spirituality, and some of the most brilliantly sustainable science and technology in history.

Whenever this kind of rebellion has occurred, the beneficiaries of the outmoded paradigm have panicked. In recent years the oil, coal and weapons barons, entrenched rich, and their minions have grown ever more vehement, violent, and streamlined in their ability to gut democracy and seize control. But no matter how complete the blindness of the "winners" in the dying system, the transcendent view, the karmically just view, the biophilic view, keeps winning adherents, defying the paradigm, and instigating positive change.

A single telling example: the dominant agribusiness paradigm keeps paving the lower forty-eight with petrochemical fertilizers and monocrops that sterilize living soil, destroy family farms and rural communities, create epidemic obesity and diabetes, and force people to consume their wretched food. The industry's stranglehold on policy-makers is replete. How strange and wonderful that, even so, the foodshed movement, organic gardening movement, slow food, locavore, and farmers' market movements have exploded across small-town America and Europe.

With little or no support from government and entrenched power, how did this happen? There seems to me to be a kind of *field effect* energizing and uniting resisters of the outmoded paradigm—something greater and more powerful than any individual or organization, hence more impossible to stop than individuals and organizations. This energy is neither a political or religious force. It's more an unspoken intensity felt by nearly everyone who is fighting for a creature, an ecosystem, an oppressed people, a small cultural good. Many have described this energy as Earth's own immune system rising up in her defense.

Does anyone besides me feel that our plight has become more *mythological* than political? And that this is a potentially wondrous thing? That, though our politics have been stolen and broken, greater and more inexorable energies have come into play? The wild appeal of the *Lord of the Rings* and *Avatar* films hints at these energies. The power of such tales is both mythic and bardic, and does not spring from some fanciful set of facts. A genuine myth is a *hyper-fact* that speaks—as Jung and others have long said—to what is eternally resonant in the body, mind and psyche as we encounter the weathers, land, waters, and creatures of our particular places on Earth. Without making contact with these resonances, we fail to make contact with what holds eternally true, and lose touch with the transcendent reasons not to turn boreal forests into profitable hellholes.

A global communication system that fails to communicate with the living globe is a sound and fury signifying nothing. The wild joy and lumens of heartlight transmitted by old bardic tellings have never been more orienting, precisely because humanity has never been more lost. To experience the resonations of our psyches encountering the weathers, places and creatures of Earth may now be a matter of life and death. For all the money in ExxonMobil's coffers, the Monster doesn't even know what I'm talking about, and cannot summon a drop of this galvanizing joy or heartlight—whereas bardic souls without two dimes to rub together often can.

I'm going to end with a transmission from some old psyches and souls.

10. The Earth Dreams of Beauty

Last year an old Irish telling made its way to me via an Irish-Canadian bard named Alice Kane, and stood my hair on end. I found the tale in a book called *Wisdom of the Mythtellers* by Alice's nephew, Sean Kane.

In this tale we meet Brigit, "the exalted one," chief singer amongst a spiritual elite of chieftain gods and goddesses called the Tuatha Dé Danann, children of Dana: the Earth Mother. Brigit is the immortal Mother's immortal child, and when I seek her songs today I catch an echo in, say, my friend Pattiann Rogers' chant. "*God so loved the world, loved the order of things, loved the earth, loved the order of the earth,*" Pattiann sings, "*loved us as creatures born of the order of things, born of the stars and the order of the stars, born of the earth born of the stars, made of stars, made of the earth…*" that I can't even finish her sentence without feeling gripped by a beauty resonant with astronomical, biological and spiritual Truths from the dawn of space and time.

Exalted Brigit's face, voice, and songs do the same. For the pre-Christian Irish her singing was a feminized enactment of the Jesus or Buddha magic, invoking realms a soul can leap into and exult, free of fear. Brigit's kin are the likes of Aengus, the impetuous young god found in countless Celtic love stories; Ogma, god of writing and eloquence and guide of departed souls; Nuada, king of the Dé Dannan; Midir, the divine judge; and the Dagda, who with his Cauldron of Rebirth brings the cyclic dance between death and new growth, and the human enactment of that dance, *reincarnation*. In Brigit's songs we also meet Manannan, the sea god who gave Ireland, Scotland, and the North American coasts and mountains their wild salmon.

I love this old European-born telling because it counters every European-born claim that the willful destruction of life is a means of pleasing some sort of White European-serving "God." I love this ancient telling because, without even touching the defiled thought that dominates our politics and boardrooms, the tale explodes the speciousness of realpolitik, and of a science that worships dams; explodes lifeless justifications for the movement of weapons of climate destruction from Asia through American wilds to the Tar Sands; explodes the silliness of claims to see an "industrial waltz" in an Athabasca watershed so poisonous that the northern pike now sprout double sets of jaws and the whitefish are mutating and the walleye exported to Midwest grocery stores and restaurants deal slow death.

I love this old telling because *In the beginning God created the heaven and the earth.* So far so good. *And the earth was without form, and void,* so far so good. And in Tir-na-Moe, Brigit was singing, and Aengus the ever-young, Midir the Haughty, Ogma the Wise, the Dagda, and all the Dé Dannan were listening. And this is what radiant Brigit sang:

> *Now comes the hour foretold, a god-gifting, a wonder sight!*
> *Is it a star, newborn and splendid, upsinging out of night?*
> *Is it a wave from Youth's Fountain, upflinging youth's delight?*
> *Is it an immortal bird winging hither in its flight?*
> *It is a wave, high-crested, breaking into light.*
> *It is a star, rose-hearted, risen from the night.*
> *It is a flame from the god world, love's unquenchable delight.*
> *Let the wave break, the star rise, the flame leap—*
> *all ours, if our hearts take each to keep.*

There was silence in Tir-na-Moe after Brigit finished.

Then Aengus spoke: "Strange are the words of your song. And stranger still the music. It was as if the voice of strange worlds was breathing on my face while you sang. Though the sound came closer and closer, and you were singing, it was not you who was singing. So: *who was singing?*"

"It was the Earth who was singing," said Brigit.

"The Earth?" said Aengus. "Is not the Earth in the abyss? Is not the Earth in the darkness of the void? Who has ever stayed to hear Earth, hear its sounds, or see the blackness of it?"

"I have stayed," said Brigit. "I have stayed to hear Earth. I have stood and watched the monstrous, writhing life that devours itself there. I have stayed and heard and shuddered in the adder pits of hell."

"Then why do you not forget that place?" asked Ogma the Wise. "Forget it, and let it be a dream that has passed away, and let it be forgotten like a dream, forever."

"Hear one thing more! One thing more!" cried Brigit. "The Earth has cried all night. It has wept all night long—*because it has dreamed of beauty.*"

"What beauty? What beauty?" asked Ogma.

"The Earth has dreamed of the white stillness before dawn. The Earth has dreamed of the star that goes before sunrise. The Earth—*the Earth has dreamed of beauty.*"

"I wish you had never sung this," said Aengus. "I can't get it out of my mind! I can't think of anything else. I wish I'd never heard of it, never known of it."

"Aengus, Aengus," Brigit said. "You clothe yourself in all the brilliance of the sun, and in all the colors the sun brings to light. Why should you not carry some of that beauty to Earth, which is crying for it?"

"No!" said Aengus. "I will not go to Earth. I would not want to shudder there. I don't ever want to see it."

"But I would go," said Midir, the Judge. "I would see it." And he stood and tossed his mane of hair till he was surrounded with a brightness like daylight. "I would go," he said, "gladly. I would go to see what is there."

"And I," said Brigit. "Because the Earth has dreamed of beauty I am going to throw my mantle, which makes beauty, around it. And you would come?"

"I'll come," said Midir. "And I'll make a way for you. I'll make a space in Earth's monstrous writhing for your mantle cloak."

"And I'll come," said Ogma the Wise.

"And I," said Nuada the King.

"I too would come," said Aengus, "if Midir would bring the Sword of Light."

"We will take the Sword of Light," said Nuada, "and the Cauldron of Plenty, and the Spear of Victory, and the Stone of Destiny. We'll take them all. We'll take them with us."

So Brigit set off, and Midir followed. He carried the Sword of Light, and Nuada the Spear of Victory. And they brought with them the Cauldron of Plenty, and Stone of Destiny, and all the Dé Dannan followed. They dropped! They dropped down to Earth like a great shower of stars.

But when they came near the great, moving, horrible, self-devouring darkness that is the Earth they drew back, shuddering, away from it. All but Midir—who dropped right into the collapse of it. Taking the Spear of Victory in hand he went down, and he trod out that monstrous first darkness the way a man treads grapes in a wine vat. He walked here and he walked there, and it moved, the darkness moved, and he held up the Spear, waved it this way and that, waved it around and made a way through the terrible dark. Then he turned and said,

"Now! Cast your cloak, Brigit! Cast your mantle, Earth's daughter, for I have made a space to throw your cloak into. And let there be beauty, and music, and lavish-heartedness upon the Earth."

And Brigit took her cloak—all silver-grey, with the slight flame at the edge of it—and cast it. She cast it upon the Earth. And where it fell, a great soft mist spread over Earth and everywhere darkness was driven away by the light-and-flame-edged cloak. Farther and farther the flame moved, the cloak spread over and over, it would have gone on spreading for a *very* long time. But Aengus, the youngest of the Dé Dannan, couldn't wait. He leapt down and began bounding back and forth in the mist, playing like a child, laughing and calling back to his fellows. And they dropped down, and the silver mist closed round, and through it they saw each other like images in a dream.

Then Dagda, the Great God, took the Cauldron of Plenty, and put his hands into it, and said, "O Cauldron that gives to everyone what is meet for them! Give me now a gift meet for the Earth." And he drew both hands up out of the Cauldron, and in them was a great green fire which he threw down over the Earth. And everywhere it spread there was a greenness like grass over everything. And Aengus ran joyous through it, and played like a child in it, and built it up into hillocks and dug it out into hollows and ran trenches and mounded peaks and dug long lanes.

Then Manannan Mac Lir, ruler of seas, saw that Brigit's cloak had spread over everything, but that great life was bulging up beneath the cloak, rising up to see what was happening. And Manannan reached for the Sword of Light, and raised it over his head, and waved it. And the great monstrous life drew back in one enormous wave, black and high, back back back into the sea. And he waved Light's Sword again and a smaller wave, violet and blue, and more gentle, drew back. And waved the Sword a third time and a small wave formed, white-crested and most gentle. And the Three Waves of Ireland drew themselves into one and broke upon the shore.

They looked at it. The changed new Earth. They looked at it all as it lay there. Then Brigit said, "I am going to lay the Stone of Destiny in the Earth and let it stay, that the Earth may have power." And she laid the great Stone on top of the Earth, and it began to sink, and when it sank deep into Earth, a music sounded. And where it sounded water flowed, and all the indentations and ruts and lanes Aengus had dug in his play began to fill, till every river, lake and stream was alive with water.

And Aengus cried, "I want to stay here! I want to stay here and build things. I want to make things. I would like in this pool to make a smaller pool, like the Well of Connla. I would like to make silver fishes, and gold ones, and humped back and pink and green ones, large and small. And I'd like to make an orchard full of golden apples like those in Tir-nan-Oge."

But the other gods said, "No golden apples, Aengus! Earth is all new. Do not make in Earth the things that are in other places. Not the things of Tir-na-Moe, nor of Tir-nan-Oge, nor of any other place at all. Let the Earth make her own things, in her own ways, till she is full of all beauty."

"Yes! yes!" said the others. "And let us stay here. Let us stay, all of us, and fashion the things Earth needs till there is nothing in all the Earth that is not beautiful. Yes!" they said, "and we shall all stay here."

"Except me," said Brigit. "I must go. There are things I must see to in Moy Mell, and Tir-na-Moe, and Tir-nan-Oge, and the other worlds. They are mine to care for."

"If you must," said wise Ogma. "But, before you go, tie a knot of remembrance in your mantle, that you may always remember this place. And tell us, before you go, what we shall call it."

And Brigit looked at the Earth, and when she lifted her mantle the gods were standing on a grass-cloaked island covered every shade of green. And the grass was studded with little flowers—yellow and red ones, purple, blue, every kind of flower. And it was altogether beautiful. And she said, "You shall call it the Emerald Isle, the Isle of Destiny. And its other name shall be Ireland."

Then, in Brigit's flame-rimmed silver grey mantle, Ogma tied the knot of remembrance.

And that is the story of the creation of the Earth.

⁂

Da Capo al fine:

Oregon, Washington, Idaho, and Montana are a weave of places, weathery forces, flora and fauna, and wild intricacy, to which people from all over the world flock like grateful birds simply to see Earth being Earth; see wildness intact; see the Earth dreaming of beauty. Today we call these places ours, but the Northwest and Northern Rockies are a weave of life-forms and mysteries we did not create, and cannot re-create once the wild's ability to weave is ravaged. These great regions were pre-American and will be post-American. They are what enable biodiversity to diversify, natural selection to naturally select, and generation after generation of kids to muck around in river shallows with frogs, fingerlings and caddis fly casings. These regions are governed not by such creatures as "governors," but by elemental and celestial harmonies as powerful as Earth's spinning yet as intricate as an orbweaver's dew-bedecked web.

These places and forces, to put it the ancient way, are our Mother, the living terrain her body, the flora her clothes, the lakes, rivers, rills her blood and arteries, the seasons and weathers her moods, the birds, fish, fauna, humans, *all*, equally, her offspring. And every man, woman and child striving to defend her life and the lives she supports—even in poverty or political impotence, even against monsters, even against seemingly hopeless odds—is not only a hero but an integral part of her, hence every bit as holy as she whom they seek to defend.

These pages are my whole-hearted thanks to that holiness.

A Short History of Montana

A Novella by

RICK BASS

It is a country to breed mystical people, egocentric people, perhaps poetic people. But not humble ones. At noon the total sun pours on your single head; at sunrise or sunset you throw a shadow a hundred yards long. It was not prairie dwellers who invented the indifferent universe or impotent man. Puny you may feel there, and vulnerable, but not unnoticed. This is a land to mark the sparrow's fall.
　　　　　　—Wallace Stegner, *Wolf Willow*

The river used to be blue. Now it's brown. Nobody can fish or drink from it. The air is bad. This has all happened so fast.
　　　　　　　　—Elsie Fabian, 63, an elder in a Native community along
　　　　　　　　　the Athabasca River

THE EARTH IS BURNING AT THE PASS. It erupts and gurgles, and here, just west of Lolo, we take our pleasure from it, in all seasons, especially in winter. We soak in the hot springs; we linger in the burning. Those of us who live on the Montana side of the pass are familiar with a phrase used by the Indian poet, James Welch: *winter in the blood*. It is the cold of hard times, heartache, loss, and failure. The stuff of literature.

Literature is the first acknowledgment, the barometer, of loss. Montana's changing fast, after putting up a good struggle, and we have to ask ourselves some hard questions about *What next?* Another story is unfolding, but whether a bedtime story or a morning story remains to be seen.

Big trucks are coming, simply because the largest company in the world has asked a lame duck governor to rent the state out for the rolling transfer of tanks and machinery to continue the big dig in Canada: the biggest industrial project on earth.

In Montana, our governor used not to be this way. But they got to him. Somehow, they found the winter in his blood.

❧

In Montana, the Blackfeet were ferocious, the fiercest in the state. They reigned terror on all who invaded their terrain, no matter whether their skin was red or white.

Over in Idaho, the Nez Perce were diplomats, peaceable warriors. In the end both the Blackfeet and the Nez Perce lost. What could they have done differently? It's not an insignificant question, because once again a seemingly insurmountable enemy approaches, only now we are all as Indians. It is true enough that history repeats itself, but is it not also true that if you know this, you can take steps to change or influence its course and arc?

I need to begin telling the story of who we are, of how we made a stand. A true story of how the least populated state in the country defeated the largest company in the world, and in the process saved the world. It hasn't happened yet but I can see it happening. I can see the few trails by which we can win.

❧

We who love Montana do so with every breath and fiber of our being. It is a love that grows stronger and deeper with each passing moment and each passing year and each passing decade, all the way to the end, to the long dirt nap, where they lay you down in the dirt of home and put the dirt in your mouth and around your body, sealing you into it. Those who are left behind may ask of the departed, *What did he love, what did she love, who loved him or her? What did he or she accomplish?*

The earth is burning at the pass. Have you ever experienced certain moments—luminous moments—that matter far more than the daily

white noise we so often consume and inhabit? Have you ever experienced the sense that certain places and people in your life seem to open you to a trail, a corridor, if you will; a hallway toward what lies beyond?

All of Montana was once this way—it well may have been the original garden, once the sheets of ice went away and dissolved into what we now call the Pacific. The garden leaping to life beneath warming skies in the flood-silt of once frigid great lakes, their terraces and hillside shorelines still visible today, as if a once-great civilization of mankind had been here, rather than ice.

And when the covers of those ice-sheets pulled back, and the ice-water lakes all drained to the ocean—carrying the breath and scent and taste of Montana through the slot canyons on out to the Pacific, Montana received the world's seeds, began to grow its forests and prairies, which became fuel for the burning; and with the old ice cap removed, the magma from below was more easily able to rise vertically, so that fire was spreading in every possible direction. The state was awakened by the ice going away, but was made by the burning—our forests as well as our prairies are the yield of those flames—and only such a short time ago.

What kind of state has the motto *Oro y Plata*, silver and gold? Be careful what you ask for. If only we had thought to call our state motto *Salmon and Grizzlies*, or *Rivers and Sky*. Gold and silver? Here, hand me that shovel, let me pass you another helping of dirt. Gnaw at the sand and soil that awaits you, awaits us all.

We had something really good here, once upon a time. Is this all we can leave behind now—a record of our rage? An inventory of our wan protests, our sputters of indignation, followed by—as happens in other states, but surely not Montana—mute acceptance?

We must win. We must leave more than a record of faint and predictable and brief protest.

In Cormac McCarthy's novel, *No Country for Old Men*, there is a passage that haunts me. "It was a cold and blustery day when he walked out of the courthouse for the last time. Some men could put their arms around a crying woman but it never felt natural to him. He walked down the steps and out the back door and got in his truck and sat there. He couldn't name the feeling. It was sadness but it was something else besides. And the something else besides was what had him sitting there instead of starting the truck. He'd felt like this before but not in a long time and when he said that, then he knew what it was. It was defeat. It was being beaten. More bitter to him than death. You need to get over that, he said. Then he started the truck."

I feel that these days we are only one step ahead of that same recognition. There is a hellhound on our trail. The trucks have already come across the sea and arrived in Vancouver; despite their impending crimes against humanity they have cleared customs into Portland, have made it onto the barges, and on up the ghost of the Snake River, once so wild and nurturing. There are days when I worry that the first wave of defenders, the Senators of the Northwest, have been unsuccessful in stopping the machinery, and that once again the enemy has made its way through the Nez Perce territory, heading this time for the ridiculous spirit-killing slackwater port of Lewiston. Would-be sailors live stranded there in a hellhole at the bottom of an abyss, an inland port at the bottom of a canyon so deep that the sun rarely shines down upon these lost souls and their big toy ships, nor upon the cold poisoned waters, where white-bellied bloated fish roil the surface in their fuzzy google-eyed death. Lewiston, where the stench of spoiled grain and spoiled milk rises through the canyon, and where discarded car batteries sit half-submerged bankside from where the locals, as if in some primitive contest, have sought to hurl them from the cliffs into the river, but have fallen short.

There is no rhyme or reason to the contents on the slow barges that make their way up the dead river, bringing things nobody needs deeper into the heart of the country, and all under the power of subsidy. Welfare shipping jobs; welfare sailors. Some crates are filled with plastic water pistols from China, while others are doubtless filled with nuggets of nuclear material, coming ever-farther into the homeland. The barges coming into Idaho and Montana are a quaint nineteenth century idea, and unsustainable without the government dole—but no matter, really, for the nuclear facilities at Hanford are breathing their slow gentle radiating breath; their buzzing fluid discharges plume slowly into the watershed, we are sipping a little buzz-juice, a little go-juice, our bones crackle and glow, our thyroids throb and swell and flutter like downed power lines.

Our lives are costly. We sign the contracts of commerce. But our best interest may be found in places left fallow and wild. Montana is one such place. We have ruined too much.

⁂

Fighting them in Montana means they have made it through the defenses of all our other compatriots, in Portland and Seattle and Eugene, in Kooskia and Clearwater. Making it all the way to the pass means that the last stand is here.

Imagine the sickening feeling to realize that all your handwringing fears and paranoias, your phobias and mistrust, have suddenly come true: the giant shadow that falls across you now is one of our own summoning. The machines have come to deliver to us that which we must have, and yet they have also come to destroy and take away that which we must have. In order to defeat them, we must save ourselves.

We must enter our own kind of burning, I think. We must be purified by fire, and right here, in a land the ice only so recently left that some nights, when you are camping in autumn and lie down on a slab of rock beneath the stars, it seems you can still feel the core of that ice, housed yet within the stone. But we carry within us a portable miracle, the fire in our heart, a burning that can warm even the coldest winter in the blood. To win, everything that is not owned by Imperial Oil—and its subsidiary, Exxon—must briefly coalesce, convene, in the handful of places where we might—*might*—find chinks in their cursed armor. They can feed themselves on anything and everything in the world—oil, coal, cattle, plastic, cotton, human lives and labor, the silica of beach sand, trees, gold, and poultry. But the thing they run best on, and the thing that most empowers them, is desire, a desire which feeds on our own.

For long decades they have been telling us what we want, even as for those same long decades they have been keeping their eyes covetously on one of the things they want most.

They want Montana. They envy the garden that has not yet been fully corrupted.

It may be that they recognize Montana is a danger to them. As long as there remains an unspoiled garden, there remains the possibility that a new story might yet form from that still-new soil: a story that does not include them. A story that dreams them out of existence. A story different from the thus-far endless loop of innocence, growth, power, corruption, betrayal, and then the fall from grace.

Here in Montana we still inhabit grace. We stumble through it, and sometimes take it for granted while the greedy, having eaten the world, turn their hungry eyes on the prize that is not only last but best.

※

There has always been a burning at the pass. The fire burned even when beneath the ice, the ceaselessly burning heart that lies at the core of the earth.

Thin tendrils of fire ascend dark miles to the surface. The burning magma lubricates the drift and slide of the continents as they shift and search, always seeking a new accommodation with one another. Wherever the fire passes, down there in the darkness, it scorches and sears and leaves in its wake a glittering residue of precious gems and minerals, vertical chimneys and rivers of underground jewels, entire palaces and cathedrals those of us in the world above would call wealth and treasure, though we will never see it. The fire rises up, as if it is seeking us, as if it loves us, and wants only to be with us.

Wherever one of these fissures opens into the daylight, bringing forth new mountains, new soil, new earth, turning over the old and summoning the most wonderful, curious thing, *the new*, with which the gardener or farmer is greatly delighted—the earth in such places is different. Such sites are—to use a word that once meant something, before it became commercialized by politicians and other vendors and consumers—sacred. There are not many such sites in the world, and if you believe as I am starting to that each manifests itself as the breath of a creator greater than ourselves, then it's possible you might start to look at things a little differently. It's possible that the entire world might shift in your perception of it. Maybe not instantly, or overnight, but quickly, suddenly: within the blink of your lifetime. As if the mountains you inhabited as a boy or girl—the ground across which you ran and played—was one day to be uplifted from the horizontal to the vertical.

Is this the rapture of which the late-night high-wattage radio Bible-thumpers speak—the tribulations they wield as a threat and a weapon to dominate you with their voices and their ability to frighten you, thereby allowing them to take control over you, or to ascend to some position slightly more elevated than you?

I believe in the rapture but I don't know what it is. I think maybe there is a rapture in every breath, a rapture in the thread of every moment; an ascent that always, for as long as the earth burns, is superior to—dominant over—the freighted gravity of the inanimate descent. I believe that the rapture of all living things defeats the brute and merciless and uninspired pull of the hungry descent back into the void, the cold lure of the abyss. I believe there is a rapture in the magma as it creeps and surges and snakes beneath the surface, seeking us—seeking to awaken us.

What matters? Not *oro y plata*. They got it wrong, back then. This is our chance to get it right.

A fire has always existed at the pass, and a fire has always been coming and going, back and forth through the pass. Sometimes new fire seems to join that original fire, and other times, ice seeks to vanquish the fire, and in so doing preserve the careful balance of the world.

Some places are more important than others, is what I mean to be saying, like the slots and crevices and tumblers within a lock, with only one species able to pass through that keyhole, and in only one way. Such rare and certain places summon and then shape that species, and sometimes summon and shape entire populations and cultures. Look at the Cumberland Gap, which like a magnet drew and directed the first waves of settlers from Europe, funneling them off the coast and southward, into the Appalachians, from which they were able to then spread, in murderous genocide, across the rest of the country.

The slaveowner Thomas Jefferson, whom it is fashionable to revere, had genteel plans for the green garden of the new continent, but often conveniently overlooked the fact that he was but a visitor, while roughly thirty million original inhabitants lived in that garden, and had been living there for about ten thousand years before he showed up so extremely late to the party, script of Manifest destiny and cutlass in hand: with those ten-thousand-year-ago residents having slid down through their own keyhole, across the briefly-frozen fire of the Bering Strait, the ocean freezing just when they most needed it to, so that the garden could begin to receive them, as they hunted their way across that frozen bridge, following the mastodons as if a god or God himself was leading them, pulling them with their desire through the eye of a needle.

Just because a thing is destined to be, or a group of people is chosen, does not at all mean that there is favor with them, or that God is on their side. The earth seeks a balance: the creator seeks a continuing narrative. For the fire to defeat the ice, the ice must at some point dominate and defeat the fire. We are each and all only a tiny part of something immense, and while we generally think of ourselves as a chosen people, it can be instructive I think to stop and consider, now and again, that monsters might lurk in our own hearts.

Why else do we find it so easy to serve ourselves, why else do we find it so hard to be pure, and so hard to spend our hours doing only good?

We want it both ways. We want to be the chosen ones but we do not want to do the work. We want to be able to befoul our nests, to shit in the garden, and have someone else clean it all up and make it be as if it never happened, so that we can do it again.

I am terrified that we are the ice, not the fire—that we are the monsters who have been summoned to balance—to drag down—what was once Eden, and I perceive that the battle here on the pass is our one keyhole-like chance to transcend and metamorphose ourselves. That we have been monsters long enough—for 234 years, blasphemy though I know this is—and that it is finally our chance, for the first time in what feels like a long time, to be angels again.

The Buddha preaches compassion and understanding, and counsels detachment from outcome. I can even feel a little compassion for the governor of Montana, who may, after all, want in his heart of hearts to do the right thing, as long as it's easy—but I cannot detach from the outcome.

The governor and his trucks, the governor and his company (which will, once the trucks are through, turn around and eat him just as quickly as any of us—will eat him first, in fact), think that God is on their side, while we who are preparing to gather at the pass think or hope that God is on our side.

Or we hope that if she is not, we might yet in these coming last days, be able to convince her to change her mind, and come over to our side and lead us, not the trucks, through that pass. That we will make it into the future as a better, not lesser, people.

⁊

It's not fair of me to badmouth Jefferson: the old slave-owner, father of our country, godfather of the West, which, like a deadbeat dad, he never saw. He's like any of us, like the governor himself: a bit player in a larger production, a cog within our immense gearing. Think how much more awful things would be if his nemesis, Alexander Hamilton, had prevailed in their various political battles. Hamilton was mad for machines and corporations; he might have invented an apparatus that would have severed the continent along the Mississippi River and ground up the West through an immense pulping machine, manufacturing widgets and sprockets out of the guts and soul of the same lands that are now our national parks. If Hamilton had put out the fire, the Pacific would now be lapping at the edges of Kansas and Wisconsin. Even our books would be gone. No *Sand County Almanac* (for Aldo Leopold would never have gone west to New Mexico, to encounter the wolves' green fire), no *Angle of Repose*, no John Muir, no *Monkey Wrench Gang*. Ronald Reagan himself would never have happened, nor either of the George Bushes. The West would have vanished, collapsing in on itself.

Jefferson was flawed, which is to say, he was a human being. Hamilton was a machine. It could have been worse. Jefferson, with his conflicting twin braids of saint and sinner, at least gave us the legacy of a fighting chance. We keep messing up, year after year, but we still have a chance.

It's a well-known story, Jefferson's earnest belief in science, and his assignation of young Lewis and Clark to explore, map, and inventory the lands west of the Mississippi, bought from the French, who convinced Jefferson that they, and not the Indians, owned it.

The boy explorers flatboated up the Missouri to Great Falls, got out and continued on foot and horseback, seeking the shining waters of commerce. The Montana plains—rejuvenated yearly by fire—were seething with a bounty the boy-explorers did their best to describe, but which is essentially unimaginable to those of us long adrift now as if on an ark with only a few examples remaining of each species.

The sun would have poured down on the remaining burned land, converting sunlight to grassland, and grassland to buffalo—a hundred million buffalo. This, I think, might well have been the heaven prophesied—the streets lined with gold, the tables set with endless bounty, as if for an endless feast—but it has all come and gone. And if it returns, as all things do, will we be here that next time to receive it?

Lewis and Clark behaved admirably for the most part—they attacked not a single native, and killed but one who, upon trying to steal their horses, advanced upon them with a gun—and for the most part were dignified ambassadors, makers of maps and seekers of science, expressing goodwill to the civilizations about to be vanquished.

Advancing earnestly, not even really considering the moral implications of the Purchase, or their jobs, their tasks, their assignations: advancing as might the front men and front women for Imperial Oil venture into the same heartland today, bone saws concealed behind their backs or tucked inside their blazers.

When they hit the mountains, the explorers ran into trouble. They had no concept of such a landscape, no idea of how to survive in the mountains, and after the easy bounty of the plains, it must have seemed as if they had been expelled from heaven. Two hundred years later, ancestors of the wild animals that sustained them have now taken refuge in the mountains, the only places left where such creatures are safe.

Back in Lewis and Clark's day, the prairies were the place to be. But to complete their master's bidding Lewis and Clark had to leave paradise, and go up into the dark west-slope cedars, hemlocks, and larch; they had to push through the veil toward the shining ocean they believed was on the other side, to connect their commerce with that of the rest of the world. And to receive the rest of the world's commerce. Be *careful what you wish for*, we want to caution them, looking backwards, but there is no way they can hear us—no way they could hear us, back then, if we had even known what caution to offer them.

It's an old story, a familiar American story. The Nez Perce found them lost and hungry and wandering in the forest—starving, and with winter settling in—and rather than letting the snows cover them up, the Nez Perce dug them up and carried them over the pass, helped them continue on their way to the shining sea, and bring back to us—like hunters, finally successful after long searching, and with the eventual gift of great good luck—our own briefly splendid history.

We know how it went. We learned the basics in the second, third or fourth grade—how, once rescued and led to the coast, the boys lingered through the winter—their excellent vacation—before returning with their maps and treasures to the Great White Father and our insatiable hungers. The predatory eyes turning to the West, the great jaws gaping open. Fuel for the industrial revolution that was coming. Roads, railways. The cost of our existence.

In the fifth and sixth grade we learned of these things—the West's supply of copper, gold, silver, timber, grassland, cattle—and finally in high school they finished telling us the real truth, that the same government the Nez Perce had rescued, supported, and gifted with trust and goodwill then turned on the Nez Perce, sought to exterminate them, and all the other tribes, and, with those last few who would not die, or who survived simply because we eventually wore ourselves out, became tired of the killing—our guns overheated, or we ran out of bullets, or whatever—we imprisoned in reservations that reserved nothing.

Our army chased the last band of them down out of their beloved mountains—men, women and children, led by the previous diplomat but now warrior, Chief Joseph. They crossed the Upper Big Hole, where many were slaughtered before dawn, and the survivors fled farther, out into the prairie, and on toward Canada, toward Alberta.

If the Nez Perce could make it across the international border, they would be safe from our murderous army, safe from our Indian-killing cavalry, but they didn't quite make it, and were finally caught and killed just a few miles short of the same border where we will one day seek to stop and capture or kill the giant trucks on their way to that same other country, should we fail to stop them at the pass.

We will not give up Montana without a fight. There will always be a Plan B. Montana will become Imperial Oil's Afghanistan, their Vietnam. Politicians' careers will live or die over these tar sands. They will have to decide whether to continue trying to suckle the thick tar from the sulfurous pit, or serve history by resisting.

Shoot low, boys, the army commanders cried as they charged the Nez Perce tepees before dawn: *they're still sleeping.* This is the foundation our country is built upon, and the only thing worse than knowing it would be to ignore it. And now the Nez Perce, having signed a formal opposition to Imperial's plans, are deigning to help us again. Are deigning to help us keep Montana as it is, in order to lend a hand to the native people up in Fort Chipewyan, Alberta.

All genocides are heartbreakingly unique; all genocides are iconoclastically the same. They start small—someone has to be the first to die—and then the killing accelerates and widens, like a river. At some point our souls flee us and it just becomes mechanical, like fire consuming dry tinder, like ice splitting boulders, like the whirl of the borealis circling the sky.

Genocide is a phenomenon of our species, an event of strange combustibility where the elements of our self-loathing mix with those of our narcissism. It makes no more sense than does digging something up in order to bury it, or burying something in order to dig it up.

⁂

It occurs to me that I am high-centered on the pass, and that I have not really begun the narrative. But narrative means movement, and I do not want to descend toward the abyss. I do not want to go down toward the lake of fire.

But the lake of fire is calling our name and the forests are burning. We must leave. We must give up pieces of the past and step forward into the future; all of our previous defenses have failed, and now they too are at the pass.

Fire rings this state, burning here on the pass at its western borders, and burning to the north in the toxins and greed and steaming tar pits of Alberta, and burning along the southern borders in the ventholes and fumaroles and bubbling mudpots of Yellowstone, where again the breath and will of gods or God seeks to make itself known: while in the center of this vast ring of great burning, the garden of Montana prospers still, chosen and special.

Occasionally the burning spills over the state lines and into the garden, but it's always for the good; it always makes the garden even more verdant, come springtime. The Blackfeet called fire "the red buffalo" for the way it passed through quickly, leaving the land nourished and rejuvenated, and likewise the forest tribes—the Kootenai and Salish—would torch the southern slopes, trying to increase the bounty, the feast, for the animals they in turn feasted upon.

As soon as the steel rails were laid along the northern tier in the nineteenth century, bisecting the ten thousand year-old migratory paths of the buffalo—the east-west rails truncating that north-south flow of sun-fueled protein, the east-west rails carrying now the carcasses and bones of buffalo back to farms in the Midwest, where the bones were ground to powder and spread in the soil to help make the corn grow, shifting the wild garden of Montana into the tame gardens of Illinois, Nebraska, Wisconsin.

The sparks thrown from the steel wheels as they squawled and hissed their way down the rails bounced into the summer-dry seas of prairie grass and ignited their own fires, which then raced along behind the trains, heating the boxcars and warming the bones and hides in such a way as to carry the stench farther, while prairie wolves and coyotes ran alongside for short distances, drawn by the alluring odor and gnawing on whatever bones spilled from the boxcars.

The trains' engines ran on coal, with black-streaked engineers shoveling it into the boilers with one man-breath after another, the fiery engines devouring and exhaling it in black ribbons that twisted and vanished into the endless blue sky. We have made mistakes in Montana, but thus far, the garden has been big enough and supple enough to accept our mistakes with something approaching tolerance if not quite forgiveness.

These railroad fires, the residue of the coal-breathing, would have summoned the faithful green fields as well, each spring, so that for a brief moment in history, that which was setting out to destroy Montana might initially have looked like something that would benefit the garden.

There is always fire, not just on the pass and at the borders of the garden, but everywhere, all the time.

Fire in the Firehole River, where some of Chief Joseph's warriors fell, blood streaming from their ribs into the steaming current, the warriors lung-pierced by those whom they had saved seventy years earlier. Fire caught burning bright and transcendent in the speckled orbs of the trout that to this day still fin above the red and green riverpolished stones, appearing as glimmering coals, their undulating movement combining with that of the shimmer of the river-current, the icy snowmelt washing over them as if in an effort to cool their magnificent burning—though still, in Montana, beneath such shimmering, oxygenated waters—in rivers like Lolo Creek, the Blackfoot, the Two-Medicine and the Dearborn—such fire undulates, survives, endures, even as the substrate of those creeks trembles and vibrates at the approach of the big rigs, the gravel-beds in which the eggs for the next generation of fire-swimmers are laid quivering into jelly at the intrusion of such unprecedented and asynchronous hog-wallow greed and poison.

Fire in the songs of the thrush, back in the old giant cedars, their boughs once sweet-smelling but now trapping the blacksmoke diesel of the big rigs groaning slowly up the pass—one, two, maybe three miles an hour in a death march, blatting out fuel, blowing it out their tailpipes and into our lungs, in order that the giant trucks can go searching for more, searching up in Canada, digging beneath the velvet forest up there, out of sight and out of mind, before bringing it, the new blacksmoke, back down to those of us here below...

The trout, their opal eyes limned with gold flecks, will see the creeping and countless caravans, as their delicate eardrums are blasted out. The rivers will still be pretty, as certain rivers in Europe are still pretty, but things will be different. Montana will be going, gone.

❧

I have a friend, a poet, who is being driven mad by corporations. This is not quite as sad as seeing a friend being eaten up by some other kind of illness—mesothelioma, Hodgkins', lupus, Parkinson's, Alzheimer's—and it can even be argued that, being a poet, he was predisposed to madness from the beginning. A fisherman, his soul is wrought by rivers and by the fleeting treasures that surge up and down them, traveling back and forth to the sea, and ever since the Columbia and Snake Rivers were dammed he has been a bit of a ghost, haunted by the stillness of flat bargewaters on which the giant tugs drift like ghosts themselves. Slackwaters, dumpwaters, oily bilgewater, fester, where once there were waves, rapids, silversided salmon surging with the kind of electricity that can keep us sane, the kind of electricity that can remind us of what it means to be human beings.

As more and more dams killed his big waters, the poet retreated to the creeks to catch bright little fish with obscure little hooks, tiny hooks with points smaller and finer than the period at the end of this sentence. The hooks are wrapped with sacred materials—the fur from this-or-that beloved pet, the feather from a red rooster raised by monks in the Himalayas, a strand of his mother's hair, a scrap of leather from his grandfather-the-preacher's old Sunday shoes. It all strikes me as a little precious—he doesn't even eat the fish!—but he's a nice enough guy, if sometimes a little strange and loony. He left the Pacific Northwest when the clearcutting by the big boys—Weyerhaeuser International, Plum Creek International, Crown Zellerbach International, Champion International—made all the soil and dirt in the mountains slide into the creeks and rivers, muddying the once-pristine waters and ruining the fishing he had once known.

His relationship with salmon changed. He moved to the first creek in Montana, to be nearest the headwaters of the Northwest's salmon, and to wait. He waits for the dams on the Snake to be removed—a true and sustainable economic recovery. He waits for the salmon to come back.

In the summer, he still goes back to his home country. In the summer, when the diverted irrigation channels of eastern Oregon,

Washington, and Idaho suddenly drop, leaving hundreds of thousands of little hatchery-released salmon fingerlings that have gotten sucked into these salmon-deserts, the poet takes a week off work and goes looking for them. With a long-handled minnow net and plastic bucket, he roams the dry West, scooping them up from their sun-warmed shallow troughs of the dying and returning them to the cool flow of the Snake, where each can resume its hero's journey through the gauntlet of dams that lie between it and the sea. Biologists have learned that for every hundred fingerlings they release up near the headwaters, two will survive the gauntlet and reach the sea, where they will live for three years before returning.

Some years the poet nets, buckets, and releases as many as nine hundred fingerlings. *That's eighteen adults that may return to the Rockies*, he crows. And waits.

Having left first home, he came to make his last stand in Montana, from which he still goes back to fish for salmon, and where—in Montana—he now he catches and releases trout.

He came over the pass, staked a claim along the first creek in Montana, closest to Idaho, in the last garden of the world. He planted a

garden, raised a family, and went fishing. Goes fishing. Writes poems, like some olden Chinese monk, in his cabin loft, late at night while the yellow cottonwood leaves flap and flutter in the mountain breezes and the horses neigh and gallop, their hoofs earth-thumping on the packed earth of the corral below. There are no salmon in his river now, but they are tantalizingly closes: so close that there could be, any day, as there were once upon a time, before the ice. Salmon so close to him that an eagle or osprey catching one near the headwaters of the Lochsa could, by flying east a few wingbeats—with the surprised and gleaming fish still thrashing in its talons—become startled by something, loosen its grip, and drop the salmon, like a bombardier, into Lolo Creek, just those few wingbeats across the pass. While still on the Pacific side of the Great Divide, the fish would find no easy way, and maybe no way at all, of making it back to the ocean.

❧

The salmon are gone from Montana, ice-stranded by the glaciers. We ourselves have come up and over the pass, up and over the high walls and into heaven, and we do not wish to relinquish heaven. Will not relinquish it, but will defend it, not just with every lawyer at our disposal, but with every angler, every river-rafter and highway-user, every tree-hugging college student, every Bible-thumping tea party libertarian who will lie down in front of the trucks at the pass, and then, if the pass is lost, we will hound the trucks for the rest of their days.

We will change the law of the land, as our state constitution allows us to do, through the ballot initiative process, in such a way as to grid-lock the trucks, should they make it over the pass, with their dynamite carving and widening the serpentine tight spots along the Lewis and Clark Scenic Byway and along the river, and with their unprecedented weights crushing old unexamined narrow bridges. Ice-sliding into the rivers, trucks would jam traffic for days, weeks, months. We would have to travel by foot or horse just like in the old days while we wait for months for a crane big enough to tug 200 tons up out of the canyon. There isn't any such crane right now, but maybe they can build one in South Korea when the time comes and ship it over here on a big boat and then drive it, so slowly, up and over the pass. Maybe it will get the job done, or maybe not. Maybe the whole road will be so blocked that we will have to dynamite the trucks into little pieces and start all over. All for tar oil.

We are going backwards in time for tar oil.

We need to remember: we have a citizens' initiative process, by which we can impose a ten billion dollar tariff per truck, payable every month, if we wish. We can decree that they paint their trucks sky-blue or pink, that they run only between the hours of two and three a.m. on even-numbered Sundays, and that they pay the state treasury a billion dollars per mile.

We can turn them back with nothing more than the fire in our hearts. We may not yet be able to stop the tar sands pit, but we can block their path along the most direct route. We can shift the fight elsewhere. We can chip away at them. We can carve away not only at Imperial Oil, but also at the hard defensive layers around our own hearts and souls, the lithification of I-don't-care.

We can win. Montana is the weak link in their chain. That's why they came to the governor.

But they—Imperial—made a mistake, just as Custer made a mistake. We may not save the world but we can defeat them in Montana. If they make it into Montana, we can defeat them.

Maybe we want them to come over the pass. Maybe it is a trap; maybe we are luring them over the pass. *Look, here is the shortest path to your gaping pit in Canada, here is the shortest route to the wound of the world: see how close it is, come this way.*

❧

There are stories in some holy texts of the dark ones being thrown out of heaven, banished. There are stories of the clashes between good and evil on the middle-ground of earth, and stories of the suffering and loss endured in purgatory. I am aware of no stories in which those who have been cast from heaven come storming back, seeking to ruin heaven. As if even prophets could not imagine such a thing.

❧

Once, not so long ago—back in the last election cycle—I was an aide to the governor. Actually, I glorify myself in saying that I was an aide. I was the one who went behind him cleaning up the mess. And there was a lot of it. To say that he was high-maintenance doesn't begin to cover it.

Actually, I glorify myself further by saying that it was the governor's messes of rubble and loose ends I patched or picked up. There were professionals who had doctorates in political science and communications who attended to all this. My task was to take care of the governor's dog. And in the year that I held that position, I think that I did good work. It was not over this issue that I parted ways with the governor, and I kick myself for having left early, before Imperial entered the scene—having completed their preliminary meetings in Seoul, the Netherlands, Ontario and Texas—came knocking. Not that I, the dog-handler, could have influenced those meetings in any way, nor dissuaded the governor from the siren-call of whatever it was he thought he was hearing. Nothing would be different; all paths would have led to the pass anyway, as they always have, and always will.

Nothing is forever, not even geology—not even the old swamps and beaches sealed miles beneath us—even they are not safe from being resurrected, then erased, laid-to-level and wind-tossed, crushed and whipped to star-dust, as if none of it ever was. But the pass will long outlast our own reeling species, will draw the best of us to it, and the worst of us to it: we will cluster on either side, and the two things within us, the self and the selfless, will do battle.

The dog-handler—the picker-up of old Shep's poop—would not have made a difference. The pass drew the South Koreans, drew the Canadians, and the White House, and it certainly it drew the bright fire of our singular governor, tiny-speck though he is in the cold universe. I gave no moral counsel when I worked for him, and I would have been unable to provide any, had I attended any of those meetings. My job, like the rest of any of us, was simply to pick up the shit.

It was exhausting, being at the further edges of the governor's orbit. In some ways, it was the hardest place to be, the area of maximum centripetal pull—and what I needed more than anything was a little rest. Anyone interested in the short history of Montana could go to college and spend years researching and coming to understand the strange legacy the state has, our odd relationship between independence and colonialism.

Power has somehow always found its seat here, as if in a mountain-and-plains fiefdom: in the fiery idealism of Jeannette Rankin, the first woman elected to Congress, and the sole consistent voice to vote against any war, every war, all wars; in the diplomacy of Senate leader Mike Mansfield, and in the working-class populism of Pat Williams, long-time House whip, from the mining town of Butte, site of what was once the Richest Hill on Earth, but which then became site of the largest Superfund cleanup on earth (until another small Montana town, Libby, vastly overtook it); and after that, power in a Senator on the other side of the aisle, Conrad Burns—a former cattle auctioneer who became Chair of the Appropriations Committee, deciding which states got how much money for every special project in the country.

Burns was the gatekeeper to every single dollar that flowed out of the federal government and into private hands—money flowing from him and through him as if through a slot in the mountains, through which all money had to pass—and needless to say, being human, he did not hold up well to this responsibility, but got tangled up with the ultra-lobbyist, Jack Abramoff.

In the mild scandal that followed—for really, truth be told, there are so many days when it's hard to be outraged about much of anything for more than a couple of weeks, or a couple of days, or a couple of heartbeats—Burns was slightly, but fatally, weakened. But it might not have been the lobbyist scandal that finally brought him down, though by that time everyone kind of expected scandal of him anyway. What brought him down, I think, was fire: specifically, wildfire. En route from Washington, D.C. one summer to cut some ribbon or another—millions of dollars pouring from him, as if plunging over a waterfall, an endless cascade of money through this one man, distributing to all fifty states—his plane was grounded in Great Falls, due to the smoke and heat. A gaggle of firefighters was stationed there, too. Most of them were up in the burning mountains, fighting the fires—hundreds of thousands of acres of fire, the firefighters laboring like farmers in vast fields whose crop was flame—but there had been one crew which, after seventy-two hours of nonstop fire-fighting, was taking a break on the airport tarmac. They were stretched out in the hundred-degree heat, still grimy-black and dehydrated, lying on the heat-soft tar as if stuck there like specimens, their exhausted bodies literally cooking in the heat, but too whipped to move. Some of them had erected little canvas tarps on the tarmac, in an effort to create a small scrap of heated shade, though the more experienced of them knew that this only gave the effect of being in an oven, and so they lay there instead exposed to the sky, craving sleep more than anything.

The Senator had spied these lay-abouts, these lounging wastrels, even as the wildfires raged, and visibly, on the hillsides above town. Approached by a television reporter who was there to interview him, the Senator thought he saw a way to make political hay of peoples' fear of wildfire. Pointing out the resting firefighters—lounging, while Montana burned!—he singled them out as being lazy.

Montana likes its firefighters. An election was held in 2006. Burns lost, Jon Tester won by a few thousand votes. The Senate had its fifty-first Democrat.

The new balance in the Senate allowed Max Baucus, Montana's senior Senator, to ascend to the Chair of the Finance Committee, which was essentially like the Appropriations Committee on steroids. If Appropriations decided what money went where in the United States, the Finance Committee was and is essentially the gatekeeper for the world, deciding issues of import and export taxation, and tax credits for new as well as existing businesses, among other things.

Montana matters—in terms of spirit, and as the gold standard, the benchmark, for the American wilderness and its effect on the American character, sure; but Montana matters politically, too.

After the genocide of native Americans, which was completed barely a hundred years ago, so recently that we have not even begun to process the reality of it—are still in shell-shocked denial about the cost of our beautiful taking—we wandered into the fragrant garden like innocents at dawn, in the gold summer light of the long northern days. There was blood up to our elbows, still wet from our taking—as a hundred million buffalo were replaced, somehow and quickly, by fifty million cud-chewing and bulbous-eyed and brucellosis-carrying and feedlot-jammed cattle, and all those millions of miles of rusting barbed-wire fence, the strands whistling as the wind raked through those sagging wires, creating a strange and lonely sound where once there had been only the singing of the larks.

You can still see a few buffalo here and there in Montana, their brown shaggy shapes inhabiting one postage-stamp-sized piece of field or another, ringed by razor wire that—if the spirit moved them, if it sparked—they could still simply walk through with no more effort than if they were already ghosts, insubstantial, ethereal, vaporous.

In Montana, we do not want ghost buffalo. We do not want any more ghost-anything. Like all good religious pilgrims of almost any denomination, we want to inhabit a period of suspended grace, should we ever be fortunate enough to attain it.

Some of us believe we can reach that destination by hard work, others believe we reach it through a faith forged by the fires of doubt and tribulation, and still others believe we are already there—that heaven is here and now—but that there are certain custodial matters to attend to, certain matters of basic stewardship.

Who am I leaving out, in this short history of Eden—an Eden so newly emerged that we are all still-changing, still being formed by these terrific forces of fire and ice, with the core of our better, more vibrant selves enwreathed, wrapped with the pulpy flesh of our protoplasm as we struggle to become better-fitted to this garden, even as the creatures that would eat the pulpy fruit of us move ever-closer, and assail us with temptations?

I am leaving out so much. Only 130 years have passed since we vanquished our native Americans, though in some ways the killing continues, if with less drama. In the twenty-first century—a century in which space travel has become so passé that we are downsizing NASA—we are still killing Indians almost as fast as they are being made. Unemployment on the reservations to which we have confined them is as high as forty-eight percent, and average family income is 25% lower than that of the rest of the country. By the ninth grade, an American Indian student is four times more likely to drop out of high school than is a white student. Eighty percent of Native youth use alcohol in adolescence, as opposed to the larger national average of fifty percent.

Walking in the garden, we are still struck by wonder at the beauty of what we have inherited. As you and I did not engage in the initial killing, this has allowed us to pass through the picket-fence swing-gate, and because the blood-up-to-our-elbows, having dried to flecks of brown crust, has since been washed clean by the dew on the broad green leaves—fronds of rhubarb and squash, lacewing ticklings of asparagus and dill—and our arms, freshly-scrubbed and absolved, drying in the morning sun—we feel or perceive that we are clean. And maybe for an instant—a breath—we are. But then we begin to breathe again, the outer world does

battle with our inner seed, and the combustion starts all over again. In the narrowness of our moral vision and in our canny refusal to open the history book, we are killing Indians again, and we know it. Talking about such things is not going to win any friends in high places, but any short history that does not mention this one truth would be blasphemy. I don't have any answers other than to point out the obvious: that unless there is forceful, creative effort to the contrary, history tends to replicate itself with the momentum of a virus.

As the Indians we confined to the dusty reservation postage-stamps must surely never have been able to imagine having such freedoms taken away, I have the sickening feeling—the foreknowledge of prophecy—that we likewise are not thinking this thing through. I fear that we are simply blinding ourselves to the idea that we, too, in Montana might one day suddenly find ourselves imprisoned where once we had a limitless freedom.

It breaks my heart that the Indians are trying to help us in our battle.

The rigs won't fit. Some kids from the university already tried it. They got together with a trucker in Idaho, Buck Lazlo, who understood that he would not get any of these jobs, with their specially-trained company drivers, specially-bonded against many though not all of the bad things that

can happen when one seeks to haul six hundred thousand pounds of iron and steel up a mountain and through a slot in the earth in order to reach another country so that the final destruction of the earth may begin.

Lazlo understood that you can't use regular trucks: that regular pistons can't bring that much weight up that pass, and no brake pads or linings manufactured by man, no material on this planet, can brake adequately coming down. Not in winter, with loose tire-chains slapping wet sparks, grinding the road up as if beneath the iron tread of tanks, and not in dusty, broiling summer. Each attempt would be a one-shot deal, each truck would end up giving its metallic best, sacrificing its mechanical life. There would be a whole chain, an entire infrastructure of Imperial and the Governor. Each truck would wear its heart out in the blind service of combustion.

"Hell," Lazlo says, "there may not be any such piston." No one's ever tried to haul so much weight up a mountain before: not in South Korea, and sure as hell not in Montana. "They're grabbing their ass," he says. "They're using us as an experiment. They're just throwing something at the wall to see if it sticks. They don't care that they're going to plug up one of the most beautiful roads in America. Hell, they're happy to do it."

Lazlo understands what machines and engines can and can't do, and understands also that in a life governed as his is by minutes and miles, hundreds and then thousands and then tens of thousands of caravans of breaking-down gut-groaning tankers, creeping at two or three miles per hour along the 206-mile route between Lewiston and Lolo, will destroy his own trucking business, along with that of all the other truckers in the region.

"Commerce," he says, "will be screwed. This is just another big fat subsidy, one more fat-ass bail-out for the biggest company in the world." Like a virus attaching to its host, infiltrating and inhabiting its host, Imperial is taking over a road built by state and federal taxpayers.

Lazlo understands also that the heavy black gates that the states of Idaho and Montana recently constructed on either side of the pass, at the bottom of the mountain—much to the initial curiosity of residents—will be closed and locked "for security purposes," whenever the big rigs (and *big* is somehow not the right word) are beginning their labors.

Who paid for the gates' construction; who knew what and when? Isn't this wildly illegal, two states conspiring to lock up a federal highway, and— salt in the wound—for the exclusive benefit of the world's largest corporation, which has decided to gut Montana as if the entire state was but a plump whitefish, or a yearling doe being made ready for the grill—gutting Montana on their way to the real feast, the banquet of tar up in Canada, where Imperial can really get down to the business of killing Indians?

Of course it's illegal, and of course it's scandalous. Does the news of it touch our souls? Sure it does, for a moment: for about as long as it takes to read this sentence. Then the world pulls one's attention away. In this day and age, more than ever, an exposed heart may feel like a heart in danger. We have learned to pass on by briskly; to avoid the groping, reaching tentacles of sorrow, which will surely pull us down into our own and very personal pit if we pause. We have spent generations teaching ourselves how not to be touched.

Art is on its last legs—yes, truth is still beauty and beauty is still truth—but in the meantime, the trucks are coming. They are on their slow boats across the ocean right now, many of them have already arrived and are in Lewiston; and though my friend the poet would disagree with me, it is no longer a time for poetry. We poets in the West had a good run—a hundred or more years of exclaiming how beautiful it all was—but look, here we are, it is time for war again. Even the ghost of Old Chief Joseph might agree, that if he had to do it all over again, he would do it differently.

ॐ

You can check it out on YouTube, it's the damnedest thing. The truck and its wooden life-sized trailer, got stuck in the second turn, bound up tighter than a tick. Lazlo had covered the sides of the trailer with dish-washing soap, to help it squeeze through the narrows—in this manner, it had just barely skinnied through the first turn—but after that, it got stopped up like a cork in a bottle. No one had even thought to run a simple mathematical model to see if a 200-foot ruler with but three segments could be placed end-to-end all the way down the canyon, and so Lazlo and the university students provided a graphic example. The traffic, such as it was—about forty cars per hour, and half a dozen tractor-trailers—got stacked up. Lazlo and the kids had to saw up the makeshift trailer and paper-mache mining equipment with chainsaws, while filming the proof of unfittedness. A teachable moment, as they say, though it taught nothing: people—including the state-house—nodded and said that adjustments might need to be made, but that the permit should be issued anyway.

Seeing is believing—and people believed, all right—but their hearts weren't touched. It's just so *expensive*, emotionally, is the thing. We try to live big lives of passion, here in Montana, but quiet, with lots of open space around our movements, though it is becoming harder with each passing day. Sometimes I worry that we are as drafthorses, asked to do the same work year after year, even as we are being led unwittingly to the slaughterhouse at trail's end.

People saw the photos in the *Missoulian* of Lazlo's stunt and read the article, viewed the YouTube clip, but then slid past. The quicksilver river of fear and despair flowed over and across but not into their hearts.

꙾

Much of the proposed route over the pass, up through Missoula, and along the Blackfoot River—a National Wild and Scenic River route along the river immortalized in Norman Maclean's *A River Runs Through It*—is utilized by the hundreds of motorcycle clubs and solo riders on their

annual pilgrimage to Sturgis, South Dakota: tens of thousands of black leather-clad locusts, as if some nearby vent-hole in the earth has opened up and they have surged up that shaft and out into the world, blatting and buzzing, rumbling and roaring. They will be there too, weaving in braids past and around the stalled traffic jams, swerving and cursing and fighting the big rigs: a vision out of the bleak futuristic film *Mad Max*.

How could our governor have let us down? He used to be something. He used to be someone. As he might yet be again. As might we all, yet. There is still hope.

⁂

The poet is losing his power. There is no television—by choice—but he and his family have a lush garden: there are apple trees in the yard, golden apples in their pies and in their jams. Wild turkeys peck at the golden apples in the fall, black bears bite into the apples with crunches so loud that they can be heard inside the cabin, where the family often sits by the fire, reading, while a pie, or an elk roast, or a quiche, bakes in the oven. Such lives still unfold in Montana. You might be tempted to ask what any of this has to do with the short history of Montana, and my answer is *everything*.

Montana is a place to come to, and a place to hold on to. The breath of still-unbroken wilderness slides down out of the deep blue furze of the mountains' forests, the air laced with the brace of cold clean glaciers, with their underwater rivers gurgling and carrying in a steady clatter and rumble a tinkling slurry of waterpolished cobbles—a sound like dice being shaken, then rolled, far back in the mountains—and even when we are warm and leisurely in our homes, the spirit of that farther, further wildness, the glorious nighttime air of the dark wilderness, comes in all seasons through and between the cabins' cracks and infuses itself into our lungs and our blood. We inhale it, breathe it and are nurtured by it, much in the manner in which a fish takes in dissolved oxygen through its gills.

This is not yet a vignette or image of myth, it is still a quiet place where lives—whether small, like the poet's, or big, like the governor's—can be lived with meaning. I'm sorry to say that converting the state's quiet back roads and scenic highways—as well as its major interstate system—into a "High and Wide" oilfield services international transport corridor—is not an action that is compatible with the lives we have carved out and still hold on to here.

In Montana, it—life—is not about money. There is not one of us living here who could not make more money doing whatever we do elsewhere. We are each and all here for a reason.

Perhaps it is amoral or even immoral of me to be so taken by the poet's plight, and his desire—like all Montanans—for a little more peace and quiet in the green garden when just across the invisible dashed line of the border, up in Alberta, the native people who with the misfortune of either chance or destiny, it matters not, are reeling in the dirt streets of poverty, choking on the benzene groundwater, the slurry and residue of Imperial's toxic breath as Imperial steam-cleans the mined sands, the tar from those sands melting into tears of oil before dripping into vats that store the precious earthly fluids, the fluids of the ages, to be shipped back south, back to us, in the U.S. Perhaps it is amoral or immoral to be wanting so desperately a little more time, a little more peace and quiet, while farther north, the Indians are dying now in the latest wave of secret and silent genocide, the Canadian government every bit as dogged and ferocious as our own in this regard, the native community in Fort Chipewyan gagging their guts out with rare throat and stomach cancers, and seeing wild visions of prophecy as new rare brain cancers interrupt their neural chemistries and pathways; stumbling, crumbling, as rare bone cancers chew away at their legs, all of them tended to by one country doctor who, when he tried to express his concern to the Canadian government, was immediately disbarred.

So far the cancer rates in Fort Chipewyan are only about 30 percent higher than normal. It's not as if they've all died in a single day, or a single hour—and with an open pit that will one day be the size of Florida, well, there's plenty of room for burying more.

Moral, amoral, or somewhere in between, the love we in Montana have for the green earth? I don't know. It is what it is. We fight for what we need and love. The haul route is wrong in every direction, as is the mining of the sands themselves.

The poet is just like you or me, then, like any of us in Montana, except for the curious matter of his poems, his soul on fire. All souls are on fire, of course, we all have our burnings, but his are made public in his pages. He offers them like a gift, and then waits to see if anyone will take them. He is driven to share them, this private man who is battling the public man. In this he is little different from you or me, and though he is the opposite of the governor, who never saw a crowd or a camera he didn't like, there are nonetheless some similarities between the two men.

Each, for instance, does not fall asleep immediately, but lies there for a while, thinking. Rare is the day when either of these artists—each working with the medium of people's hearts and needs—is entirely satisfied with the way the day has gone. There is always something that could have been controlled a little more tightly: a word, a collection of words, an image, a message, a theme, a meme. At the end of the day, each wants just a little more light in the day.

Except for that, the poet is not so different from any of us. The other day he helped bury a friend's favorite mule. The animal had gotten out onto the scenic highway, a black mule on a moonless night. Farther up the road, closer to the pass, there is a moose crossing, which funnels the giant herbivores down from the north into the Selway-Bitterroot wilderness. The hot springs near the pass have a complicated, little-studied and still-unknown system of natural piping and plumbing—like veins and arteries—that warm the earth in this area and produce numerous pools and pockets of warm water and snowmelt, and which percolate salts and other minerals back up to the surface, as if spreading a thin feast for the animals. At night, driving past such sites, you'll see their red eyes glinting at the edge of the forest. You'll see them licking and pawing at and sometimes eating the earth itself, scalloping out little troughs, so hungry are they for these certain minerals, tiny trace elements they cannot live without.

The poet is losing power, here in middle age—or rather, the power is going deeper, is going back underground, and seeming to disappear. What once flowed through him with the ease of each day's sunlight, rising and flooding him as if with the unquestioned availability of electricity, is too often fragmented these days. It does no good to lament or long for those younger days of innocence, when there were fewer if any responsibilities—those days in the garden, when nothing but light poured through him. Life is *supposed* to get harder as you get older, and, like Chief Joseph, possessing the heart of a diplomat, a peace-lover, yet the ethos of a warrior—he has already had to retreat from one homeland—he will not leave another. He works harder, longer, later, slower, as if in his own internal exodus through the snow and over the mountains. He begins early and works late.

There are so many distractions. First and foremost there are the children, fast-growing, with the most precious commodity of all, time, flowing past, traveling faster than even the river itself, just outside his window. There is his passion, fishing—he stands in the river, insinuating himself between its braids and currents as if separating strands of muscle, to either deliver energy to that muscle, or to extract energy and strength from it.

The poet does not own any cats. There are birdfeeders for hummingbirds and picture windows looking out at the mountains and the river. In the spring and summer and early autumn, the quietness of the days is punctuated by the thunkings of birds flying hard into the thick triple-paned glass, sending a concussive vibration all throughout the cabin. Reflexively, the poet and his sons leap up at the sound of each window-strike and rush outside to protect the stunned bird, before any wild cats or hawks can prey upon it. They'll be sitting quietly at the table, eating, or standing in the kitchen, cooking—so often, they are preparing meals—and then that *thunk* will come, the irregular but frequent announcement of the outside trying to pass through to the inside, and they will drop what they are doing to dash outside and mediate this confusing space on the other side of the veil. If you think that a gentle heart belies a weak heart, this would be a significant mistake in perception.

It's a tough way to make a living, but this does not mean the poet is without resources. He has friends in low places, tens of thousands of such friends, who send him letters daily, some of whom have been writing him for years. The poet's disciples, or if not disciples, then friends and peers, are everywhere: he seems to have almost as many devotees as birds in the sky, and they will do as he requests. Not unlike Tolstoy, he has even written a little religious tract, and you can imagine the devotion of that readership: the acolytes, each far more intent upon hewing and polishing their spirit than anything else. Willing to not just lie down in front of trucks, when the time comes, but to do more: to do whatever the poet asks.

Again, what has any of this to do with the short history of a big state? Truthfully, this is mostly the history not yet written, the history-to-come: the history that will be read after we are gone, and with none of us yet knowing what the outcome will be—new peace, or the return of war.

Loss, or gain. Captivity, or freedom. The odds are that the old stories of captivity, fiefdom, colonization, will repeat, but there is still just enough chance for a new story to emerge to make the battle, the war, interesting. As the old warhorse Pat Williams said, *We may take glory in the struggle when the cause is just.*

Make no mistake, though, we are playing for more than glory. Imperial is playing for money; the governor is playing for corporate glory and power; and we are playing for the preservation of a safe harbor for our souls.

If we lose, we lose everything.

The poet has been successful in these matters once before, is the thing. Do not automatically despair, thinking, *What chance does a poet in the garden have—or an entire state of poets, or an entire state of gardeners—against Imperial?* While not quite a battle on the scale of David and Goliath, the state has, through the citizen initiative process, defeated a multinational corporation before, and not that long ago. The international mining company, Phelps-Dodge, as well as Canyon Resources, was hoping to dig the guts out of some mountains in Montana and douse the rubble with vast amounts of cyanide. The state legislature—under the administration of another governor, who had eagerly declared herself "a lapdog of industry"—seemed to believe that cyanide was just what Montana needed, and had issued the permit. But we the people took it back. We passed a citizens' initiative that said you can't saw the tops off mountains and douse them with poison. The poet-angler and other people who honor and live near the creeks and rivers were, needless to say, engaged in the process. So there's a little bit of history, one brick's worth, and not so long ago at all.

❧

We know what is coming. The first truck is due this icy winter; after that, there will be no end until we end it. They say there will be an end, but as long as there is tar in the sands below the boreal forest, they will keep coming, clawing and digging, boiling the sand in a witches'-brew vat the size of Florida, redirecting the mighty Athabasca River—as if the river itself is now nothing more than a garden hose—into the steaming, toxic vent.

None of us are pure. Every time we turn the car key, we are scratching, chipping at the pit ourselves, worrying a scab that will not heal until we stop picking at it. But we can stop the trucks. We can set our largest temptations beyond ourselves. We can preserve what is best about us—the place we live, the place we love. The gift we have been given.

We know what is coming. Once the permit is issued, Imperial will begin trying to coax and entreat and sway and soothe us. They will seek to seduce us with the usual unimaginative one-trick ponies of their profession, billboards and newspaper ads and radio spots. Open houses with smiling men and women—robots, really—in suits. Pumpkin pie, ginger cookies from a grocery store, apple cider in plastic cups, reassuring promises, bonhomie and fealty.

They might even set up a web page, they might even tweet and blog. They will identify the maddened anarchists and will task them with demonizing the Hollywood elitist tree-huggers and other environmentalists—the most-reviled demographic in Montana. They will pour millions into the state: radio ads will run round the clock, the sound waves drifting often uselessly through the pines at night, invisible, with the cold stars casting icy light on the forests—the shimmering lies snaking their way across the snowy mountains. It will be a very good time to be the owner of a radio station, or a newspaper, or both. The governor and Imperial will talk about jobs, and the economy. They will proclaim their concern for the workin' man.

And after they have spent their wan imagination in the attempts to seduce us—gathering a few corporate converts, in that manner, such is the nature of the human condition—they will become less sophisticated in their efforts, and will begin to batter and bludgeon us with repetition and force. While continuing to seek to identify the issue as one opposed exclusively by knee jerk handwringing liberal elite not-in-my-backyard enviros, they will extol the economic virtues of their project—how it will create a job for two truck drivers and two pilot cars for eighteen months, and seventy-five part-time roadside flag-holding jobs. As if someone had put an ad in the newspaper, *Western state for sale, cheap, good riverfront acreage. Asking price, seventy-five orange flags or best offer.*

Not in my back yard? Damned straight. Not in my back yard, not in my front yard, not in my side yard, not in Montana. Take the long way around. Take the boats to Galveston and send the equipment up that petrochemical corridor, if they must be sent at all. Shift the battle to Texas and Oklahoma, then seek to cut off those tentacles, too. But first things first: not in Montana. They may not have the shortest, cheapest route. We must make the route more expensive for them. *No paseron.*

We know what is coming. They will manufacture giant funnels and back them up to the state's borders and begin pouring cash, like grain, into the media outlets. We saw it with BP in Louisiana and we will see it here with Imperial, and we must be ready for it. This is our first as well as last uncontested shot at framing and identifying the story before the infidels arrive.

They will pour so much money into the advertising that we will each and all be up our ankles, our knees, our waists, in their lies, and still the money will keep pouring in.

They will back the funnels up to the hungry babybird mouths of any state legislator willing to support them, or even to defer responsibility, as they have asked the governor to do.

The governor is good, or good at what he does. If they were to make a movie about all this, they would use Robert Duvall to cast him; he has that kind of bristling, bustling, physical presence, that coiled-to-bursting persona; that raised-hand, *pick me* charisma. The child who cannot stand to be ignored—who will not be ignored, even if it means doing something outrageous. Especially that.

He's good. I was with him when he started. Even then, you could see that the sky was the limit. In the first half of his career, he delighted in smacking down bullies, corporate or otherwise, and in so doing, giving power to the oppressed and longsuffering workers. He made people believe in the power of politics again, and with Old Shep roaming the halls and snapping at the ankles of anyone who stepped out of line, he delighted them, as the voiceless or underrepresented have always been delighted by the belief that one of their own, against all odds, has made it into the halls of power.

He wears a bolo tie and expensive but scuffed and well-worn cowboy boots. Rarely does he appear without a blazer, often navy, giving him a nautical look, which makes the horseshit country aphorisms that come out of him all the more potent and endearing. They are no longer surprising—we've come to expect them. The dressing-up makes him look capable in an era where financial acumen is more important than it's ever been, as state budgets all around us plunge in freefall, and yet his coarse agrarian sensibility never fails to calm those who would otherwise have feared he was at risk of becoming corrupted by the trappings of wealth and power.

Not our old straight-talking governor, no sir. No cityfolk, no Beltway lawyer, no corporate shysters, would be able to pull the wool over his eyes. He would conduct himself well; he would represent his state in such a way as to draw notice, positive notice.

No longer would the little man be forgotten or unheard. When our governor walked into a room, everyone noticed and tensed with anticipation.

He had a limitless gift and a bottomless hunger. Less than a week after his election to the statehouse, he was on the front page of the newspapers, quarter-page photo above the fold, celebrating the re-opening of a hunter's bar in Butte, sharing a shot with the bar's legendary owner, the 87-year old Skank Davis, at ten a.m., on a workday, no less.

It was quite a photograph, shot from floor level looking up, so that Skank and the governor, already larger than life, looked even more so. The bar was dark, but had that exquisitely lonely ten a.m. sunlight coming in through the small dusty windows (the bar had been abandoned for twenty years), and that weak light, that soft and elegant and almost *futile* light, just barely reached the governor's raised shotglass, just as he was throwing it back, so that the shot glass caught perfectly that dull struggling early winter morning light, so familiar to all of us—such weak winter-light, so desperately hoped for and deeply requisite yet ultimately unsatisfactory, that even if you *didn't* drink, just the image of that pale and ineffective sunlight itself was enough to make you want to.

A week into his career, and he already had a photo that defined him, an image that comforted, entertained, and educated the voters about the force they had directed to pass through the gates and represent them.

∂℞

The governor is good—he is great—but I think he has made a mistake, as the great ones always do, eventually. In leaving Helena and intruding on the poet's home ground, the poet's home waters, I think the governor is suddenly on thin ice. The poet in middle age is losing power, literally—the giant earth-thumping trucks have not yet crested the pass but already the poet's power is being cut off, as is that of his neighbors, as the rural Montana co-ops—supposedly owned by the people—are falling over themselves to make the garden ready for the Behemoth, even though the permit has not yet been issued.

Like groundskeepers at a country club preparing the way for the banquet, or the wedding, the rural co-ops are tidying up, removing all overhead powerlines and burying them, so as to make way for the high overhead clearance that will be required for the giants' passage. They are digging and hiding, burying and obscuring the lines, disconnecting them to do so, and in this manner as they prepare for Imperial's feast, they

disrupt the poet's computer; even as the poet has been composing his poems and manifestos, and collating his list of fishing guides from around Montana and the West, who will, when he asks them, show up with their driftboats and trailers a thousand strong, to blockade the big rigs. But he labors on, working now by hand.

In Montana, story is more important than money. It's why we're here.

The governor used to share this view—and there were few if any better at crafting, shaping, presenting story, than he (I am thinking now of the time when, during his first campaign, the governor commandeered a bus full of rest-home seniors and drove them—illegally—across the border and into Canada, so they could buy their prescription medicines more cheaply as well as protest the rising costs of healthcare)—but I worry that the governor is in a strange place in his life right now, that he sits as if on a high divide, perfectly and precariously balanced between salvation and ruin; I worry that he finds himself tempted, more than ever before, to the point where even his essence, his instincts, are at risk of becoming corrupted.

The thing is, back when I worked with him—or back when I worked with Old Shep—the governor believed in story as an article of faith. He woke up in the morning ready to shape the story of our state, and the day-to-come, the world-to-come.

He followed no one, was owned by no one, and we loved him for this. But then the money found him—what a thin and ultimately unsatisfying substitute for love!—and for the first time, I think, he allowed himself to be led. He followed their little crumbs up to the divide, carrying his soul loose in a bucket, with all the state below him. Whispers from another, now, deals and proposals. *Seventy-five flagging jobs.* I don't understand it.

The greater the politician, the more flagrant and baffling their fall. But that inevitable fall from power is such an old and unoriginal story—so tediously predictable—that I always believed the governor was immune to that cliché. And I still have hopes that that may be the case, though I know I am increasingly among the few who believe or even hope for that.

He stands at the edge of one of the greatest betrayals of all time—his puny, paltry soul, in exchange for the whole of Montana, past present and future—and there are days when I, who perhaps knew the enigma of him best—who saw him at his most unguarded, saw how he was with his dog—am made sick with the fear that, being mortal—his greatness laced by necessity with a proportionate flaw—he might make the wrong choice, is making the wrong choice, and I am frightened further by the fear that we the people may not be able then to assume our own leadership in this matter and escort him away from Imperial and lead him back to safety.

I am terrified—as is the poet, and a lot of other people in the state—but not so much that I find myself paralyzed by my fear. Quite the opposite. We are assembling what the poet calls "the Mother of all phone trees:" a sometimes-underground, other times above-ground coalition of names and numbers of people who are willing to make one stand in their lives—who are actually hungering for the opportunity to make one stand—and who know they will be called to do so, and who are waiting, and ready: grandmothers, schoolchildren, teachers, hunters and anglers, politicians, celebrities, Hell's Angels, Tea Partiers.

It will be a public relations train wreck for the governor as well as Imperial, and while we hope we never have to activate this list, we are building it. And the list is long; the list is willing; the list is excited.

The means of activation—the summons—may be the receipt in the mail of a single gold aspen leaf, like a coin, with the time and place on a square of paper. The defenders have each and all agreed to make themselves available, for one battle; they are massing in the secret place just beneath the heart, where the heat first kindles when one is most frightened, or ecstatic, and their numbers are growing, secretly, just beneath the surface. The red-haired Scottish poet gets to make the call, though because he has a temper, truth be told—he has promised he will not push the button without consulting others first.

I hope that too is the case. Sometimes he can be a bit of a crazy mofo. There's this deafness that comes over him sometimes, when he gets too frightened, or too angry, too ecstatic or too lonely, and when this happens, he can't hear anything. It is a time when reason flees him and he follows his wild heart down the slope, rather than leading it carefully along the rocky path.

Who among us is not this way at times? There are so many ways, really, in which the poet and the governor are similar. If only everyone would chill the fuck out, we might all yet get out of this alive, and keep Montana Montana.

We are trying to chill. But we are also gathering thousands for the impending battle, day by day. Thousands.

So even the great ones make mistakes. Especially the great ones, and reliably, at the zenith of their power, or in the first hour of its dimming, perhaps—before anyone recognizes it. The Chair of the Appropriations Committee, so secure in his old power that dizzyingly hot day with the firefighters out on the tarmac, saying the one precise thing he should not say: what strange power, strange contrariness, surges beneath and around our very existence?

Surely there is a balance in the world, power must yield to frailty, just as the meek must one day ascend. Montana cannot kill Imperial and cannot stop the tar sands singlehandedly, but we can cut off one tentacle; we can keep the garden intact for a while longer, yet. No fire lasts forever, nor any one glacier, nor even any mountain, nor any sea—but we can hold the trucks off a little longer. It is our charge. It is what is expected of us, those of us who have been fortunate enough—blessed enough—to have been given custodianship over the garden. It is a hard thing to imagine, but our hearts have changed.

The poet flops and thrashes like a caught fish, and it is no barbless hook, nor even any single hook that binds him, but the trebled claws of the past, the present, and the future. He gasps and burns in the agony of the bright air. The world he once knew—the world we all once knew—before the trucks began to approach, the air itself vibrating and trembling, was so magnificent, and he loved it so.

The poet is not a fan of the governor, and maybe even fears the governor a little, I think. Certainly, I would imagine the governor—though he might be a fan of the fishing-poet—fears the poet a little.

It doesn't have to be this way. There doesn't have to be a war. The governor can save the state, can still call off the trucks—can be the first to lie down in front of Imperial. There is still time.

I do not understand how a man who likes to cast for wild trout—I'm speaking of the governor—can trash an entire state, and turn it into a waste-bin for what can only be called oilfield trash, and then, term-

limited, retire, having consumed Montana. Only a great burning beast of a soul could do that. Such is the nature of the corporation, the business entity, that we have allowed to amalgamate—Imperial—but surely that cannot be the nature of any one man.

⅋

The poet is not a fan of the governor, nor of any politician. He is overly harsh, I think, on all matters. He tries to traffic in pure words, and pure waters, and with pure hooks, pure dry flies. The poet wants the world to be perfect. He believes in a life of service to a higher, purer cause, he considers the life after this one, and sometimes, in the evening, at the end of a long day of service, he likes a glass of scotch with two or three ice cubes rattling in it, the tang of oak and Scottish peat burning.

In a perfect world he and the governor would share such a glass; in a perfect world, the poet would guide the governor on the Lochsa, the Lolo, the Blackfoot, the Dearborn, the Sun and the Teton Rivers—all soon to become oilslicked trash-heaped slurries, victims to the corridor— and at the end of a day or a week of spectacular fishing, the poet and the governor would drink their Scotch and look up at the stars and plot about greatness for the state of Montana, as the great naturalist John Muir and President Theodore Roosevelt once did.

We can still—just barely—get out of this jackpot.

⅋

Old Shep had to be let out every few hours to do his business. I soon began to develop a sixth sense about when he needed to do which function, and because of his breed and temperament, he needed exercising often. He simply wouldn't have been able to survive without that daily burning-off of energy.

On our walks, Old Shep's mind-view was expanded from the state-house, so that there was a greater world available for him to herd and control, to run and lunge at, and to refashion.

Even for a border collie, he was relentless. Squirrels, pigeons, old women, cars, tractor-trailers, clouds, sprinklers jetting sprays of water into the sunlight: everywhere he looked, he saw the imminent destruction of order while he boiled with the irrepressible desire to help mold it all back together, rescuing it just in time with the singular intervention of his muscular will alone.

After our walks, he was more manageable in the statehouse for the next hour or two. He would lie in repose beneath the table at the governor's booted feet, and though the governor was always supremely centered and in control, I was often struck by the feeling that the dog's behavior nonetheless helped protect and maintain the governor's.

The vast gaps and abysses that Old Shep perceived—perhaps he saw them as glimmering polygons of bright light—must have appeared everywhere he looked. I think that he saw the world as a vast fabric not of interlocking miracles, but of absence, loss, incompletion. I think he saw the world as an emptiness that could never be filled.

⁊

The students—only so recently, they were still children, really—at the university are making another giant papier-mâché construction, a scale model of one of the Dong units. It's not life-sized—they couldn't transport it, there's no room for it—but it's big, about half the size of a logging truck, and, at the poet's request, they have also constructed a life-sized governor, who, tiny against the missile's mass, is waving hat and hand in the air, howling with apocalyptic glee, boots and jeans and bolo tie recognizable.

Imperial can ruin a state. But no one man, no one woman, can ruin a state. Least of all one who knows and loves it. The governor does love it. The poet disagrees with me on this, but it is the truth, or was the truth, for I saw it with my own eyes: the governor loves, or did love, Montana. I saw it.

Maybe something in him died and rotted. And maybe if that is the case it can yet be born again. If only he could go for a hike into the Scapegoat or Bob Marshall wilderness and look down at the plains below not yet clotted with an endless streaming of service trucks and trailers bound to and from the Pit. Maybe he could remember love.

He could still be a politician! He wouldn't have to give up his power! Doesn't he know that generosity and courage are the things the state is hungriest to see in him?

Is he not still so strong—so incandescent—that he can stand up to the trucks?

Everyone in the state believed this about him, and wants to believe it again.

❧

The governor can still save the state, and can still save his soul. He would be respected for changing his mind and standing up to Big Oil. He would be loved. He has always prided himself on being slightly ahead of the zeitgeist. Why is he wobbling so, now, why is he falling behind? He would be loved as few politicians ever are, for awakening from his fevered dream—for announcing that he has awakened from his fevered dream—and announcing to the state that he has changed his mind, that the trucks shall not pass.

❧

The poet stands outside the governor's mansion some nights, calling out to him. Some nights the poet, when he is in the neighborhood—fishing the Smith River, or the Madison, or the Gallatin, or the Yellowstone—stops off at the governor's mansion and calls out to him: calls him out. The poet howls to him, and the governor either pretends not to hear, or truly does not hear. The old dog hears, and cocks an ear, and whines, troubled without knowing why.

❧

For two years Exxon met, out of the public's eye, with the governor. For two years, the state highway department diverted taxpayer funds into the upgrading and widening of roads and bridges—some extraordinarily obscure—along the route, working in lonely little out-of-the-way places like Augusta, Choteau, Bynum, Dupuyer, and the port at Whitehall, which could be an alternate port of crossing. After federal stimulus money committed eight million dollars—real money, in Montana—to various industry-friendly upgrades on the U.S. side of the border, the Canadians announced they were closing their side of the border at Whitehall, rendering our expenditures a big fat waste. Only five or six souls per day crossed at that empty port, out in the middle of the prairie—and by closing it, the Canadians were able to send more resources and traffic to the Imperial-desired port at Sweetgrass, within sight of the three holy hills of the Blackfeet tribe, the Sweetgrass Hills—where, ironically, the state of Montana recently defended the site against the depredations of a Canadian-based gold-mining company.

There is gold beneath those three sacred hills. They are so named for the medicinal grasses that grow on top of them, which the Blackfeet bundle and burn in religious ceremonies. So we saved them only to now ruin them—defile them—with an international energy transport corridor—dirty energy, rather than the clean energy our state could produce—while the earth burns.

I just don't know what has happened to him. Simple greed, or lust for power, doesn't even seem to explain it, because again, in Montana, he could garner more power by standing up to Imperial than in rolling over. I just don't get it, there's some piece of the puzzle I'm not understanding.

We're all increasingly in the same boat, in Montana—out-of-work logger, out-of-work book-writer, out-of-work coffee-pourer, out-of-work mall-clerk, out-of-work waitress; sure, a part-time flagging job sounds great—but once we go down that road we can never turn back, and there is hardly anyone in the state who, in the cold light of the next-day, after the money is gone, would not regret having made that choice. We'll leave Montana, get a job somewhere else, before we'll kill it.

❦

Montana summers pass more quickly than any other. There is great sweetness and intensity compressed into them. Some years it seems summer consists of but one single perfect event. The confluence of longer sunlight, the sound of riffling water, riverbank blossoms, great food and fine drinks at dusk, music, cool nights beneath cold stars with the day's last glow fading until after eleven o'clock that night—will eventually create one perfect take-away from the entire season. Autumn arrives in a rush, with the plunging-away of those days of long light.

In the fall of that year, an off-season between election cycles, the governor and I went hunting at least once a week for many weeks, from the time of heat-crackling dry-wheat mid-September light on into the snowy, bitter cold that preceded Christmas. We hunted birds exclusively, mostly the brightly colored rooster pheasants, their species having been introduced to the state only a little more than a century ago. Other times we pursued the beautiful native sharptail grouse, not ostentatious in the least, but plump and elegantly camouflaged to fit like the perfect piece in a puzzle the landscape that had so long ago shaped them, and was still shaping them with finishing touches too minute for us to see in our lifetimes.

It was the governor's idea, and his press folks agreed, that a season spent hunting as much as possible, in the big wide empty lovely open country along the Front Range, the seam between the rough stony waves of the mountains and the rolling swells of the sea of grass and farm country, would solidify his image and identity as a Montanan first and foremost—Montana before anything else.

A Shotgun Listening Tour, is what he called it: getting out into the country, visiting his constituents. Folks in places like Fairfield and Dupuyer, who had busy lives and weren't going to come to Helena to talk to him; folks he would have to seek out on his own, to find out how they felt about the issues of the day.

It was as glorious an autumn as Montana was capable of having, which is to say, the best in the world. The Front Range, from Augusta up to Babb, already had its first snows, which the blue skies of September made seem even whiter. We hunted the farm country below the mountains, the yellow fields of leftover dryland wheat toasting in the heat. In the beginning we took tons of media along with us, print journalists and radio and TV crews, with big growling trucks painted with bright sunrise logos from around the state, and bristling with antennas, plated with satellite dishes, armored not unlike the great Cretaceous dinosaurs that had once prowled this same route beneath the mountains at the edge of the shallow tropical sea, leaving footprints, here and there, that still linger, three hundred million years later.

In September, our outings were all about the photos—the governor in his orange safety vest, grinning hugely, the panting black-and-white Shep in his lap, the gleaming shotgun—an Italian gun, a Guerini, one that any hunter would envy, broken open for safety.

There was very little hunting. It was almost all maddeningly labor-intensive setup—waiting for sunrise, waiting for sunset, working this or that shadow, visiting with a farmer sitting atop his huge tractor, or sitting at the kitchen table with the cherry pie in the sunlight and cup of coffee steaming—all the feel-good archetypes necessary were found to keep a wild animal like the governor moving deeper, further, farther, into the heart of the government and the seat of power.

It was, I imagined, as it might have been in Russia, back in the late nineteenth century, when a sportsman such as Turgenev, with sympathy for the common man, and longing for agricultural reforms that would return land ownership and dignity to those farmers, had strode the countryside looking for woodcock. At the end of each satisfying day, inviting himself into the cottages and cabins of those distant and far-flung hamlets, where he would spend the night drinking and visiting, listening to the poor, whose confidence he had gained by being a man of the earth himself.

There, his hosts would begin to unburden themselves about the long difficulties of their lives. They would have solutions—simple, practical solutions that would yield greater crop production, healthier and more dignified lives, stronger communities, a stronger nation—political impossibilities, but agricultural and land reforms that would be easy to implement otherwise.

How could the governor possibly have been having these conversations with the farmers in Fairfield, while at the same time having those below-radar meetings with Exxon?

In September, with the fire season winding down in the mountains, the fires popping and then sizzling out beneath the first snows of autumn, the news media swarmed him that first week as we had known they would. There was hardly any hunting, and very little talking or listening. Instead, it was all babysitting, all crowd and media management, trying to control the crackling radiant sphere of the governor's charisma. It was a pain in the ass; it was like driving around with some freak meteorite on the back of a flatbed trailer, so that you always had to allow extra space for your maneuvers.

It was like driving through small towns with an entire circus in tow, elephants chained to the wooden decking of flatbeds, and tigers in cages behind iron bars, growling and rearing.

The media loved it, and the juniors in his staff loved it. But it wasn't what I'd envisioned, not by a long shot. It wasn't real. They all crowded around him at the diners and cafes in the evening. He ate pie and basked in the novelty of chatting with waitresses who had been waitressing for forty years or longer. All that week in September, he fired only three times, hitting one dove, which Old Shep ate.

Then they went away, the media's own attention span being not so dissimilar from that same flaw or failing for which the governor was so often criticized.

It was smart politics to go out into the field and tour around with his dog and gun in the autumn, living the life that so many Montanans—or middle-aged white male Montanans—would choose to live, if they were in the governor's mansion—but it was also smart for the oxygen-burner, the air-eater, to re-establish contact with some terra firma, and to take a little rest.

That's pretty much how it worked. We had one whole day, one perfect Saturday in September, in which he knocked on doors and visited with farmers who were winding up their year's work, harvesting the last of the wheat and plowing under the stubble (though others now left it on the surface, in a new-fangled way, as farmers had once done in the old days) before readying to flee the coming winter, traveling to the Southwest or sometimes farther: Mexico, and the Caribbean.

At one farmhouse where we stopped, a young man, already afflicted with Parkinson's syndrome from all the herbicides he'd applied, came hobbling out and invited us, Shep included, into his dark trailer home. So many of the farmers owned thousands of acres, and co-owned, with the banks, several hundred thousand dollars' worth of machinery and big American gas-hog power-trucks, but they never put any money into their homes, partly because there was never any money left over, but partly too because they were never in their homes. Instead, they worked from dark to dark, coming inside only to shower and eat and collapse asleep before re-entering the unending scroll of the next morning and the next: and then when the harvest was over, they fled the country, soaking their aging pesticide-laden and wind-whipped bones in the shallow gulf of some faraway place, if it had been a good year for crops and prices, or taking a travel-trailer and staying with relatives in Phoenix if it hadn't.

The wind rocked their mobile homes, sent tumbleweeds rustling past the cinder blocks on which their homes were perched, the tumble-weeds rodent-rustling beneath the trailers. The wind, utterly powerful and unharnessed, unwrapped the aluminum siding from the homes, peeling it away with claps of thunder. Plastic Big-Wheels would be wind-tipped out front, and plastic slides and swing-sets, with the nearest consolidated school forty or fifty miles away: this stubborn allegiance to the land, this almost pathological addiction to staying connected to the passing of the seasons.

The young farmer with Parkinson's spent most of his hours in his trailer now because the bright light of day jolted his nerves, set their frayed and frazzled newly-exposed endings bristling with pain. The heat had the same effect upon him, so he had two window units humming, rattling the little trailer, but the air they were circulating was lukewarm at best. He could work only at dusk and dawn, tried to sleep in the middle of the day, but the nature of the disease disrupted his sleep patterns.

For whatever reason he was glad to see us—*We who had failed him*, I couldn't help but think, but he didn't see it that way. He just seemed glad for the attention, and glad too that at least we were healthy and fairly strong—strong enough, for a while—and enjoying the earth. He knew who the governor was, and while he, John, hadn't voted in the last election, hadn't ever voted, he said—he was still glad to see us, if only to bear witness.

He knew there wasn't a damn thing anyone could do for him at this point. It seemed to me that a tiny aura was around him, an invisible and pulsing electrical field. It seemed to me that he was wrestling, grappling as if with an invisible anger, with what it meant to be a human being, not in rare happenstance occasions of deep thought or stargazing, but in every crackling, pain-scribed, illuminated second—and that even here, on this hot bright September day, frying in his own short-circuiting body, he found the experience more than worthwhile. That in these last moments, it was holy.

Not from a church-going standpoint, but another one. The solitude of pain.

"You're the one who tried to get us free medicine," John said, his words slurred slightly, as if he had been sipping beer all night. As if he were still a very young man, and had simply been out all the previous night at the saloon. He smiled. "Thanks for trying."

The governor grimaced. There weren't any cameras, no reporter, just a sick man who was still working, and his wife, who—if a fleeting impression based on gestures, silences, facial expressions, can be trusted—seemed to be a hostage caught in the imperfect and shifting space between love for her husband, and the ever-changing manifestations of the illness.

Waking up, looking out at the hazy light of dawn, the scrim of first faint light, and wondering, *Will this be a good day, or will this be a bad day?*

Betty let her husband tell his story. Surely there were days when she had to be the caregiver, but today, thus far, he was still capable of caring for all of them, just as he had been when they had gotten married ten years ago. The children were still asleep in their dark rooms, lulled by the near-useless rattle of the air conditioners. I didn't want to think of the electricity bill. The tremors weren't too bad in John's hands, but they weren't too good, either.

"We had to get divorced, so that they would treat him," Betty said, and again the governor winced, knowing exactly what she was talking about: the transfer of assets in order to qualify for treatment; in order to keep the farm from being sold out beneath them, to pay the medical bills for a treatment that wasn't working, and which wasn't going to work.

It was just us. There was no need to turn on the Governor Show, and so he didn't. He gave John the dignity of his testimony, listening to him not as a governor but as a man, and as a Montanan.

"I guess it's from all that spraying," John said, knowing damned well it was. "I guess I should have taken better precautions."

The governor just listened. He had owned a hay farm outside of Livingston for a while. He knew the deal.

John should have been angry, and Betty *was* angry, though not at us. They received us there in the dark, which was slightly less hot than outside, as if they had been waiting long years for us to pass through, and had known that one day we would, though in that waiting had known also that we would not be able to help them.

The governor sighed and looked at the cluttered dining room table, loose papers and ripped-open envelopes scattered everywhere, the daily and accruing detritus of debt. Empty prescription pill bottles, their transparent red plastic glowing, gathering the dull blades of light that were able to seep through the curtains. The governor reached over and patted John on the knee, and in the same motion, picked up the empty bottles and slipped them into his coat pocket, stood straighter then and went over and shook Betty's hand. There just wasn't anything to say, and he didn't sully the space or the moment by coming up with some aphorism. He was humbled—he knew plenty about living, but nothing that these folks didn't—and he said he would keep them in his prayers.

"There's been a flock of sharptails watering up there at the tank on the hill, early in the mornings," John said. "Then they work their way back down toward the house." He laughed. "Can't keep 'em out of the garden, most days."

I had noticed that garden on the way in—a sunscalded withered caliche scabland, the tomato plants and corn stalks looking as if they'd been hit by nuclear fallout—soil that had clearly not been turned or watered or composted in a couple of years, so that surely the birds had long ago picked through the last of any leavings, and returned now only out of habit, and to the memory of abundance, rather than the actual thing itself.

"I used to keep a little pan of water out for them," Betty said. *Back when I gave a rat's ass*, she might as well have said. *Go ahead, kill them all. Take no prisoners. Fuck those days, when I had so much tenderness for the world, such an overflow of it, as to be able to bestow it upon birds.*

"If we go up by the tank," the governor said—"we'll be careful to stay far enough away where you can't hear us, if we shoot. Hell," he said, "I don't care anything about birds, I just want to get out and give Old Shep a run."

"Is he a good dog?" John asked.

"Oh, hell no," the governor said. "He's a scoundrel. He's an old egg-sucker from way back. Look at him," the governor said. "You can just tell he's crazy."

Even Betty smiled at that.

"Go on up there," John said. "I saw them up there yesterday. Don't worry about the kids, they'll sleep through anything. You two go on up there and shoot 'em up."

The governor smiled, nodded, rose and shook John's hand. John reached for the governor's and almost missed it, so that the governor had to help guide it, catching John's hand with both of his—and then he gave Betty a hug, whistled to Old Shep—"Come on boy, let's go find some birds"—and we went out of a dark trailer into the brilliant yellow light of September.

We drove out into the field, up toward the distant rise, the trailer behind us becoming slowly smaller, until it was far enough away for us to feel unconnected to it again—in the mirror, it glinted, looking like a beer can lying perfectly on its side—and we parked and got out to walk the rest of the way, with Shep whirling in wild circles, dashing and feinting, herding nothing more than the imaginary glints and motes in his mind: snapping at the air, dashing back and forth, and with his thrashings leveling the tall grass before him, as if passing through the field with a scythe.

The governor had left the empty pill bottles on the front seat. We had all the information we needed. We would need to make a few calls, but was the least we could do. We couldn't heal John—he wasn't going to get better—but at least we could keep his medicine filled. The state is small enough that you can still help people one at a time. It's a strategy that works politically but it also works from a standpoint of simply helping people.

I lived and worked in the oilfields in Texas and Louisiana, and in Colorado and Utah. I understand why Montana is different, even if the governor no longer does. There are some things you can't manage or control. He has no earthly idea of what is coming.

The first birds got up directly in front of us, before we were in any way ready for them, and certainly they were unscented by Shep, who with his huffing, panting exertions had passed right over the top of them, so that in their flush they actually frightened him for a moment, as if he thought he might have provoked a hive of giant cackling bees.

"Ferfuck's sake," the governor cried, fumbling new shells into his gun as birds continued to get up all around us, like a deck of cards shuffled clumsily and spilling into the sky, birds everywhere.

We fired, missed in our haste, and the sounds of our shooting made more birds get up, and once again we fumbled with new shells, spilling them into the grass, then loading them backwards."Ferfuck's sake!" the governor yelled again as Shep nosed the remaining birds into the air, snapping at their tailfeathers, and finally, praise Allah, the governor hit one, the loose white belly feathers separating from it at the sound of his shot, the bird folding miraculously back to earth. White feathers drifted faintly from right to left and clean as snow against the blue sky.

I broke my gun open for safety and ran to where the bird had fallen, to search for it before Shep could find it and worry it. I found it lying on its side, limp, and when I picked it up it felt as warm as a coal; as if it had just come from the oven. I carried it back to the governor, who accepted it proudly, slipped it into his game vest as if he did this all the time, and we pushed on, farther up the hill, where, as John and Betty had said we would, we encountered still more birds, and were able to bag, after much shooting, another one each. It was the vaunted home covey, John's and Betty's ex-pets, and I wondered if, down in the distant trailer with the air conditioners rattling, they could hear all the shooting.

I wondered if they were listening for the shooting. There was no mistaking what they had done, giving these birds to the governor like an offering, *bequeathing* them to him—the King of Montana. The Imperial Ruler.

We reached the pond, which was only half-full, and saw from the dampness of the mud-ring around it that it had been dropping quickly, would likely be gone completely in a few more weeks. And what could the governor do about that? Send in a water truck from the state, filled with barrels pumped from the Sun or Teton River, to gush back into the muddy pit, the drying crust cracking into polygons that curled more with each passing day? Or send one of the firefighting bombers on a low run overhead, to dump a thousand gallons or more into the mud pit, so that they might last another few weeks?

The tracks of deer and antelope stippled the mud at water's edge, as did the tridents of countless birds. Sweat was roaring off of us, and our arrival at the parched flats of the mud cracks sent up a clacking horde of grasshoppers that sailed away like little musical toys, their wings the shifting colors in a kaleidoscope. They seemed utterly mechanical, void of brain or soul or even spirit—their response was simply what they did when you approached; they whirred away—and like children, we stood there and watched them until they were all gone and had settled back down into the grass.

The sense of timelessness was staggering. John would die soon, and then, some years after that, maybe long years, Betty would, too. The farm would become overwrought with tumbleweeds, drier than parchment, and in only a few hundred years this very spot where we were standing would be well on its way to becoming a sandy desert that would rival the Sahara.

Our own knowledge seemed to give us a kind of freedom, but it was such a vast freedom, standing there on the open prairie, with the blue and white mountains not so far away, that I didn't have a clue as to what might be the appropriate response. Quite possibly the only sane reaction was to be kind to others afflicted with that same predicament or adjudication—which was to say, be kind to all.

Who could give Montana away in such fashion, turning it over to the rush and roar of Exxon's corridor? What man?

We stood there with the hot birds in our vests, beholding the mud pit, which some might characterize as ugly, but which we beheld as a great and soothing beauty, that day. *Everyone has wounds,* I realized. *Everyone is sick or injured, or why else would we know the sensation of being soothed?*

The sweat was roaring off the governor. He called Old Shep over and gave him some water, pouring it into his cupped hand for Shep to lap. The governor splashed some onto Shep's head, before doing the same to himself.

"We're going to have to give Old Shep a haircut if we keep doing this," he said—*we* meaning *me,* of course.

"It'll be different in October," I said. "In October, especially in the mornings, he'll be glad for it. And November."

"Hard to picture, isn't it?" the governor said.

You know how your heart slows and then becomes still sometimes, when you're in the presence of great wide open space? How you feel almost as if you're getting doctored, receiving some kind of medicine that a part of you has been needing, even without your realizing it? The day was like that. Every day is like that, out here in Montana, and there for you when you most need it.

How can we get our governor back? How?

⁂

I used a harsh term earlier, oilfield trash. So much for my fledging attempts at tolerance and compassion. But that's just the way it is; it's the nature of the beast. As I mentioned, I worked in the oilfields down South for a decade, and so I know what is required of the profession: you are reaching down into the earth and pulling up old rotting hydrocarbons, the liquid putrefaction of the ages, in order to burn it, in order to attain a quick sugar-burst of power. The work is hard and dirty.

And the odor is acrid. As the sky accepts the polluted residue of the burning, the world grows more heated. The company and the industry drives you harder and harder; you have no time to rest; you quicken your steps to the pace of production, the pace of consumption; and the company uses up the best of you, and discards you at the end of each day, like a Styrofoam coffee cup. A generation passes, and then another, and the world keeps turning, the world keeps sinking deeper into the tar and mire.

I was there: I lived in the oilfield camps, the cinderblock honky-tonks and shanty-town lifestyles—Rock Springs, Wyoming; Houma, Louisiana; Fort Nelson, British Columbia; Farmington, New Mexico—and I understand that while oilfield trash is a derogatory term, it is, alas, the most accurate one. It is a world the governor has never inhabited and he does not understand that it is inseparable from the oil. You can't have oil without oilfield trash.

Something else he doesn't understand is how often things break in the oilfield. Every piece of equipment breaks, every week—tongs, sonic tubes, logging cables, drill bits. Pipes bind and need fishing out of the hole; pipes fail as hidden blemishes in the steel corrode. Motors break down almost daily; hydraulic hoses burst under pressure and spray viscous drilling mud everywhere, slinging the heavy and toxic mud all over the landscape; welders come and go; trucks break; pumpjacks break; wellheads fail; blowout preventers fail. The earth quivers just beneath us; it throbs with pressure. It is physically impossible to work in that underground realm without taking on that pressure directly.

It is a pressure that will always defeat metal, rubber, or flesh, and as such the oilfield life is one of haste and expendability, and of pieces and lives increasingly cobbled together with wire and band-aids, until finally they can go no further. It is the nature of the endeavor, and is not something that can be managed or regulated. It's messy, far messier than a slaughterhouse. The blood in a slaughterhouse can be washed down the sinks easily enough—the floor can be hosed down, the morning light can come streaming back in through the dusty windows—but the blood of the earth, whether in rivers and lakes of steaming oil, or in coagulated clots of tar that must be steamed out with the chemicals of the dry-cleaning industry, is nowhere nearly as neat.

In the manner that the westward wagon routes were once littered with the bleached bones of settlers and the broken-down carapaces of their wagons and snowy bones of all the slaughtered buffalo, as the government sought in calculated fashion to exterminate that which fed and sustained the natives—and in the manner in which dilapidated little

trading posts, slums of alcoholic squalor and mercantile misery that mas-
queraded as communities but which were nothing more than temporary
brothels and jails, stippled these corridors—so too will the governor's and
Imperial's High and Wide corridor be a trail of tears and misery amid the
ceaseless daily and nightly racing traffic that attends to the development of
any major oilfield: in this case, the largest oilfield in the world.

We've seen such tragedy strike in other states. Consider Montana's flat
and distant cousin, Iowa, also sometimes known these days as Methland,
where the ascendancy of Big Ag and the push for profits has, with cunning calculation, created working conditions (particularly in meatpack-
ing) that only a ceaseless and ever-replenishing supply of disposable illegal
aliens can fill, and even then only under the influence of meth and crack:
an unholy trinity in the heartland, all serving the one remaining seed in
the garden, genetically modified and patented corn, where once, and not
so long ago, there was biological as well as community greatness.

In Montana, we want to believe we are smarter than that. In Montana, we want to believe we are too smart to take that hook.

Just the other day the governor was quoted as saying, "What's the big fuss, the modules are just high and wide, is all, they're not *toxic*." And one of the Imperial shills, over in Idaho, in arguing before a federal judge that no studies were needed, pleaded that appropriating the Lewis and Clark Scenic Byway for purposes of servicing the tar pit was utterly in the spirit in which the byway had been consecrated, for just as Lewis and Clark had been seeking to establish a path of potential commerce, so too was Imperial and Exxon/Mobil carrying on in that proud tradition of exploration and development of routes.

※

Where is my dog in this fight? Much of it has to do with the solitude and silence—or if not silence, then the natural sounds of the seasons, and a country uncorrupted by man—that I was looking for when I came here thirty years ago, as a young man fleeing the oil and gas industry: in the last sweet breaths while I was still young. (I cannot imagine having had the good fortune, the great luck, to be born here, and wonder what hikes I would have taken, what mountains I would have climbed in those first thirty years; but it is fair to say that in the subsequent decades I have made up for lost time.)

Still, I'm reminded of a passage by the great Texas writer, John Graves, writing on similar matters: "To grow up among tradition-minded people leads one often into backward yearnings and regrets, unprofitable feelings of which I was granted my share in youth…and easy enough with hindsight—to damn the ancestral frame of mind that ravaged the world so fully and so soon. What I myself seem to damn mainly, though, is just not having seen it. Without any virtuous hindsight, I would likely have helped in the ravaging as did even most of those who loved it best. But God, to have viewed it entire, the soul and guts of what we had and gone forever now…"

My dog in this fight, then, is the Montana landscape—the high and wide lonely lovely country, beyond the brief clots of the towns, villages, hamlets and communities that keep us clinging here, all of us hundred-year newcomers in a harsh and beautiful land—the mountains we can see when we look out our window—and, specifically—*be still, my heart*—the elk that live back in the farthest, wildest places, and which in the autumn lure us, ever-deeper, into those wild places—up through the slender bars of the bone-white aspen trunks, the aspens' shimmering leaves gold against the blue sky—through willow marshes and swamps, with the singular smell of giant cottonwoods, their yellow leaves already down on the ground, creating a slightly hallucinogenic effect as we hike, moving higher and closer to the siren-call of the bull elk squealing, groaning, bugling in the cold morning sunlight, the elk and the man, or elk and woman, glorying in being alive, and, unlike fishing, with only one of them continuing on into the future, still alive, still living, just a little longer.

Sometimes, climbing the steep mountains—pursuing our passions far beyond the limits of our abilities—we fall and break our backs, or slip and sprain our knees. Other times we get lost, find ourselves aldered out, down in the bottom of a dark hole of a valley late at night. Sometimes we get rained or snowed on and lost, and perish from hypothermia—in the last moments of which it is said the warmth we have been seeking and craving finally returns (I have been at this edge, have experienced it, and believe it to be so).

The governor's corridor—bad as it will be—is not just a corridor, any more than an artery is just an artery. As the artery becomes clogged, the lesser oilfield traffic will seek alternate routes. When Lolo Pass is blocked by a wedge-slid trailer, or a spill into the Lochsa, the nearest detour for everyone else—whether servicing Alberta or simply conducting normal business—is a 300-mile detour through the Idaho resort towns of Stanley, Ketchum, Swan valley environs. Tell it to Schwarzenegger, who owns a second home there, and to Tom Hanks, and to Demi Moore, and the Kennedys, and all the other swells in that sweet mountain hideaway.

When the artery plugs up, the veins will labor to do the work of carrying the poison farther into the body.

Push an elk hard enough—for days—and eventually it will seek to return to the place where he was first jumped. Perhaps all stories must reach the end to find their beginning again. Montana—beautiful though it is, and young though it is, so newly made by the ice—rests on nothing but bones, already, anywhere you look: not just the bones of one hundred million buffalo, but of all the miners underground, in Troy and Libby and Butte, and the bones under the tall waving grass along the Little Bighorn; not just bones beneath the Indian reservations, with their illnesses and social stresses; and not just the bones in drinking-and-driving wrecks, in which we lead the nation; it's all part of our myth.

The ground rumbles and shakes, so loose is our foundation still, the bones not yet lithified to make stone or mountains themselves. The bones nourish our garden, the garden is green, but what an expensive crop. What will we grow next?

⁂

I've only seen him do little bait-and-switches before this—nothing this immense. I know how he moves, what he will do next. After a while, there is nothing new under the sun.

We saw it when he sold out the state's lease on its dirty coal at Otter Creek, down in the Powder River basin. When I say dirty coal, I don't mean figuratively. Montana's coal has 90% more sulfur and lead in it than other coal, but he built a private railroad across some Montana ranches— once a great populist, he suddenly became a temporary fan of imminent domain—so he could send the coal to Asia, where burning dirty coal is not a crime.

In so doing he blocked off a producing mine west of Colstrip that was shipping to the steel mills in the Midwest, but no matter, what are a few more manufacturing jobs lost in a swing state? By selling the coal beneath the state lands in Otter Creek—*The country east of Billings doesn't matter*, he is reported to have said—and selling it cheap—he was able to get a one-time bump to the state treasury, which is his obsession in a way that is unbecoming.

There are many who say he has national ambitions—again, just because I am disturbed by his increasingly erratic behavior does not mean I think he is not a great politician, a great campaigner—and certainly, being the one kid on his block, the only governor to be operating in the red during the Great Recession, would appeal to a lot of folks who might not have the time to look under the hood of the car they're thinking about buying.

So I've seen him bait and switch before. It's as if I can watch his eyes, downcast at the line of scrimmage before the snap, his stance giving away nothing, and yet know as if with the certainty of prophecy the route he is going to run.

Push an elk hard enough, and it will circle back to the place it knows best. I have hunted a lot of elk, have killed a lot of elk. Their bones lie beneath the thin forest soil, now, lush thickets growing in a patch of sunlight in the forest where I cleaned the animal, faint blazes on the trunks of lodgepole marking my way out of the forest—tiny scrimshaw, temporary hieroglyphics, the schematics of desire, the schematics of clean meat, of sustenance and success.

In the autumn, the light of the days is tumbling toward the long winter, the sunlight becomes denser and more compressed, and butter-rich in that compression, and you move toward the rich scent of your quarry, sometimes following the tell-tale sign of fresh tracks in new snow, the imprint of their hoofs making perfect ice-casts so recent that a speck of dirt or moss is still loose within the cast, though other times you track the giant animal by scent alone, following the braids and rivers of its rich musk. You move so stealthily, and draw so close to the animal that you can begin to know it even before you see it. Then you do see it, the polished mahogany tips of antlers back in the tangle of forest, the dark wet eye beholding you with alarm and surprise, and you have only a moment to lift the gun and put the scope on the heart, the delicate crosshairs performing the signature once again, and your own heart no longer racing but seemingly perfectly stilled, as if in meditation.

The noise of the rifle-shot is loud; the blast separates the day into before-success, and after-success. It's best and easiest if there's snow. You walk up to the fallen, magnificent animal—it's as big as a horse, and the antlers are so large that you marvel it was able to even carry them—the king is dead, long live the king—and you sit there quietly for a while. No matter how many elk you have killed—two dozen, say, in as many years—you never get used to it, never quite completely believing your luck, being alive in such a world, with the senses so inflamed—every fiber having been forged anew by the incandescence of your desire—and with the beauty of the forest sealing back in over you.

I watch the governor from afar now. I can barely remember who he once was, and I wonder if he, too, seems a stranger now to even himself. I fear that as he grows larger, immense, that self-loathing will lead him to seek a new punching bag as he draws ever-nearer to the end of his lame-duck term; and in this state, the easiest punching bag of all is the environmentalists who, though they have helped preserve the scenic beauty that is the spiritual foundation as well as economic driver of the region, are, nonetheless and truth be told, not always that likeable.

Some of the environmentalists are a little too earnest while others are hard to take seriously—dressing up like giant salmon, lashing themselves to the tops of trees and giving themselves names like Treefrog and Beaver and Wood-Owl. The governor cleaves the state when he goes after them, and it is hardly an original page in the playbook—for a brief while, his Republican predecessor made a pretty good living threatening enviros. I remember one particular public meeting in the Bitterroot, where, when a burly logger-type threatened the handful of enviros who were there that they should be careful for their safety, his predecessor, instead of admonishing such tactics, chimed in, to the applause of the crowd, and taunted them, "You're not *afraid,* are you?"

This new unoriginality by the governor—the predictability of his choices and responses—confuses me. He used to be smart; he used to be creative. That business about smuggling the bus full of seniors up to Canada to get their meds cheap, back before health care was even on anyone's radar: that was good. But now it's as if he's traded good for blunt, and mind for muscle. As if he has been taken over by some inner bully and walks around searching for weaker opponents. As if feeding some beast—some magnificent self-loathing—within.

The nature of such a wound may be deep and immense, a gaping pit. It can never be filled, yet the sufferer is doomed to try always to feed it, until, in his final self-destruction, he takes on someone far more powerful, who administers such a drubbing that the bully is never a bully again—or, just as destructively, the bully—bloated with accrued power—makes a mistake so foolish that it leads an observer to believe that it was the bully's own destruction that he or she sought all along;

that the wound, the pit, was simply too great, and the bully had finally become weary of feeding it. Of being hostage to that pain.

What makes me think the governor is in trouble—that he perceives his goal, whatever it might be, to be drawing near enough for him to reach out and grasp, yet while at the same time beginning to enter the mythic wobble that will prevent him from attaining that goal—and there are those who say he will be unsatisfied with anything less than the Presidency—Imperial's candidate—is the fact that never before has he been behind the curve.

Governor Oil? How old school, how *Texas*, is that? In the age of global warming, why is he hitching his wagon to oil and coal?

And yet: perhaps the governor—who has always done things differently—is taking, at the last instant, steps that he believes will protect himself from himself, steps that include tucking himself in, at just the last moment, beneath the protective wing of the world's largest corporate bully.

This is not the same man I went hunting with, in that autumn of his first re-election. For a brief while his opponents on this issue sought to create a safe space for him to make a graceful exit without risking humiliation, but it was futile; he appears to have thrown in his lot completely with Exxon. No entreaty by man or woman can turn him now. Only the wilderness can save him now.

❧

The dog ate a lot, therefore it shat a lot. There was an awful lot of it on the statehouse lawn, and in the surrounding parks where I walked him, trying to cut his manic, ceaseless energy. He was totally unmannered and had on occasion defecated in the marble halls of power. When this happened, it was I who received a scolding, not Old Shep. Nothing was ever Old Shep's fault, it was all always someone else's. I don't miss that job at all. They say you can tell a lot about a man or a woman by the kind of dog he or she owns, and the governor's dog was crazy. I don't mean just border collie one-eyed crazy, which he came by naturally, but crazy beyond his breed, afflicted with too much intelligence and, I have to say it, too much power. The governor let him roam the halls of not just the mansion in which they lived, but the statehouse in which the territory's business was conducted. I use the olden term *territory* because nothing had changed that I could tell, the same struggles were in place that had been present during statehood a scant 121 years ago. The same interests that had first flocked to the country, seeking to claw as if from a vault the timber, furs, gold, copper and silver were still hanging around, squabbling over the last of the crumbs, even while reaching for more treasures: Montana's coal, which represented ten percent of the world's supply, and the wild blue rivers, with their increasingly-brief snowmelt charge in June for hydroelectricity, and even the sky itself, as new barons sought to set up giant wind farms out on the prairies along the base of the mountains, to capture and sell each day's crop as the night-cooled air slid down off of the dwindling ice-caps. There is plenty of power in Montana. He doesn't have to carve out the guts.

It was still all for sale, and the governor who relished both the deal-making as well as the bare-knuckled brawls of resistance—he understood that both were part of the same dynamic—was a busy man. He strode the gilded high-ceilinged halls quickly—the most beautiful statehouse in the West—like a man going from room to room in a burning building, checking to make sure all was well despite the smoke and flames, and Old Shep trotted along with him, the black-and-white pattern of his breed making him look like a Rorschach in motion.

As with all border collies, Shep's herding instincts were maddening, maniacal, obsessive. Whenever he saw two or more people not moving in the same direction, he would break from the governor's side and lunge at the ankles of the offending irregular, be it a spindly, ancient secretary bringing coffee into a conference room or the burly ex-Grizzly lineman who served as an aide to the Natural Resources Director. There were none among the staff who had not been walking down those wide hallways with the Persian carpets and marble columns, their heads deep in a quick read of one briefing or another to be absorbed and processed in the ninety-second walk between one's office and the next conference room, only to be pulled from that intellectual reverie by the primitive and archetypal sensation, complete with chill-of-spine and hair-on-neck bristle, that something ominous and even dangerous had just entered one's sphere.

Shep was a force of nature, and the staffers were not. I am not sure how much mirroring was involved, but he and the governor moved together, each a shadow of the other.

The dog was great for photos, of course. There was something about the orderliness and control of the process that appeared to briefly soothe the savage writhings of his dog brain. Lying there at the governor's feet, staring into the camera with seeming wisdom and an utterly false patience, knowing that after each snap of the shutter, the governor would slip him one of the dog biscuits he carried in his coat pocket. In these photos—in all photos—the dog looked preternaturally wise and engaged, even soulful, staring into the camera with an intensity of expectation that no viewer ever dreamed was but food-based.

❧

Sometimes I worry that our governor will follow the arc of Louisiana's Huey Long: that the governor came to power by running as bold new blood, and yet will one day come to be seen as establishmentarian, old-blood himself, and boring. It seems impossible to imagine, but the world likes a full circle.

He was, and is, the best, the most naturally-gifted politician I have ever seen or heard. His charisma is radioactive; his is a card shark's renegade mix of intelligence and coarseness, a workingman's vernacular and mindset that can skate near the edge of vulgar.

As with almost all greatness, there is an element of anger within him. His critics call him bombastic, or a bully, but he is not those things. The governor is as seized with an electric power, and more intelligence and ambition than anyone should have to bear.

❧

In the days of paddlewheelers and coal-belching steamships on the Missouri, the railroads were king, denuding everything along the zippered scrawl of their subsidized signature, hauling mostly coal but also every other commodity out from the farthest, sweetest reaches of Montana, and back to the state's masters in the East: ferrying all the furs, fertilizer, gold, copper, silver, timber, beef, and hay that the trains could pull, black smokestruck billowings writing in cursive against the blue sky the names of the masters, Anaconda Copper, Marcus Daily, Northern Pacific, Union Pacific, Plum Creek, while trumpeter swans, whiter than any white ever witnessed—birds as large as small dinosaurs yet as graceful in flight as if traveling through one's dreams rather than one's hard life—rose from the water and, disturbed, flew up and down the river searching for a newer and quieter place. As they search still.

The trains used to run east, especially the coal trains, but I have been noticing an increasing number of them—far more than the state is reporting—running west, up and along the Clark Fork. What's that about? An enterprising journalist—if any independent newspapers remained— could ride one of those trains back to their source. Camping in the open-topped car amid the mountainous rubble of glittering brown-black coal-diamonds, sweet-scented riverside air swirling his or her hair, eagles and ospreys perched on giant cottonwoods, clickety clack, one part of the rider's soul lulled by the peace and joy of the adventure and every cell vibrantly abuzz with the realization that the rider, like the poet, was doing something that mattered, was like the village hunter who goes out into the forest to search for that which will sustain and nurture his or her tribe.

Past Trout Creek and Noxon and Heron, and into Idaho, past Sandpoint, and onward, along the Canadian border, to the port. How much dirty coal is going to Asia now—far more than last year's reported? This frantic, frantic race to balance a budget—admirable, on the face of things—but this is no balancing, it is executive power run amok, and it is liquidation: selling the state's treasures at a dime on the dollar. It is not balanced. The other 49 states will look at the numbers and say *Aha*, Montana was in the black, there must be a fiscal conservative at the helm; but in reality it is just a resumption of the one-shot looting that was our First White Story—the pattern, the cut-groove, of our first story, and because it was the first, how very hard to step completely away from the endless cycles of our lesser histories and craft open to the new.

We know where the old stories go. They take us back to the beginning. Bleached skulls and bones, the depauperate trail, while the East sucks hungrily at the straw. I will drink your milkshake, indeed.

It will take a real force of will to step up and out of the same old tired story the governor is following with muscular resolve—with the largest company in the world now shoveling resources, like coal, into the boiler-engines of the train—but if we can win this battle in Montana this time, we can do anything, can win anything, can even—it sounds so funny to say it—save the world.

We can begin to put a patch over the damaged left lobe of the earth's lungs. We can put a firmer foundation beneath a sinking world, as the rising waters lap higher at all edges. We can mop our burning brows with a dampened washcloth, and we can cleanse, for the first time, the grit and soot from our grimy coal- and oil-blacked faces.

※

The Colossus approaches. The modules and cylinders, having left South Korea on their short five days' ocean journey, bob now in the port at Vancouver, waiting the next leg of their earth-killing sojourn—cold, sterile, dispassionate steel, cylindrical as bullets or missiles, so implacable and without soul or emotion or meaning that to look at them is to feel the human race never existed, never mattered. What are our lives really about, if anything?

Imperial's spokespeople are beginning to admit that the modules—the world's largest cylinders—have a "slightly unusual center of gravity." They discovered this on the ocean voyage, and will need a few extra chains strapped onto the trailers. As if they are transporting bull elephants for the circus.

The poet rages. "The governor's big head has a slightly unusual center of gravity," he says. Some nights he goes out and lies down on the dark and empty road down which the big rigs are threatening to travel. In the end, when they come, will there be five or six others who join him, or five or six thousand, with CNN camera crews and helicopters whirring overhead, National Guardsmen and smoke grenades, tear gas, rubber bullets?

In the long run—in the arc of history, and the ark of history—the number really doesn't matter. His protest will be recorded, and the governor's choice will be recorded. Montana will stay wild or will be tamed, sterilized, lost to the dusty, olden story of how a thing, a great thing, once-was. The poet knows this, and strangely, despite his fervor, fights without thinking too much about the outcome, and the consequences of losing.

ॐ

The population of Montana is graying: it is the third-grayest state in the country. But its very fullness beckons, and more and more young people will start up their farmers' markets; they will climb Montana's mountains and raft its rivers and chase wild elk and cast to bull trout and rainbows—seeking to be re-born, to make new lives, they will come to know the joy of inhabiting a home where the shape and substance of the land is for once in synchrony with the joyous burning, the strength and wonder and mystery, in their hearts. They will continue to come here seeking, in the words of Wallace Stegner, "to create a society to match the scenery"— and if the governor does not clog and cut off the supply-lines to their spirit, this magnificent spirit-route from Lolo Pass to the Bitterroot and along the Blackfoot and then up the Rocky Mountain Front—then they will one day succeed in finally creating that society envisioned by Stegner.

But in the meantime, a lot of us are getting old. It is getting to the point where some of us in the age group of the governor and myself are beginning to see the mountaintop tips of the hereafter appearing from within the blue glow of the receding ice: the land and time beyond these days of our youth.

The poet's perspective about working not for himself, but for a further, greater force, is not an inappropriate one, at this late stage.

Do we not spend far more time in an afterlife than here on these gold-lined streets?

You can live a long life, a life that by almost any standard would be described ambiguously as "productive," or even "good"—whatever that means. But no matter how long you live, in the end there are really only going to be one or two sentences used to describe you. The river of history, and all the billions of us in it, shoulder to shoulder and seething and surging, are hurrying past, even if we wanted to slow down and savor and examine the subtleties of any one life, there is no time, there is only that one sentence—if even that—and for my own part I would choose that sentence to be something along the lines of *He made a stand*; and while the governor and I have parted ways over this issue, I still have a remnant affection for him, and would hope—for Montana's sake, but also his own—that that sentence is not *"He was once a popular governor who fell from favor when he sold out to Big Oil."*

We do still get to make choices in these matters.

※

Would things be different if I hadn't quit my day job? Who can say? It's not so much that I think I could have intervened with the governor— once he gets up his bull-rush on a project, he's pretty tough to dissuade— but still, I have to wonder, I spent as much time with him as anyone. I'd like to think there was something I could have suggested (for no one can tell him anything) that might have gotten his attention, or captured his fancy—something that might have served as a rock upon which he could stand and defend the state, when Imperial came rushing in.

Maybe I could have had some influence, back in the early days, when Imperial first started talking to him—whispering to him—but I didn't know they were even meeting. No one did. The journalists have Freedom-of-Information-Act (FOIA) notes that would curl your hair, notarized minutes from meetings where Exxon states baldly that they want this route to become their permanent "High and Wide Corridor," while the Montana Department of Transportation Director—who was in those meetings—declares that there was no discussion whatsoever of a permanent route.

But beyond these two—the governor and his highway guy—nobody knew anything. If anyone noticed that Exxon was in town, they would not have connected them to the tar sands, would not have thought anything was unusual. Even if they had walked into the mansion with big satchels bulging with ten thousand-dollar bills, no one would have blinked; no one, back in those days of innocence, would have even been able to imagine the scale of what was coming.

A lot of people in Montana right now are concerned about the return of wolves, saying that the wolves are eating too many deer and elk, too many sheep and cattle, but in my opinion the real wolves have already come and gone.

I left without knowing. And even if I had known, back then, I'm not sure I could have stayed on any longer. I needed a rest from the governor. Being around him 24/7 was like standing next to a high-powered propane generator or tornado: the ceaseless roar, ceaseless radiant thrum that created a kind of strange magnetism so forceful that it seemed the paper clips on his desk would twitch, trying to align polarities. Even when he was smiling and laughing, and you were smiling and laughing with him, you would realize afterward that you had been gritting your teeth, slightly on edge in preparation for whatever pyrotechnics had been coming next. I needed a rest from the governor, and because I was once fond of him I can say without having it sound mean-spirited that I think the governor himself needed a rest from the governor.

Hell, after seven years, maybe the whole state does. Everyone wonders where he's going next. He says he and Shep are going to Patagonia to live in a stone hut and fish, and while the gullible, human, storytelling part of me mostly believes that—he is sometimes just loony enough for that to sound right—the intellectual part of me notices that there is one tiny thread that might not quite match up with that assertion: for how could one sign a deal betraying the wild trout of Montana in order to go pursue the wild trout in South America? For when trout—like elk—are your religion, you are not capable of parsing out which ones get saved and which ones do not. You seek to guard them all. You are inflamed with love and stewardship. You burn exquisitely. You cannot parse.

ॐ

It's the craziest thing. The bond between a man and a dog is strong. The thing he started out as a gimmick—Old Shep in the statehouse—has, I think, over time, surely worked some small bit of magic, has become in

some small way something real. Over time, I saw him be truly affectionate with Old Shep, even when the cameras and reporters weren't around. A man who can be kind to a dog surely still has some thread of the possibility of redemption within him. Indeed, such small kindnesses might be one of the first signs that such salvation, such transformation—such resurrection, such metamorphosis—is beginning: though I have to say also, that since Imperial came to town, I have not seen Old Shep in the news as much as in the old days.

꙳

Think about it: why protect the Rocky Mountain Front—buying up and permanently retiring millions of dollars of federal oil and gas leases, as Montana and Congress has done—only to then gut it—eviscerate it—with an endless supply chain of oilfield equipment? The route runs down past the poet's house, toward Missoula. For a couple of years we had been seeing road work, but we didn't think anything about it. We had lives to lead. We were hunting, going to soccer practice, cooking burgers on the back porch. We were gardening.

꙳

The governor has made a stand before against Big Oil, is the thing—it's why I can still believe in him. I've seen it—we've all seen it. At the Democratic National Convention in 2008, he brought former President Clinton leaping to his feet with his rousing, barnburning red-meat populist hyperpatriotic delivery. A journalist, Steve Hawley, who is involved with the non-profit group, All Against the Haul, reported on the governor's convention speech.

What's changed in eighteen months, then, and why? It's disturbing to realize that even as the governor was bringing down the house—the stadium—in Denver, the governor was in the thick of his meetings with Exxon, on behalf of Imperial. Steve Hawley, who has far less hope for the reclamation of the governor's soul than do I, writes: "I watched this speech with the farmers in Fairfield in mind. I don't think they would include American energy independence in their description of what happened there. A Canadian oil company got American stimulus funds and was granted American right of eminent domain to shove a pipeline down American farmers' throats. Same with business owners in Choteau, who all see the big trucks as a threat. They also see the governor as the man who has taken up waiting on big oil hand and foot as his main political strategy. Big Oil will not be kind to the Rocky Mountain Front."

ʒ⋲

The governor went to Iowa once, and to New Hampshire as well. He went to a couple of fairs there about a year ago, and spoke, then came home. It went okay.

ʒ⋲

One of the governor's new arguments on behalf of Imperial is that government and people of Saudi Arabia are our enemies, though he worked in Saudi Arabia for several years as a soil scientist, and has in the past spoken kindly of his hosts and that culture. He studied the Arabic language, history and religion. Something is different about him now, something sudden and even erratic, and I just can't put my finger on it.

The governor says our wars in Iraq, Israel, Afghanistan and Pakistan are about oil, and that buying tar sands oil means we don't have to fight wars in the Middle East: that we can walk away; that by developing the tar sands no more Americans have to die over there.

You can see, perhaps, how perplexed I am—how confused. How can a man change so fast? And how daunting our challenge, our thin hope, is, here in Montana. You can see how everyone in the state says that he is lost.

ʒ⋲

He is a student of history. On our hunting trips, that was all he would read—that, and the daily newspaper articles that mentioned his name. The fact that he reads history may in the end be all we have going for us. That, and the hope that he will turn the pages and read the next chapter, the one just-written with invisible ink, the unknown. How cool would it be for the governor to be ahead of the curve, and stand up to Big Oil?

The poet says *He is on the other side of the river, at night, without a lantern.*
Yes, I agree. But if we call out to him, might he yet hear us?

۽

Even if the governor fails us and leaves us here to battle Big Oil without
him while he goes on elsewhere to feed on the bitter fruit of that harvest,
we who remain can learn, and still change the ferocious centripetal pull of
the only history we have ever known, the despoliation of colonization.

The orbit of our lives has been established and we find ourselves
replicating it almost without even trying, without even having to look
up from our gardens, our weekend football pools, our high school vol-
leyball tournaments, our hunting seasons, our Fourth of July parties, our
lives drifting by, and while it is a good enough orbit, and we are grateful
enough to be here, there are few of us who do not want something better
for those who will follow behind us.

The poet, in particular, is adamant about this. It is simply good man-
ners, he says, to leave something better than the way you found it. It is the
Montana way.

The poet wants to cut, to score and scour new grooves in the mountains and plains themselves down which the rivers of time—and us in it,
like fish—will move. There is still time, he says, here in Montana, with
the garden still so new, to shape and fashion such paths—though with
each generation in which the old selfish ways repeat themselves, the
other-scorings grow ever-deeper. That story becomes more entrenched
and polished until it is all we know and, worse yet, all we can imagine.
Some days, in Montana, it seems to me that what our state's beauty and
mystery requires most of all the awe of a witness.

As if there could be no greater loneliness than for such beauty and
uncorrupted power to exist without witness.

۽

The man I knew before Imperial came through the gate knew how
to inhabit those good times in all seasons—the great times that were
bequeathed to us as if with no more thought than vapors that might rise
from the soil on a cold morning when first struck by the sun.

Back then, the governor inhabited happiness, even joy, and did not appear to be haunted by insecurity or frantic for love or power, nor owned by the giant shadows of darkness.

❧

I am remembering something strange about the governor now, something that surprised me at the time, and which I remember now in my telling. He could never get warm. He was always cold. Even in summer, in the evenings he'd be wearing some sort of vest; and in the winter, well, forget about it: whenever we'd drive somewhere, he'd have the heater cranked all the way up, so that it would be almost melting the plastic on the dashboard. And if there was a campfire, he would tuck in so close to it that it seemed he was about to step into it: that he *had* stepped into it, and was standing there in the coals, while the sparks rose all around him. And while it might seem undignified for a governor, he had on occasion warmed himself with fires made of roadside trash. He'd stay in the truck with the engine idling while I went out and scrounged whatever I could: Styrofoam, newspapers, plastic Coke bottles, what-have-you—and put the trash in a steel barrel we carried in the back of the truck for this purpose. I would splash a dollop of gasoline onto the trash, light it with a *whoosh*, and like a salamander scuttling from a log, the governor would come hurrying out of the truck, would tuck in as close as he could to the burning barrel, shivering like an old man.

He was not an old man—he was robust—which is what made it seem so strange. He was the last person in the world I would ever expect to be vulnerable to the cold. But for as long as I knew him, he could never get warm. It was as if he had been born from a glacier.

I would have guessed the opposite: that he would have run hot, and if anything, would have been perpetually in need of great cooling.

If the governor gives Exxon the state of Montana—the poet will be waiting for him. Students at universities all across the country will set up a resistance against him: in Madison, Wisconsin; in Ames, Iowa, where the poet sometimes teaches; in Seattle and San Francisco, where some of the governor's money sources lie. In New Hampshire, in Colorado, in California and in Florida. The poet has only one life to give for his country, and he will give it.

After the governor had warmed up again, we would be heading on, back to Helena, and the business of running the most beautiful state in the country. It's funny how similar certain words in our language are, with just a single crooked letter altering the meaning of a phrase entirely. Back to the business of running the most beautiful state in the country; back to the business of ruining the most beautiful state in the country.

I can't remember now what the price tag was—whatever paltry few million he gave the pass up for—but if he thinks Exxon is going to support him and only him, when he decides to run for whatever he runs for next—president, vice-president, king, whatever—then he is not as smart as I thought he was. Is no longer as smart as he once was, back in his innocence, and the beauty of his instincts.

Usually we stayed in a little trailer-court hotel along the Hi-Line; went to the bar, watched Sunday Night Football with the locals, talked crops, price supports, the weather. Once, however, we camped out. We had intended to stay in Shelby but all the rooms were taken, and when we called ahead to Conrad, they were full there, too, as was Valier and Chester. It was crazy, it was ridiculous, it was utterly Montana; the governor couldn't get a room, not even a fleabag dive! What I didn't know then was that all the construction crews were already busy along the proposed High and Wide route.

Hell, I wasn't an accountant, I didn't know or ask where the money was coming from to upgrade those little bridges-to-nowhere. I just thought that was what Western governors did. I was a *naïf*; I was busy wondering about where the next pheasants were, the sharptails, the Huns.

"They say you can never shoot too far in front of a pheasant," the governor said, there by the fire. He had shot well that day and was feeling pretty good about it, was willing to dispense advice. "They'll fly into the shot string. You can't lead them enough. They're big birds and big birds always move faster than you think."

We had six of them in the ice chest, three each. That was my job also, to clean them, and as I sat by the fire plucking them—their fantastic color rendered drab and mute by nightfall—the feathers swirled everywhere in that breeze, great fistfuls of feathers, which Old Shep watched depart with mild interest, as if within all those scented feathers there might yet be another pheasant, hiding.

I watched Old Shep as I worked, and after a while I saw his ears perk up, and thought at first he was hearing some high-pitched whining from the fire, a sound we could not discern, or that he had heard some faint rustling of an animal out in the grass. But then I did hear it, a faraway grinding that reminded me of the sound an iron manhole cover makes when it is being lifted from the top of a storm sewer and slid across the concrete.

I had heard that sound only once before—the shifting of tectonic plates along the Rocky Mountain Front—and it was as thrilling to hear it again as it was to see the northern lights, or to watch a foal being born; it was a phenomenon, as opposed to so much of the rest of our days that were filled with the white noise of unremarkable things—or rather, things to which we had become accustomed, and viewed now as unremarkable.

The shape of your dog's head under the palm of your hand. The ability to go out in your garden and pluck some leaves of lettuce for a salad, or to cut some flowers. Turning on the radio and listening to the news without worrying that a bomb was going to fall on your head, or fretting about your upcoming lung surgery for the mesothelioma that had just been diagnosed. The unremarkable skein of one day after another, without ever having to think about leave-taking the green earth. As if a spell of narcolepsy has been cast.

The grinding got our attention. To hear the actual sound of the earth still being formed and shaped and sculpted by a force and logic different from our own got my attention. It was like being in the garden in Day One or Two of Genesis—like being carried back to the time when the garden was being made ready for man and woman, but before anyone had yet arrived. It was like walking into an empty stadium late at night and beholding nothing but space, where soon—the next day—there would be motion, fury, speed, ecstasy, despair.

"What's that?" the governor asked, with some concern.

If I had known then what I know now, I might have told him, *It is the sound of the bonesaw or hacksaw: of Imperial and Exxon sawing in half this quadrant of North America, beginning at the mouth of the Columbia and travers-*

ing straight west, then quartering along the mountains, up into Canada. It is the sound of the first and last bite. An eclipse not of the moon but of the earth itself. We are down in the belly of the beast, we will know sunlight no more.

I didn't know anything, back then. "Talus in the mountains," I said. "Or maybe those underground missiles we've got aimed at the Russians are jiggling around. Maybe the underground engineers are having races with them on their rail links. Seeing who can get his warhead from Bynum to Conrad and back the quickest. Listen," I said, "put your ear to the ground, you can hear the steel wheels on the tracks."

"Shee-yit," he said, "those things are *mothballed*. Their firing pins are rusted, their powder is rotted. You couldn't light those things off with a *blowtorch*. Mice have gotten into the wiring. What a con job. We've got *nothing* down there. Just a bunch of radioactive duds simmering below, helping our wheat grow tall." He turned over and faced the fire and asked what all men and women have asked themselves, when in the presence of the mountains, any mountains, "Ever wonder what it was like a hundred years ago, before we fucked it all up?"

I knew nothing, then. I thought—assumed—we were going to be able to hold on to what we had. I guess it's a common enough mistake. Maybe the Indians felt the same way. Maybe anyone who ever loved something felt that way.

I started to answer the governor, that night. I started to wax rhapsodic about how damned lucky we were. I started to ask him, "I wonder what the rich people are doing tonight?" But he had rolled over on his back and was sleeping, was already snoring lightly, a gurgling, grinding sound, while beyond us, the mountains shifted and ground against each other, as if calling out to him in a similar language.

᠅

The state loved him, back then. How can love go away? Maybe it wasn't love after all. Maybe we were hungry for something big, something as remarkable as the landscape itself. We saw a greatness in him, and trusted him with even more. At any rate, he's lost it now, though not yet so much that he can't yet circle back and pick it back up. The cycle of forgiveness is a critical one in any epic myth, and forgiveness of failure is always an element in the path of the greatest of our politicians.

If a person can be hungry for fame, or love, or power, then cannot that same person come to know a hunger for doing good?

The Nez Perce are not waiting for him to change. Exxon is not waiting, either. It occurs to me that although this is a Montana battle, it is also a world battle: that if we are ever to turn away from hydrocarbons, we must do so now, before carving open—further—Pandora's last box.

In some ways I don't even blame the governor! Who would want to shoulder that burden—literally, the weight of the world? Who would want to be the first—who would dare to be the first—to turn his or her back on oil, and choose the harder, longer path to freedom?

I worry for him. I worry for our state and our world far more than for the governor, but I worry for him, too. I was once his friend. He does not take my calls now, nor does he answer my letters—but before the men and women in black got to him, he was my friend—I believe that he was. It is not that I want the friendship back—water that has flowed past does not return in this life—but it is important to me that he reclaim himself while he can. He has walked right into the fire, and it is not making him stronger.

⁂

We stopped off at the Pishkun Buffalo Jump once. We stood there in the wind and watched Old Shep run casting and weaving into that wind, the shortgrass tickling his belly as he surged, thinking at first that we had stopped to hunt.

Standing there with the wind in our faces, and the shape of the land so clearly the shape of our history—facing a past we had chosen to destroy—I could feel the governor's acknowledgment of that history. We were standing there not as governor and aide but instead as two white men, uncomfortable with dull shame, having to look at the shape of absence, and feeling the loneliness of the outsider, and a little weary, I think, from what another poet once called "the tasks and burdens of an inauthentic life."

Maybe Old Shep could still scent the faintest odor of the buffalo. Some of the boulders out in the meadow below the jump were polished as smooth as the marble in Greek temples. Buffalo for millennia had rubbed against their rough edges, itching and scratching. We walked over and placed our hands on some of those boulders, and looked up, as if from the bottom of a pit, at the high cliff that blocked already the sun of early afternoon.

It took no imagination at all to envision the buffalo—pursued hard by the Blackfeet—hurtling over the edge in black swarms and tumbling, manna from heaven for the hunters below. An endless rain of meat and fur, falling from the sky like a blessing. A blessing without end.

We didn't say anything, didn't wax poetic about how things must have been a hundred and twenty years ago. The governor just looked up at those high cliffs, and out there in the big wind like that, with no photographers and no witnesses save me and his dog. He looked vulnerable and lonely, but not frightened of his loneliness, and almost at peace with himself—or if not at peace, then in a place where the dynamic tensions within him, the creating and the destroying, had found some safe place of stillness. He laughed to see Old Shep's wild energies continuing undaunted as he worked farther into the wind, barking as if herding something only he could see.

જ

Driving back, then, I could feel the greatness leaving him, could feel the other thing—not the great stillness, but the frenzy—entering him. It was always that way, and even before the men and women in black—the suits—had found him. Or maybe they had found him, and no one knew it yet.

Old Shep rode between us, taking one of his too-brief naps. Recharging. When he could exercise, he was fine, but when he had to be still for too long, he just flat unraveled. Often he would snap at imaginary flies, and whether for self-entertainment and amusement, or from some fevered madness within, I could not say. The sound of his jaws chopping, there in the truck, on the drive back to the capitol.

જ

What a tangled web we weave, when we accept that first check. I'm still about four years behind on my sleep patterns, just from my brief spell in the oil patch. The hours and the traffic never end. I cannot tell you

how much above-ground traffic—at all hours—it takes to service the sour black tar lying below, which we suck at like butterflies drawn without differentiation to either nectar or roadkill. I've been trying to caution the state about it, but the future is a hard sell. Folks who are used to the wide open spaces simply can't imagine it. There's probably some mathematical model you could run that correlates truck-traffic hours per barrel of oil, per gallon of oil, a number that is never included in the true accounting of oil's costs, and with the extremely labor- and machinery- and energy-intensive processes for the tar sands, that number is surely in excess of even the ceaseless clot of traffic associated with more traditional oilfields: day and night, coming and going, holidays and weekends, ice storms and blizzards, no matter: chains slapping snowy pavement, trailer-loads of pipe spilling like matchsticks and marbles, fluttering flotsam of trash, the entire Rocky Mountain Front a groaning black ribbon of diesel, a river of trucks and diesel and ice-slide, and with the agrarian towns that stipple the plains there, milking snowmelt from the mountains to irrigate their fields and farms each summer, being converted into squalid pleasure-ghettoes whose sole purpose is to provide the drugs and alcohol and rental units to those who are servicing the tar; to those who are bringing to us the tar our leaders have not been able or willing to set beyond us.

We all share culpability, but it is our very culpability that gives us the greatest authority, not the least, to insist that our leaders—our proxies— set the pit beyond our reach; lock it up and throw away the key; and that first and foremost, we do not use Montana for the injection of big rigs into the bloodstream that stretches from the Pacific to the boreal forest of Alberta.

You see it already—the ravening, the summoning. I have tried to tell the governor, have tried to tell the state. A second company, Conoco Phillips, is petitioning to use the proposed High and Wide corridor, to deliver giant equipment to a refinery in Billings, and there are other, still-secret plans to create a haul corridor down the southern end of the Rocky Mountain Front, to service not just the coal in the Red River desert (to hell with antelope and mule deer wintering grounds) but the Niobara shale play in Cheyenne and Denver, the aging oilfields of Rock Springs, and all the way down to Albuquerque and beyond.

The governor plans for it to all be one glorious incandescent blossoming of the last of the continent's hydrocarbons, with Montana at the center, glowing, briefly—for another fifty years—like an ingot, and from the night sky looking like the planar grid of LAX or Atlanta-Hartsfield, the hub of dirty carbon use, as all travelers approach that central glow in the night, drawn to the burning.

Already, the center of the governor's main untruth—that this is just a one-time deal, cowboy—is unraveling. The 200 loads he says will be permitted—nothing more—have ballooned in the last few weeks to 257, and Conoco Phillips has already barged their giant modules up the dead Snake and has them idling in Lewiston, awaiting but a single friendly judge to wave them on farther. Now a third company, Harvest Energy, a subsidiary of the Korean National Oil Company, having learned of the High and Wide proposal, has applied to bring its own giant equipment for the tar sands through Montana, and that's just in the last week, and before any permits have been issued.

Three will become one-hundred-and-three. The only thing that can stop them is the citizen's initiative. Once the first permit is issued, there's legal precedent, and all the others will follow like water through a burst dam, like an ice-age river eroding a busted glacier: carving anew.

It's reminiscent of the furor over NAFTA, which, ironically, the governor and his administration opposed with full-throated red-meat American isolationism. And—for a moment to put aside the job loss of that boondoggle—millions of lost jobs—anyone who's ever tried to drive not just the interstate but even the back roads south of Houston, with the ragged trucks racing over hill and dale, eighteen-wheelers pounding the shit out of the sun-heated highways, rattling the roads into such disrepair that already they look like relics from the 1940s—anyone who has seen the before-and-after of that outcome would know better than to allow our governor to do the same thing up here, where the scale of traffic would be even greater, as the world serviced the death star. And again, how ironic that the governor was once—pre-Exxon, pre-Imperial—so adamant that we not do this sort of thing. Lamenting NAFTA's giant sucking sound to the south, while to the north, that same song now sounds to him like that of the Sirens, calling him.

ॐ

Hunting, that autumn, the governor and I stopped once at a big farm outside of Dutton, where we saw cars and trucks parked all up and down the driveway and stretching out to the road. Wedding, funeral, bar mitzvah or family reunion, it made no difference to the governor. He had had a good day hunting and the walk had been useful to him in helping to clear his head, but he had been too long now without either an audience or a podium, and could not turn away.

The balloons and hand-lettered posterboards soon told us it was a reunion, and most of the license plates were from Montana. As we drove in to park as close as possible, we could not help but tally, from the various registries of those tags, the different voter districts represented: Billings, Butte, Bozeman, Helena, Missoula, Great Falls.

The field in front of the modest ranch house had been irrigated through the summer—the snow in the not-so-distant mountains the source of that water, to be distributed across the plains below, much desired and fought over, the water a guarantee of who would succeed and who would fail—and the lawn had been mown only a day or two earlier, so that the cuttings still rested atop the green, curing and dried already to a paler, desiccated green.

A group of teen-agers was playing Frisbee out in that grass, barefooted and wearing shorts, and in their joy of the game, they focused only upon the next throw, or the next catch, and upon each other, with an intensity of absorption in which they took everything in the world for granted.

We drove past them and found a parking slot. I had cleaned our birds and they were in the ice chest, plump as chickens, protected from the day's heat. It seemed to me now that our hunting was over for the day, and while I wished we had kept on going, I understood that there were some temptations that the governor could not resist, and had perhaps unerringly and at some unconscious level sniffed out and been drawn to their gathering: as if the feast had been prepared for him and no other, despite how it might appear otherwise.

We parked and walked slowly toward the big tent, where the blue smoke was coming from: a barbecue, corn and ribs being grilled, with watermelon cut in bright wedges and glistening, all of it arrayed on folding card tables covered with plastic checkered tablecloths.

I could feel it, as we walked down the gravel drive toward the noise and heat and light: the waves of electricity entering into the governor, and then his own internal dynamo generating a pulse that radiated outward.

They recognized him immediately: the most-recognizable person in the state. A small fish in a big pond, but at least not as small as the other fish.

They recognized him, and certainly, they recognized the famous black-and-white dog trotting at his heels. Immediately they began to point, heads rotating almost mechanically toward us, so that after only a few paces he was in the center of everyone's attention. The way their heads turned to face the one object, making it central, reminded me of the way the heads of flowers will turn to face the sun and follow it all the course of the day.

Some of them were pointing with animation, while others whispered, speculating on which branch of the family he might be. They all wore smiles. Part of it had to do with who the governor was, of course, but part of it was simply the way he presented himself, striding eagerly with chin up and shoulders thrown back and grinning, as if he had only that moment fallen into possession of the most marvelous news, that the world found favor with him, was delighted with him, and here he was then, an emissary for greatness, and just in time to rescue people from the traps of boredom or ignorance, those two weirs as dangerous as any ever constructed.

It was a simple equation and I am not quite doing it justice. It wasn't just that he made people smile by initiating the smiling, and it wasn't just confidence. It was the other thing, the radiant thing, which we call charisma, but which in the case of the governor was more powerful and complex than mere charisma. And no matter whether he was the honored invitee or a party crasher, I never saw him without it.

He strode toward their midst as would a bear. Every eye swung to him and followed his every movement: and he was keenly aware of it, and something in him fed on it.

Some of the bolder of the reunion-goers came walking over to meet us. He would give no speech that day, uninvited as we were. The electricity was in him, though, and when people came up to him to visit, he unleashed the same electricity upon each one of them that he would have delivered to a crowd of several thousand or, in the case of the convention the previous year, millions.

He could speak to one or two with that earnest intensity and specificity, or he could pull in the whole nation. And watching him do it there at the barbecue, as an uninvited drop-in, I had to ask myself, why *wouldn't* he run for president? Someone would have to do it, eventually, and it seemed a fair guess to say that after the long national nightmare of Bush and Rove and Palin, we preferred an unknown, someone to whom we could affix hero-qualities over the monotony of dynasty and name-brand familiarity.

A little girl was playing with Old Shep. The governor reached down and tousled her hair. A young mother holding a baby was standing next to him, laughing and listening. It had been done this way once upon a time and never would be again, politics was all corporate glide now, except in Montana, and the hell of it was he was just treading water, he didn't need to be doing any of it, we could have been out hunting.

What was he going to accomplish, raise his approval rating from eighty-four to eighty-five percent?

Bill Clinton was the same way. He would turn his back on the eighty-five percent to go after the fifteen percent he didn't have: his strength becoming his weakness. It happens to all of them and it would happen to the governor some day. I didn't want to be around to see it, but here I am, looking right at it, and trying now—with the poet—to help take it away from him. To show the governor a room where he could have more than Imperial could ever give him; but if he does not choose that room, then to transfer the accountability of the cost he and Imperial seeks to place upon us, and the land—back upon them, politically and financially. Servants of the tar.

I stood there in the sweet-smelling newly-cut hayfield with the odor of barbecue swirling and mixing, and the brutal heat of the day that had leached the land seeping back into space, and the evening's first crickets beginning a slow chirp. I watched as the governor, not yet corrupted, worked the crowd, watched the men and women who had gathered around him gave him their hopes and attention and everything else that was good about them, piling these things on him, or pouring them into him, as if sending him on a long journey, an arduous journey, for which he would need all of our collective resources, and with him our best hope for pushing through the disturbing approach of darkness, back into the light that we hoped if not absolutely knew was on the other side.

Children were chasing one another through the crowd and laughing, and over the easy lull of adults talking and laughing, I could hear the growl and grind of an ice cream maker.

The governor was speaking. He had a cold bottle of beer in one hand and a rib in the other, and had tucked a large paper napkin into his collar. He waved the half-eaten rib as he spoke. "I'll tell you one thing," he said, "the man or woman who figures out how to get rid of orange hawkweed will end up being a billionaire."

There was a band setting up on a trailer out beneath one of the larger tents. I caught the governor's attention and gave him the same signal for leaving that we used for planned or scheduled events—nothing fancy or discrete, just a glance at my watch and then a feigned incoming call on my cell phone, or a wasp-buzz at my hip: the latter two affectations ridiculous, I realized midway into them, for that fact that there was no cell coverage out there.

Still, he caught the gesture; he missed nothing in a crowd, and already, we were wired tightly enough for him to pretty much know my thoughts, and for me to know his.

We left before he could get sucked too far in. He understood that it was far better for his myth-building for him to drop in and then dash off than to stay over-long, like someone with nothing else to do. This brevity of his appearance would make it all the more improbable, all the more myth-worthy. *Was it but a dream*? He understood that. We said our good-byes and thank-yous and good-lucks and were out of there within five minutes of his having gotten the signal.

He was the best I ever worked with, in that regard, like a commando; eager to declare his mission completed, and eager, also, to be traveling on to the next one.

It was still barely light when we got back to the little trailer court. Summer was not long over, but was gone; no lost tourists were checked in, nor were any highway crews. We were the only ones, a dozen empty little clapboard cottages, their white paint peeling and flaking, the cottages prob-ably never to be painted again. We could have packed our gear and headed for Helena, could have gotten back before midnight, but instead we decided to stay the night, to get up early and drive at dawn, or even a little before.

I had drawn the birds but not yet plucked them. We sat in the white plastic chairs in front of our room beneath the giant leaning cottonwoods with their fig-green leaves that were just starting to turn yellow and drank another beer and I plucked our birds, dropping the feathers into a paper grocery sack, though not all of the feathers made it back in. The loose feathers drifted away slowly as I worked.

We watched the mountains, and because the evening was so pleasant, I brought the clock-radio from my hotel room outside, and we listened to the Griz game. They were on the West Coast, playing some piss-ant team from central Washington, and were beating the daylights out of them. It wasn't even close. I finished our birds—Old Shep lay by our feet, a perfect gentleman for once, napping—and we listened to the game, and to the cool rattling of the leaves overhead, and stared at the distant blue moun-tains with their scrim of ivory already along the highest ridges.

After dusk had gone and it was the beginning of true night, we saw a few flickers of heat lightning to the north, but where we were, it was quiet and dry. I thought about cooking the birds over a little fire, there in the empty gravel parking lot—it was too nice a night to go inside—but I was too tired, and in the end we just opened another beer and sat there listening to the end of the game.

Our cottages, side by side, were the only ones with their little yellow outside porch lights burning, beneath which fluttered a number of moths. The breeze settled down and the crickets started up with greater vigor, and then we said good-night and went to bed. The whole time, after we had gotten back to the hotel, we hadn't spoken of politics once, which was unusual, and not unpleasant.

Feathers fluttered around our ankles when we stood up—*the governor is a man who kills his own food*, I thought. It seemed like something from a century or two earlier. Montana is different from Wyoming or Colorado, from Nevada or Arizona. Montana is better.

Power, or peace? Most will almost always choose power, and it strikes me as odd that those who possess the least peace, and who are the most frantic, should choose to turn their backs on it when given the opportunity. We killed all the Indians, took their land from them, and for a long while after that, knew a beautiful peace. Now an enemy capable of blocking out the sun is encroaching upon us, and the Indians want to help us defend ourselves against it. Go figure. I guess they really mean it when they say they love the land.

�֎

Black coffee just before daylight, with the orange lip of the sun cresting the flat prairie half an hour later, and we were already driving. Young rooster pheasants crowed out in the fields—it would be another month before the season opened for them—and for a while, we were too far out to pick up any of the public radio stations, which aggrieved the governor, news junkie that he was.

He fooled with the tuner, finally settled on an ag station from Lethbridge, and listened attentively to the day's quotes on feeder calves, cows-with-calves, and bulls—and he whistled appreciatively when the quotes for corn and wheat were read out, with the food crops now almost as valuable as the oil and water it took to grow them.

The hayfields, the open space, *Montana*—the healing place—flashed by. Such beautiful country out here on the east side, preserved so far not through any forethought of man, but only because it has thus far resided always just a bit beyond our grasp. The late cuttings of hay glinted yellow and green under the softening sun, the mown cut fields shiny and flaxen.

We were drifting out of range of the Lethbridge station, but still a little too far out to pick up Great Falls' public radio. Choteau, where cattle grazed amidst fossils and dinosaur bones scattered in Jurassic clutter. The town's wide sidewalks looked like those in movie Westerns depicting

the previous century. A passerby on one of those sidewalks caught sight of the governor, did a double-take, then waved excitedly; and casually, the governor waved back.

"*Gawd, Shep!*" the governor cried, and hastened to roll down his window, dabbing at his eyes before looking at me with half-apology, half-accusation. "Did you feed him a corndog?"

It was sulfurous, the odor that I imagine attends the burning rivers of hell. "No," I said, rolling my window down, and again I marveled at the seeming distance between aspects, or sides, within a man; a man who, if he didn't sell out to Big Oil—if he remained a man of the people, and avoided antagonizing warriors like the poet, could be president one day was shooing a farting cow-dog out of his lap and sticking his head out the window to breathe the clean fast-rushing air as stray bird feathers swirled in the cab of his truck.

And when we got to Helena, I let him out in front of the mansion just like any other man: not as if he was governor of the secret pulse of the world, but as if he was just a man coming back from a hunting trip with his dog at his side.

His Blackberry and palm pilot beeping and buzzing, the world was telling him where to be once again in three-minute increments. But back then he was just a Montanan, and still a man, capable of making choices. He was not yet owned by the black rivers below, nor the black rivers of tar in Canada.

❧

The governor is lost. Before Big Oil got to him, he had such fire. It was a thing to see. He was incredible. He would stand up to anyone. He was afraid of nothing. He had nothing to lose, or thought that he had nothing to lose. He perceived that he had only everything to win. And he did. But now—what paradox!—he stands to lose more than he could ever have imagined.

There are so many ways to skin a cat. South Korea is the second-largest trading partner with Montana, importing huge quantities of beef and grain. The U.S. ambassador to South Korea is from Montana; the United Nations' trade ambassador, likewise. We don't have to accept South Korea's mobile refineries.

The entire world is wanting to dig up Alberta, and wants to come through Montana—our little backroads, our scenic byways—to do so.

It doesn't have to be this way. We stand at the edge of converting to electric cars. A scientist in Montana, Janine Benyus, working with the Biomimicry Institute, is discovering all sorts of elegant designs and formulas in nature that save vast stores of energy. There is an economy in every living thing but us. These silly oversized mega-loads, for instance: Imperial claims the cylinders can't have any seams in them; that they have to be manufactured whole and shipped all that distance: that the refined tar oil will cling to and cake any seam or irregularity. But in Montana there are scientists working on developing substances that imitate the way that whales use sessile cells to keep barnacles from forming on their flukes, which would otherwise destroy and sink them. The same chemicals could line the seams of cylinders-assembled-from-smaller-parts. *We don't have to let the giant mega-loads creep through Montana.* This is all a waste, all ridiculous and errant, all too much of a rush, the way so many of our largest mistakes are. *War and peace.*

There is a scale going on here that transcends our individual work in our individual gardens. I do not see how the world can eat itself. There is a force going on beneath us, a grinding of immense gears in the center of the earth, that will surely balance and position the good before the bad.

How strange that even as we try here in Montana to scratch out a new story, all the old ones continue to come to the surface. The idea of one's name being written in a Book of Life, for instance. That which we once had the luxury of believing was distant prophecy realizing is now suddenly—or seems sudden—upon us, emerging as if from beneath the surface: the dream made real.

It's strange that this short history of Montana contains so much more space devoted to the governor, my former friend and now nemesis, than to the poet. But in a way it makes sense. The poet is on the perimeter of everything, resides on the literal borderland, while the governor is the dark seed at the center; dark, though he craves light.

The poet will be the first to hear the trucks; to see them coming over the pass and into our trap.

When we call your name, please answer. When we call your name, please give us your name; please sign your name. It will be the greatest story in the world, a story a poet could love: a story of how ink, drying on paper, saved the world from its burning. A story of how the names of ordinary folk shut down kings and villains and the most powerful forces on earth—as if dreams were to defeat geology, as if dreams were once and still are the ultimate force of nature.

⅋

I remember this about the governor, too: he was fascinated by the cost of things. Not just big things, like the jet fighters at Malstrom Air Force Base, or the reconstruction of the Going to the Sun Highway, or the cost of the helicopter hazing of those buffalo unfortunate enough to wander out of Yellowstone, where the state would begin shooting them—but in the cost of *everything*. A piece of pie, a quart of oil at the gas station, a round bale of hay. As if it was important for him to know the price of every little piece of the state. As if in his mind even then he was calculating some sum total. Knowing always the cost of a thing, but not always the value.

⅋

We'll need luck but first we have to stand up and position ourselves in such a way as to be able to receive that luck. It'll take a miracle, and a little bit of cunning, but one of the things that would help us is if the beast would begin to eat itself. It's hard to imagine a corporation out there that's not already owned. horizontally and vertically, by the largest company in the world; and if another corporation *did* possess enough temerity to resist the beast, Imperial could simply buy them up, the way Imperial, or any other corporation, foreign or domestic—thanks to the Republican appointees on the Supreme Court—can buy politicians.

But there are still a few cracks and crevices of daylight before the boulder is shoved over the tomb once and for all. Travelocity.com is currently in a spat with the governor, who is nothing if not diligent about trying to add to Montana's treasury. The governor is claiming that through its e-commerce, Travelocity has avoided paying certain taxes to hotel rooms in Montana, and is seeking to recoup those fees, which the governor calculates number in the high thousands of dollars.

Travelocity in turn seems to me to be suggesting that if Montana waives those fees, Travelocity will make Montana one of its featured Web destinations, with a whole bevy of discounts aimed to steer tourists toward Big Sky country.

You understand the paradox: even the good guys' economies—the seemingly non-extractive industries—are based on fossil fuels. We've got to change, but it's going to take time. If we bite farther into the tar sands, there will be no motivation, no urgency, for change. We'll just keep on sinking. We'll sink for another fifty years. Same deal for the big pipeline east of Billings: if we put it in, it will justify the sucking out—the benzene fracturing—of every shred of deepwater hydrocarbons beneath the high stony frozen waves of the Rocky Mountain Front.

The world will keep burning, so hot that nothing but time—call it ten thousand years of silence—can extinguish it.

The governor sold us out so cheap! The Natural Resources Defense Council has just discovered, by translating Korean documents, that South Korea has already manufactured $1.5 billion worth of refinery modules— that the 200 loads they told the governor were coming are but the tip of the iceberg, the Trojan horse. Now is the perfect chance for the governor to step in and say to Exxon, to Imperial, to South Korea, *Whoa, hold on, not so fast, big fella…*

Travelocity's investment in the Montana tourist and travel industry alone is more substantial than the $66 million, or whatever pittance Imperial bought us for, which was one-one-thousandth of Exxon's quarterly—not annual, but *quarterly*—profits. Which in some ways is irrelevant, for this is not a negotiation—we are not for sale—though in other ways the numbers do matter, in that by increasing them in certain pinch-point bottlenecks—by refusing to shoulder the weight of all the costs that Imperial seeks to externalize upon the taxpayer and the consumer, through secret subsidies, and delayed or accountabilities—we can force them back from the pass, can keep Imperial/Exxon out of Montana.

Travelocity could present a package to the governor that is positive, promoting Montana, and brings in huge revenues, or which is negative, boycotting the leading tar-sand state (and the governor's forthcoming, unpredictable, massive traffic jams—which is not the reason people come to vacation in Montana), taking away huge revenues: hundreds of millions.

There are cracks of light.

Google, likewise, which has just invested $1.5 billion in offshore wind energy development—and which is a huge consumer of electricity— could come to the governor and say *We want to help you, governor; help us to help you.* They could forge an agreement predicated on clean energy—a wind collaboration—but an agreement that is contingent upon renouncing the tar sands and the pipeline.

In some ways, this struggle is pure as ice, is about nothing more than simple math. Certainly, in every sense of the word, it is about power. In other ways, though, it has nothing to do with math, is only about each Montanan's soul: whether we stand up or not. Whether we are for sale or not. It is the last battle.

It is terrifying, and yet it is exhilarating, to even still have a chance, at this late date, to secure a soul, and to witness the affirmation that a single human soul is more powerful than the largest corporation in the world.

It's almost like a dream. Except for the beautiful specificity of this world—the first big October snow in the Mission Mountains, the sounds of the geese and the sandhill cranes heading south in the fall and yet always returning, cracking open the long and otherwise silent end of winter; the scent of summer hayfields in their first June cuttings—except for the specificity of where we live, Montana, it could be a dream.

❧

The governor and I chased sharptails up into a forested draw one time. Instead of flying down farther into the grasslands, the birds wheeled and pitched upslope toward a little thicket of chokecherries and aspen. There was a spring up there, and good hiding cover. It was a steep hill and they must have thought we wouldn't follow them up there—they had probably discovered that other hunters wouldn't follow them up there— but we did.

Old Shep ran too far ahead of us, flushed them wild just before we could get to within shooting range—the governor fired twice anyway but didn't cut a feather—and, huffing from the climb, we walked on over to the spring to see if there might still be one or two stragglers, as sometimes happens with sharptails.

There was nothing, however, only the rich pungent smell of dark moist earth, the tiny oasis in an arid land. Wheat below us and to the horizon. We've traded buffalo for wheat, I thought. It was still beautiful, if tame—pastoral, not wild, but still easy on the eyes. A person could look out and think about one's life, and about what it means to be human, and to have some space around you that is not governed by the Man.

Big country always arouses in me that joy, and the governor and I both felt it there that day, I'm sure, looking out at our state below. The distant tiny thread of U.S. 89 along the Front, without a single speck of a car on it, only emptiness, silence, wind.

The aspen grove in which we were standing burned gold beneath the blue sky. There were already damp gold leaves like coins stippling the dark earth around the little spring, and as we stood there, more of them swirled all around us in fantastic whorls and spirals, pressing and pasting themselves against the governor as if seeking him.

Up in the hills above Missoula, on the south face of Mount Jumbo, a kind of modern-day petroglyph appeared one morning, the white-scrim iconography, the represented artwork of a big rig—not life-sized, but big enough for people to see from town—bearing down upon a single stick-figure person standing before it with outstretched hand, *stop*.

I know that when I tell you your life is at stake, that our lives are at stake, you want to not believe me. You want to think it is poetic over-speak. You know that one day our lives *will* be at stake, but not now; it is not convenient right now. You want to wait a little longer. I understand this. We all want one more season in the garden. We want to ignore the summons. We want fiercely to believe that the time is not right now. We want one more hour, one more breath of freedom.

You think there is no hope: that once a politician is augured in on a matter, he or she cannot extract himself, cannot change. I don't believe that, however; for how can we profess to seek change, and cling to the feeble hope of one distant day turning away from oil, yet not allow in our hearts the hope that one man among us can change?

Maybe it is this simple. When the folks in the suits came to meet with him they did so in a room without windows. If there had been windows he might have had more courage—the hand on his back, the support not of those of us here now nor those-to-come, but of all who were here before him. He might not have yielded.

I know it's not that simple: *a window*. But the man I knew, the man who followed his dog out in the fields, was once free. He knew freedom. Who among us, given the time and space to make a decision based on charity, would not turn toward freedom, rather than away, if given a second chance?

I was lost once, myself, out in missile-land. It was winter, I was coming back from pheasant-hunting near Glasgow, and had gotten stuck in a drift. The road had simply vanished, had turned to undulating hills and mounds. I was young and bullheaded and should not even have been out—all the roads were closed—but I had wanted a pheasant badly; had wanted my dog, Colter, to get some more work. I drove around the barricades and continued on, into the snow.

And just as foolishly, once I was stuck, I got out and started walking. It was nighttime and thirty-five below, with high winds; nobody would be coming through for days. I didn't want to die in the car, roadstranded, one of those poor folks you'd hear about a week later. I wanted out. I wanted to walk. I wanted freedom.

I left the dog in the car with a blanket and put on everything I had and then started walking, heading north into the wind. I was on an obscure county road, but I knew also that the Hi-Line was out there somewhere to the north. It would probably be closed down too, but I might get lucky and intercept a town, or a cabin, a ranchhouse, in which I could take refuge.

It was more like swimming than walking. Often I found myself in swirling drifts up to my armpits; but then just as suddenly the wind would swirl away all the snow that had been pressing against me, so that my way was free again, and I could travel farther on. It was like a dream but was not a dream. That's what I like best about this life—and if I was going out, it was a good way to go out, with the hot little spark in my heart bright if unseen amidst so much cold and howl.

Obviously I made it. I got lucky. After only a couple of miles I bumped into an electrified chain link fence. I was knocked to a sitting position by the voltage. The voltage was warm, it jolted me out of the sleepy dreaminess I'd been entering. I couldn't go any farther but I had found fire. It was one of the underground missile silos, out in the middle of fucking nowhere. No one manned the silos, but there was a locked gate and a bunker, an office. The fence was too high to climb, I was too cold and tired, and I never could have broken in anyway, even if I had made it over the fence; but I pawed beneath the snow until I found some of the cobbles, the glacial moraine, that had been excavated when the fence had been built, and I began lobbing them over the fence at the big NORAD satellite dish: pelting the dish with cobbles and stones, setting off all kinds of alarms.

The snowy night sky became filled with the swirling red and white strobes of the alarms, as if aliens were landing. Had landed.

I curled up and waited then, right at the front gate. When I awoke, there were tanks and half-tracks around me, National Guardsmen were lifting me and carrying me into one of the heated half-tracks, handing me thermos-cups of hot chocolate. Rock-and-roll music was blaring on the radio, the blizzard was still howling, I was a million miles from nowhere, but I was allowed to stay in this life, was able to keep on keeping on. We went back and got my dog, a shivering German shorthair, and the tanks and half-tracks growled their way down the snowy road back toward Shelby.

What does this story have to do with the short history of Montana?

Listen more carefully. You are not paying attention. We are warriors, we are survivors. Part of our short history is that we have always been, and always will be, until the end, warriors. It was Chief Joseph who made the mistake of peace, over in Idaho. His descendants will not make that mistake again, and here in Montana, we have never yet made that mistake. There are times when the homeland must be defended. We are not a peaceful country but I think that we still crave peace.

⁂

It's October, and the poet labors on, searching the ingots in his heart—too hot to touch, but touch them he must—pulling up words and images from a burning river. He arranges and re-arranges them on the page, as if trying to fashion a hand-made key with one specific pattern of ridges and grooves, which will release the one lock that has been clicked and hasped over this world. The poet senses dimly that only the deepest prayer, and the deepest good, might soften the hold on that lock—might release it completely—but then the taste of the burning peat at the bottom of the glass each evening reminds him that we are made of fire, and that we will live or die by fire: that we were put here to burn, and only in that burning are we truest to ourselves, and the larger plans of the world.

Many days he works on through the setting of the sun and into the night, working in his loft, dimly aware of the passing of time and the sound of his family moving around down in the kitchen: the small and regular movements of those daily paths, patterns, and gears.

Some days, however—knowing that he must at least attempt to moderate the burning—he takes a break at dusk, and just before dusk emerges from his cabin as if from a dream. He looks up at the red sky and takes in the scent of the pines, and the scent of clean water, the river nearby. He listens to the dusk-stillness, no sound of the trucks' approach yet, one more day in paradise—and he takes his fly rod—bamboo, in the old style—and goes down to the water.

People think that he loves fish, and that he loves the muscles and mind of the river, the shimmering secret electricity that is generated by its gurgling currents, in the same way that sentences and ideas sometimes generate a certain current, a certain glow, in his mind, and from that, a shuddering current in his soul.

But some days, and some nights, what he loves most—what he is fascinated by most—are the insects: the delicacy of the mayflies, blue-winged olive duns and green drakes, lighter than springtime cottonwood fluff, and utterly helpless and vulnerable, utterly beautiful, and mere fuel for the appetites of the great trout below, hidden within the current like monsters. Some nights he crouches there on his heels beside the stream and is so mesmerized by the shimmering curtain of insects that he does not even cast, does not even enter the water, but just hunkers there watching, and listening to the river, and—soon enough—to the sound of the trout feeding.

Other nights the caddisflies and mayflies are not yet aflight, the sky-drift of them has not yet begun—the mysterious lock-and-key fit of temperature, light, nutrition, and oxygen—and he examines instead their curious, clumsy progenitors, the nymphs in grand armament as they sledge themselves like miniature tanks across the graveled bottom, carrying their lives with them like beggars, little bits of twig and leaf and grains of sand adhering to their shells, partly so as to be camouflaged, and partly for protection: as if, the harder their self-made shell, the less vulnerable the soft parts within are.

Do they not know they are doomed anyway? The poet, of course, though nymph-like in his life, much prefers the winged courage of the mayflies, refined, finally, of all impurities.

He can't watch insects forever, however. He emerges from his reverie, his dream of purity, and steps into the water, delighted, and no matter that it is for the ten thousandth time, by the cold press of the river against the bloodwarm shin and shank of his ankles, and then deeper: the mountain river hardening his legs as heated iron is forged by similar immersion. Casting lightly then to the little brown trout that are spawning there at that time of year—aliens, really, newcomers to western rivers in only the last hundred years or so, though beautiful, and voracious.

In this small river, they don't grow nearly as large as the salmon over on the other side of the mountain. Nothing does. He knows he should probably keep them and eat them—they're not native—but they live here now. He plays them, then turns them loose again, even as in his freezer there is a forty-pound Chinook salmon, encased as if in a glacier, awaiting the grill some starry night. The poet wants to be as pure as ice, wants to burn cleanly, but thank goodness he is not, thank goodness he does not. How boring that would be, and how inaccessible, his poems!

He fishes on as the curtain of night falls, fishing by sound and touch now, feeling the trout tug in his spiderweb line and listening to the hungry sippings of the fish as they follow their blind instincts.

None of us are pure—this may be why each of us is here, set down into a land of fantastic purity—to marvel and bear witness, with our daily findings, our daily flutterings upon the water's surface. What refineries, I wonder, might be built for our souls, not just here in Montana, but in this country, to burn free finally the sticky impurities, the flaws and contaminations, toxins of greed and cruelty and most harmful of all, denial? What would such a refinery look like?

Perhaps it would shift shapes, appearing sometimes as a classic phalanx of illuminated towers glowing in the night, a city gridwork of incandescent burning, skyscrapers and neon pulsing; while other times taking the shape of any of our bodies, of each of our bodies, isolate and chilled, for a moment, doing the one thing that most makes us live: standing in a river casting, or kneeling in a garden, preparing a way for the next meal and the next season.

Following the tracks of an immense antlered animal high up into the mountains, with the traveler's back turned on the humanity, the village, he seeks to feed. The intoxicating scent of his quarry growing stronger, as he draws, with cunning, endurance, skill, and resolve, ever closer to it, with the quarry sometimes knowing that it is being followed, and other times oblivious.

In times like those, the hunter—like the gardener, the fisherman, or the poet—is glowing and burning, and all flaws are burned away, and there is greater membership in a world that is ancient and miraculous. In times like those, it is possible for the one who burns cleanly to believe that there is a purpose and a reason for everything, and that we—improbably—are chosen to be here, and that the greater good within each of us is going to prevail over the lesser parts of ourselves.

୭⊀

A smoldering, smoking soul can still be rescued; a soul which burns yet generates no heat can still know purity, and the power of that purity, again. A smoldering soul that is asked to become vulnerable before the fire, and to burn more brightly—to burn without reservation; to choose one way, rather than two ways—will be terrified, standing at the edge of fate, understanding that such a soul will either become case-hardened, tempered by the new burning and the new courage, or consumed entirely, like summer grass. As if there was never any substantial or durable core within than summer grass.

Say what you want about the governor, everyone has already written him off, but he had spit, once upon a time, something more there than dry grass. And yet may have it again. *The man who stood up to Imperial*? Wouldn't that be a story? It is our job to put a hand on his back, and to build a fire within, once again.

୭⊀

There are other Indians out there. Two of them—one in Canada, and one in the U.S.—are traveling the route of the existing pipeline that sends the tar sands' refined gasoline underground. Clayton Thomas-Muller is a Cree from northern Ontario, while Marty Cobenais is a member of the Red Lake Band of the Ojibwe (Chippewa). Day after day they speak to communities along the pipeline route about the dangers. The quarter-inch flexible steel tubing—thinner than elkskin—so thin that a boy or girl with a hammer-and-nail could puncture it—is sending tar sand oil southward at 72% capacity of the maximum pressure that the tubing is rated to withstand before bursting.

Exxon has filed a petition to run the pressure even higher, to send more oil, faster oil, southward: to go to eighty percent and, in surges, higher. Even at 72%, the tubes are swelling with a pressure of 1600 psi. Put your ear to the ground and just four feet down you can hear the oil singing, rushing.

Marty is tired. He's a big man, but is getting ground down by all the tens of thousands of miles traveled, meeting with reporters all day, every day, and in the evenings showing his documentary, H_2Oil, to any community group he can interest in watching it. He's warning municipal governments (and the keepers of towns' water supplies) that this pipeline is going to fail—with or without terrorist attack. People listen to Marty, but they don't know quite what to do, they don't know where to sign their name, they are a little like lizards flipped over on their back and lulled into sleep by the hypnosis of the sun's mild warmth.

There is nowhere to sign, there is nothing to do. The pipe's already in the ground, the oil is already flowing. We can't really tell them to stop, can we?

❧

The economics of the tar-sands' steamed oil—as though a toxic latte—is predicated on a world oil market costing around $120 a barrel. They're currently selling it to us at a loss, just to keep us hooked. Just to develop the market, and the transportation corridor that they know or believe we will need or want. As if they possess the ability to prophesy.

We could put a carbon tax on the dirtiest fuels. We could still stop this. A carbon tax doesn't change the price or availability of energy. A carbon tax forces the suppliers to give us a different, cleaner kind. It provides an incentive for the corporations—which, like the governor, work for us. It provides the motivation to change. It turns bad capitalism, fake-capitalism—corporate socialism, corporate welfare, and corporate subsidies—into good capitalism. Due to the current Supreme Court, the corporations have been gifted with the rights of individuals though none of the responsibilities. The Supreme Court said corporations—no matter whether foreign or domestic—need to exercise their free speech (and their right to vote, and bear arms, next?), but those corporations don't even have to sign their name to their "speeches." They get to make anonymous donations in unlimited amounts. You can see why the left and the right have united against this.

Missoula doesn't matter, the governor is reported to have said, but this isn't about Missoula. (A *little* bit of it is about Missoula. The trucks are supposed to roll right through the school crosswalk at C.S. Porter Middle School, now and forever. Imperial has agreed to construct a little crossing bridge that the children are free to use, if they wish.)

The corporations will tell us that a carbon tax will crush the little man. The corporations are so protective of the little man that they awaken each morning wondering what they can do for us. They look after us when we are ailing. They are like our parents, our god. If they tell us the carbon tax is bad for us, they must be right. I feel myself getting sleepy. I am going to lie down and take a nap for a while. The corporations will take care of Montana. The governor will take care of Montana. I'm sure of it. I just know they will.

❧

China wants the tar sands' oil, too, and is getting it, via yet another slender crooked pipeline that crosses western Canada to the Pacific, where the oil and gas is loaded onto thin-hulled tankers that ply their way through the rough waters, past reefs and shoals, toward Long Beach, California, before departing for China.

But those spills that people worry about really aren't even worth fretting over yet, right? They will happen—we kind of know that—and California, Oregon, and Washington will get all upset, the way Louisiana got upset for a while. We'll hold a Congressional hearing, right?

❧

Marty looks so tired. There are different ways of lying down in front of a big rig. Each morning, he gets up and does it again, one man versus the world, but with each passing month and then each passing year he looks more and more haggard, while Imperial never ages, never grows old.

Another truck has gone off the road, up in Canada. A regular-sized tractor-trailer carrying diesel has slid off the road on U.S. Highway 12 in Idaho, spilling fuel into the Lochsa and jamming up travel for several hours. A few more hunting and fishing clubs have signed on to the protest, and a few hundred thousand more people who skim the newspapers have noted and filed away in their busy minds. *Oh, another lie, the corporations were mistaken,* and—perhaps they note this—*the governor, entertaining though he is, was mistaken, was not in control.*

This is not a familiar cognitive association: people are used to being confident that the governor is always on the right side, and is always "for the little man." Imperial will come in later and spread some public relations salve over this region, like roadworkers applying patchwork asphalt to a pothole—the twenty or so advertisements sociologists tell us are all that is required in the deadly alchemy of our times to spin lies into brief truth. You have to hear a lie twenty times before it becomes the truth. I find this amazing.

But a few will remember that spill. Our lives and our minds are filled to the brim and often to survive we all decide to hear only what we want to hear: but like it or not, already, the trucks are sliding, and it's not even winter.

Up in Canada, still another truck has gone off a road up there, in the rolling hills of the region formerly known as the Great North American Boreal Forest. Again, no ice, just a winding road and that pesky human error. The Royal Canadian Mounted Police, who investigated the spill of the Mammoet equipment at milepost 161 on Bretonne Road, reported that the driver received a broken leg and was cited, and that the accident was being investigated. Traffic there was blocked for only a couple of days, because there was a crane nearby that was capable of clearing the obstruction, and commerce, and the world's work, was able to proceed.

Still, and already, the rivets are beginning to pop at the seams. Imperial's too big to fail, but might the project be too large, too lunatic, for even the largest company in the world? The tar sands of Alberta are not all that dissimilar from the asphaltic deposits around and beneath Los Angeles, where perfectly-preserved Ice-Age mammals—saber-toothed tigers, North American rhinos and camels from 30,000 years ago lie trapped and forever anguished in the bubbling seepages of La Brea. Activists report that Imperial drafted plans to excavate there, too—that Imperial is taking hundred-year leases on the ground beneath the city, and will excavate there when Alberta is finished—though there is no nearby water with which to flush and steam the tar of Los Angeles, other than the ocean itself.

There are tar sands in Utah, as well. After killing Indians we will move on to the Mormons. Instead of flushing the tar with the Athabasca, we can use the Snake River itself.

What seems unthinkable now, they know, we may well be clamoring for, insisting upon, and soon. As the world burns further—the crackling of flames so loud it makes it hard to sleep, and even the nights so hot that we must run our air conditioners ceaselessly, to try to mute the burning—we will be asking for, demanding, more. Whether a governor in some obscure Western state was once upon a time called Governor Oil or not really won't matter to anyone, everything will have burned or sunk back down into the earth anyway, there will only be fire, and sky.

※

The trucks are failing already. Montana is the weak link in the supply chain of this fevered dream and the trucks—improbable as elephants laboring to cross the Alps in snow—are failing already, even without the burden of their mammoth loads. I wonder if the governor ever wakes up troubled, understanding that for the first time he is exposed to the vulnerability of having made the terribly wrong choice, and considers an exit, an amendment: if he ever considers turning away from Imperial's power and going back toward his own self-generated power, his populism, his purer burning.

The governor is on the wrong side. He has his spokespeople saying that this issue isn't a two-by-four of a problem, but a toothpick.

Think about it—how problematic can a toothpick be? It's just a toothpick. He says everything will be fine. He says the big oil companies who asked him to make the corridor permanent didn't really mean it, that they don't really want it to be permanent after all. He tells us to relax and forget we heard that. Everything is under control.

For now, Imperial has his back, is pumping money into the wound of his ambition like Congress pumps money into automakers, or banks, or what-have-you. Right now however—before the money begins to move—is our brief uncontested shot, our one chance to tell the story of what Montana is like, and what our lives are like, here in the garden, before the spell is cast over us.

We will know they—the devourers—have arrived, coming as they will in a first-wave advance of the trucks like a plume of poison spreading loosely and slowly toward us, when the television, radio and print ads, and *faux*-grassroots agitprop, begins, the rhetoric about the tar sands' mining being necessary so that we can stop having our soldiers killed in Afghanistan: a murderously disconnected piece of political usury. If the governor wants us out of Afghanistan then he should work to that effect. Killing Indians in Canada and checking *Yes* on the box that asks if we want global warming to be irreversible, with its trillions of dollars of damage and untold hundreds of thousands of lives lost, is not a matter of choosing to fight in Afghanistan or not. Hooking us ever-deeper on Canadian oil and a petro-economy increases the degree and duration of our relationships in the Middle East, no matter how much oil we steam from the great pit in the north.

We will know that we in Montana—the weak link in the chain, the one best place we can battle to a standstill the monster of Imperial, and monster of our own procrastination—are winning when they begin to change their names—finally, no longer arrogant; finally, knowing (and for the first time) just the least little bit of concern. The modules' transport ship, the *Exxon Dong Bang*, will change its name to the Hope or the Patriot, and Imperial itself will spin off and splinter into various mercurial divestitures, each as temporal as a mayfly. They will form nonprofits for Indian health care even as they are killing the Indians, killing everyone, and will keep pumping money into these new divestitures, more difficult to track—much less corner and capture—than any wild-spooked elk herd thundering in twenty directions down off the mountain and into the thick ravine below. It will take a sturdy and willing heart to follow them and find them.

Imperial will continue to pump money into these divestitures, and into their secret politicians, redistributing their power as if through giant cables filled with shimmering electricity. They will change the names of their companies to words like ConAgra or Altria or Nutritia or Sweetia.

They will ask us to accept them. They will negotiate with us—will tell us that they will accept and feed us if we will accept and feed them.

They are shoving us around like they own us. They are naming themselves when really, though we never exercise this power, it is we who possess—again, through our charters—the power to name them.

You may operate in our state, we can tell them, *though you must do so under the name of Adolf Hitler, Satania, or Putrid, Inc.*

We know what's coming. Right here, right now, is our first and last uncontested shot. They had a two-year jump on us, in those secret meetings with the governor, but now is our time, in these coming weeks. They have been planning this for a lot longer than two years, and I think they were surprised when in 2004, a Democratic governor won in Montana, in the reddest state in the country. But in time, it came to be a pleasant surprise for them. A lap dog, some would say, but what a politician! Good enough to carry wildly a wildly red state.

Needless to say this is not a red or blue issue. Like war, or a garden, life is not red or blue.

⁊

All my life I have leaned heavily, hungrily, on what's real. I've reached down into the ground, in Mississippi, Alabama, Louisiana, and Texas, and have pulled up oil from three thousand feet below, cracking into the brittle sand reservoirs of old oceans-turned-to-stone. I have reached into the forest, into the mountains, and summoned—extracted—bull elk, as well as mule deer bucks and whitetails. It is the destiny and identity of each of us to be a taker—no living thing can exist independent of this real and made world—but being human, we are perhaps uniquely gifted with the compensatory mechanism, the ability to give back, or to try to give back, in some accordance with our taking.

To know the price of our existence is the foundation, I think, of all morality and religion. Ultimately, such knowledge is a path to peace, if any is to be had.

I used to think that when the world finally changed for the better, the central pivot-point for that long-awaited slow turn of history would somehow be visible as a vertical structure, like a landmark rising from the plains, visible from hundreds of miles away: a real and positive space on the landscape—not just culturally or imaginatively, but a real and symbolic thing—toward which we could all travel, committed to make a change, to turn a corner and pass beyond.

How strange it is for me to consider that that massive landmark—the point around which we must all pivot, and now, if we are ever to change—does not rise above the horizon at all, but is a gaping pit, a negative space, and one which, despite being the largest in the world, isn't visible until you're right up on it, standing at the edge.

The Alberta tar sands are such a threat to life as we know it on this green earth that the damage there will make the BP oil spill in the Gulf of Mexico look like a broken fingernail, a sneeze, a modest cough, a hiccup, a blink. Further development of the Alberta tar sands will by comparison make the BP spill in the Gulf look like a shot of multivitamins, good for the earth. When pressed on this point, the governor and his spokespeople dodge the issue that they could stop this, and with the malice of a drug pusher rather than the courage and foresight of leadership, taunt us, saying, *Don't put gas in your cars if you don't like it.*

My governor, what word, what words, could awaken you from this dream? It is as if you have fallen asleep, or as if a hood has been placed over your head. What falconer owns you, now, and can you not uncover it yet, and return to who you were, and where you came from? This life is such a short one but you still have time.

❧

The shape and the measure of things is getting beyond us. The list of things that are slipping from our control—yet for which we are accountable—is growing, to the point where we are going to need something larger than our own selves to get us out of this jackpot.

Every bent and twisted fish, every sick frog, every vanished bird species, every dying Indian, is on our increasingly perverse wish-list, as we dodge and weave, trying to avoid looking at the real cost of tar oil—and as we grow still and quiet and humbled and shamed by our affluence as well as our inaction, we are coming slowly to realize how very much we could use a little magic.

We sure don't deserve any, but that's part of what makes it magic. Some people call it grace, no matter; I'm talking about the same thing.

And it is close. It is close. It is so close that if you listen you can see it, and you can hear its breath: as when you are in the woods on a cold morning, and are sitting very still, just listening. It is close.

All we have to do is have the courage to speak our name. The one thing given to us when we came into this world, and the one thing Imperial and Exxon cannot take from us. Not even Imperial can take that. All we have to do is write our name on a sheet of paper—pass a citizen's initiative—and they go away.

❧

I get weary of words. They are useful—they are the building blocks of democracy, and of revolution—but without action, they are nothing more than the relicts of ancient civilizations, crumbling across time. They can be the foundation of history but without action, they are—even in the moment of their first-being-created—like mansions uninhabited by any residents, or like a man or woman uninhabited by a soul. They need the spark of action, they need the breath of the living.

I am getting weary of them, important though this short history is, and this issue. Imperial and Exxon may seem patient, but they aren't. The shark must keep swimming, must keep eating. Not a day may pass without the largest possible bite. They are a ghost, a nightmare, are becoming a phenomenon unto themselves, like the ice age, like the northern lights, like a volcano, an asteroid.

Imperial is not at all about words, only action. Now they have brought more modules up the deadSnake to the so-called inland flat-port of Lewiston, in defiance of the court cases that are still to be decided. As if knowing already the outcome—Imperial's success, and our demise. As if so accustomed are they to always getting what they want, rolling over everything, that they cannot and will not pause for anything—not public opinion, and not rule of law, nor court of man. They are busy, after all, they have oil to deliver to a waiting public. They are not patient. The refinery-tubes sit down in the pit, the dark canyon, of Lewiston, in the eight-foot shallows of the dying deadSnake River, where there has been discussion of laying a set of railroad tracks down the center-spine of this once-great river—which can be great again—so that after the water has dried up Imperial can continue to truck the tar sand equipment northward in that fashion.

What few beleaguered salmon remain in the Snake will be writhing in the mud-cracked shallows. Eagles will feed upon them and Indians and non-Indians alike will be able to walk down to the dead river's edge and pitchfork the last of them into wicker baskets as was done in the old days.

It would be tempting to say the salmon won't ever be coming back. But nothing, really, is forever. Ten thousand years from now, the ice itself might come back. A hundred thousand years beyond that, it might melt again, and gigantic ocean-going silver-sided fish might tentatively explore the ice-carved canyons—gliding over the sutured lattice of those tracks, and the sunken carapaces of barges and refineries.

Along the Rocky Mountain Front, shaggy ice bears, weighing in excess of a thousand pounds, might glow burnt umber in the morning sun. Who knows what world lies beyond this one? We are each alive for only a few more days, hours, years; is it not richer to live these last hours with courage and resolve rather than under the brown-nose kiss-ass sell-out of being owned by Imperial?

❧

The falconer has the governor in his grips. The falconer has taken hold of our governor and is squeezing his spine. The falconer has hooded the governor and put him in a cage, only lets him fly when the falconer is hungry. I think that the governor has given up on this world. I think we have to save him from himself—that we must intervene.

❧

The thing about history is that even though it goes in cycles and circles—the robber barons arrive, squander horrifically, then prairie populism arises from the ruins and kicks them out, though yet they return—the thing about history is that despite, or because of, those cycles, it never ends.

You can pretty much tell what is coming next. It's not that hard for even a novice to be able to predict what comes next. And yet, here in Montana—where we will make our last stand, to the best of our ability— we who believe we live here and now in a peace very much like heaven on earth, and who stand also as the last-guards at the entrance to the gates of hell—we know enough natural history to cling even now to that most human of emotions, *hope.*

Even here in the garden, we are guilty of succumbing, through too many days, to the plague of numbness, and to the chronic disease of failing to notice how remarkable our world is. We are guilty, even here in Montana, of doing as we are told, and walking quietly forward into the future with our heads down.

But we have seen geysers erupt hundreds of feet into the sky, have seen giant bull buffalo butting heads, and seen winter nights cold enough to crack trees. We've seen glaciers and wildfires, have seen so many remarkable things intrude themselves upon our sleepwalking lives almost every day of our lives in Montana. Any failure to be struck rhapsodic by witnessing the remarkable is our own failure.

Hope will leave us last. That which many others would view as miraculous, we still accept as commonplace. We do not take such miracles for granted—they're why we're here—but we accept them, to the point where, even though we are surprised and amazed by them, we always expect one more, and then another, beyond that. As if where we live is the source for such things—that they come flowering up from below, as if from some shaft or fissure, and are cast down upon us here; that it is we who first receive them, and for as long as we treasure them, we will continue to receive them. And that it is we who are in charge of safeguarding them.

As such, there are none of us who cannot yet imagine a way out of this impasse between the governor and the poet: between the governor and the blind history he cannot quite yet see.

Will it be the old mistakes and sins, or will it be something wonderful and new? Damn this hope, for even at this late date we can—despite evidence to the contrary—imagine the latter. This is a land to mark the sparrow's fall, and we can imagine it. We can imagine yet the lion of the governor lying down with the lamb of the poet; can even imagine the lion of the poet lying down with the new lamb of a governor who has come to his senses just in time. Who has chosen not to destroy the state, destroy the earth, destroy his career.

In the meantime, the refinery tubes rest on their boats. It would only take them five days to turn around and go back where they came from. Melt them back down and turn them into wind turbines, or geothermal tubes, or wave energy generators, or backing for solar panels. We have all that, and more, in Montana. We don't have to kill Indians any more. We can write a new chapter. We can stay in the garden, this time without shame. We can demand of a gardener as gifted as the governor that he not sell out to Big Oil. We can tell him that everyone is deserving of love and that he needs not do this to get our, or the nation's, attention.

That although the riches of heaven are stored and waiting for him, they are not to be sold—that they are a gift—and that when he remembers this—for I believe he knew it, once—a great light will enter his soul and his heart. He will remember. He was not cut out to repeat the mistakes of others. He was made for greater things, but he has forgotten this.

We have seen miracles before. We can see one more; and if it does not arise on its own, seeping up from beneath the earth's plates, or up those fissures at the burning pass, then we can still lift it up ourselves. We have never made one ourselves before, but we have seen how it is done, and we can make one ourselves, if we must. We absolutely can write a different chapter for the history of ourselves.

And if we do not make the miracle—if it does not happen; if the governor, being mortal, chooses the old path—the easiest path, the path chosen by so many others before him—then we will have to put down our hoes and rakes and fight. And when we do, or if we do, I believe that we will win, for I simply do not think the earth can take any more such burning, and that the ground we stand on would be on our side. That, although outnumbered and facing the largest company in the world, with the earth's burning at stake, Montana would win.

It would not be easy—will not be easy—and it would be like no chapter I have ever read before, no verse or psalm I know. But when we go into the woods in the autumn listening and looking for the elk, if we put in enough miles and work hard enough at it, we do find the elk. The mountains and the plains give them up to us, so that we may travel another year, one more year, fed and strengthened.

We will surprise Imperial, will surprise the governor. It's nothing personal—it's not about either one of those entities at all, if they decide to proceed. Instead, it will be only about giving glory and honor to our home. We will defeat them, if we must. We might actually welcome them in. It may be that we have them right where we want them—that it is part of the story for them to come here, in order to be defeated.

Okay, so it's time to give your name for your country—Montana—time to sign your name, time to arm-wrestle, one by one, with the governor. You have to make a choice. It's time. Not signing your name is the same thing as throwing in with the governor and his bosses. We know his talking points. He will bully, he will wax patriotic, he will talk about the Montana wind turbines he has supported. He will bring his fastball, sometimes what he says might make you waver, but if he does not turn back, do not be frightened of him, and do not be fooled. Do not let him defer this decision to the legislature—he knows and Imperial/Exxon already knows their decision. Deferral is the same thing as ratification. Insist that he change his position. Do not be bought and do not be sold.

Stop the trucks at the pass. Your one name is stronger than the governor's. Your one name is stronger than Imperial's. All you have to do in the citizen's initiative process is write down your name, and the trucks stop at the pass, then turn around and go back down the hill to Lewiston. Your one name stops the trucks.

And once the trucks are stopped, we still have work ahead of us. The world is still warming, and the Indians are still dying. The pit, the abyss, grows wider and deeper, day by day.

But first we have to stop the trucks.

Forty years from now, young people will be calling upon us to tell them what it was like, in this crucible-forged time when democracy was attacked from abroad as well as within. When everyone, or almost everyone, was suddenly for sale, and when politics was flooded with money—corporate money, secret money: and how we won anyway. How we defended the sweetest of homelands.

It was a long campaign and though it could have been more organized, in the end it was perfect. The first protest was the largest—three thousand Northwesterners lying down in the road, and cars parked catty-wampus everywhere, clotting the highway, so that it took two weeks to clear. (Always, they left a narrow lane open for emergency vehicles. But not a twenty-six-foot wide lane).

The television crews couldn't get enough of it. But still Imperial kept coming, though always, they were ambushed. Sometimes it was two or three protesters forming a blockade—other times fifty or a hundred. Elk hunters set up tent camps in the center of the road and built huge bonfires of beetle-killed pine. Blue-haired seventy-something birdwatchers, their guidebooks clutched like purses, joined with river rafters to stop the trucks along the Blackfoot River. Activists from the BP disaster in the Gulf came up to stop the trucks, and for a while, they did. Imperial never knew where the next blockade would be coming from.

It was the year of the big snow, La Nina, which stopped the slow trucks often. They slid off the roads frequently and crashed through a bridge once, as had been predicted, and—also foretold—could not be pulled out. The giant refinery tube almost looked like art, the orange module brilliant in the green pool of the roadside river. Scientists found employment measuring the leaks from the secret chemicals being transported in subsequent loads along the corridor—benzene, mostly, and other toxic cocktails used for fracturing tight sands, trade secrets of the petroleum industry.

Nor were the blockades limited to the pass. Farmers along the Rocky Mountain Front blocked Highway 89 with their tractors and sprayers. And Reserve Street in Missoula—already the most congested road in Montana—became the site of many epic battles. Even those who had initially supported the haul changed their mind, after being stranded behind one of the mega-loads on Reserve.

After a while, the t.v. and radio crews stopped covering the story, as they eventually do in all wars; instead, it had become just the way a thing was. A quagmire.

The poet was involved in many of the blockades. He could be found in one or another of the blockade tents late at night, often playing a pennywhistle. As if believing he could win. The governor scolded his state, but could not control his state. The blockades had become a form of entertainment. Instead of bingo or Sunday night church services, people would say to one another, *Let's go stop the trucks.*

The blockades aggravated and slowed the trucks on their important missions to the tar sands, and costs politicians their careers, but did not stop the trucks completely. All this was the chipping-away. What did stop them, in the end, was the last thread of democracy.

We wrote our names down. The citizen's initiative passed, with three times the number of required signatures. Imperial and Exxon had wasted years of time and shareholder investments. The High and Wide corridor remained open, wide, lonely, lovely. It did not become an international industrial thoroughfare, despite the governor's wishes.

❧

What was it really like, young people will ask us, some day. They will want to know how close and intense it was, when the trucks came but then were turned back. They will want to know how we achieved our victory: their victory.

We sharpened our knives, we will tell them. We were frightened, and we were fearless. We chose courage rather than silence. We turned our back forever on the myth of self and selfishness; turned our back once and for all on the myth of utter independence.

That myth, we will tell them, was no longer compatible with the genius of democracy.

We were frightened—terrified—of the seeds, the sprouts, of dictator-ship—secret decisions, anonymous corporate donations—arising even in our own homeland, we will tell them—but we cut it down, just barely in time, by throwing everything we had at it—body and soul, intellect and intuition, everything.

We sacrificed our fears, we will tell them, and chose action, one more time.

We wrote our names down on a sheet of paper. We chose democ-racy—we made democracy. We stood by our names. Our names stopped the trucks. The earth was on fire, flames were licking all around us, but we shut them down cold, sent them away. We sent them back.

It was terrifying, we will tell them. It was glorious. Our lives have been full and glorious. We changed the world.

End